THE WYOMING BLIZZARD OF 1949

SURVIVING THE STORM

JAMES C. FULLER

FOREWORD BY SUE CASTANEDA

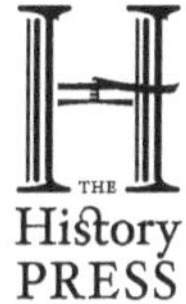

Published by The History Press
Charleston, SC
www.historypress.com

First published 2018

Manufactured in the United States

ISBN 9781625859358

Library of Congress Control Number: 2018936087

Notice: The information in this book is true and complete to the best of our knowledge. It is offered without guarantee on the part of the author or The History Press. The author and The History Press disclaim all liability in connection with the use of this book.

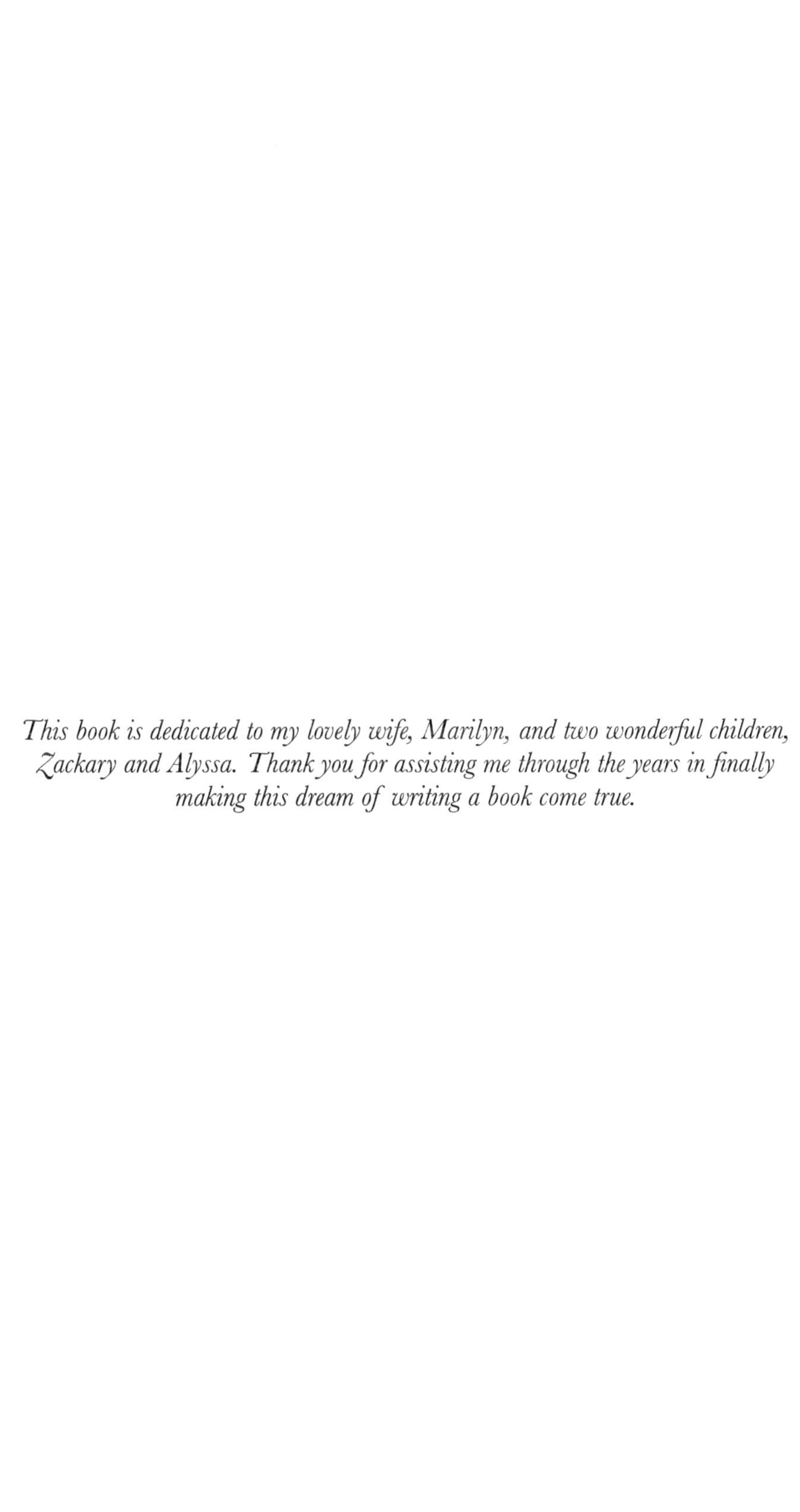

This book is dedicated to my lovely wife, Marilyn, and two wonderful children, Zackary and Alyssa. Thank you for assisting me through the years in finally making this dream of writing a book come true.

CONTENTS

FOREWORD

I've often thought that history is just really good gossip. We go through our days barely remembering what we ate for breakfast, but we can vividly recall the incredible tales of an event that affected us many years ago.

In 2008, as an oral historian for the Wyoming State Archives, I had the opportunity to interview one of Wyoming's centenarians. Vera Walling was a lovely Cheyenne woman who distinctly remembered the treacherousness of the Blizzard of '49. She and her husband, Ken, lived out in Durham, a little railroad station along the track east of Cheyenne. They came to town on a Friday night to spend the weekend, but when they tried to return home the following Sunday, snow drifted their car nearly to a halt at what is now Pershing Boulevard and Ridge Road. They managed to turn around and drive to the Cheyenne depot and waited for a passenger train, which finally arrived around midnight, to take them home.

"When we went through Durham, the engineer didn't even see it, so they let us off at Hillsdale to catch a westbound train that never came," Walling recalls. "One of the railroad section men and his family attempted to get to their home east of Hillsdale, and they froze to death in their car. I was glad we hadn't gotten off in Durham or we would have never made it home."

Fortunately, the Wallings were able to stay with another railroad employee and his wife for a few days and finally got home on Friday behind the railroad snowplow in a "motor car." Even better, they thought their dog would have died in the frigid temperatures, but some kind neighbors had managed to take care of him.

Foreword

As in any blizzard or natural disaster, there are those who simply endure or wait out the event. But for the ranchers and farmers in Wyoming, the loss of cattle and crops is financially devastating and can alter the future, not only for them but also for consumers who depend on them for sustenance.

I feel it a great privilege to know the author of this book, James Fuller, who, like me, didn't start out as a historian. We may both be what I call "accidental historians." We came to love history and Wyoming's historical events later in our careers; James served in the military, and I was a marketing specialist and fundraiser.

My book, titled *The Hitching Post Inn: Wyoming's Second Capitol,* was published in 2012, which was how I came to know James. While completing his military service in Cheyenne, he served on the board of directors for Wyoming's Historic Governor's Mansion and as chair of the Cheyenne Historic Preservation Board. Together, we enjoyed talking about all the great stories that Cheyenne and Wyoming had to offer and coming up with book ideas that we hoped would be interesting reads. James is a go-getter! Originally, the contents of this book were made into a feature film presentation on Wyoming's PBS station and received statewide acclaim. In book form, the reader will enjoy in-depth stories about the Blizzard of '49 and how it affected the lives of so many in the area.

I heartily applaud James for the many hours of research he did and the numerous in-person interviews he conducted to pull such a book together. As the Hitching Post Inn was a mainstay of Wyoming's travel industry and legislative history, the Blizzard of '49 will long be remembered as a cataclysmic occurrence—even more so now that this book has been published.

I know you will enjoy it. I would also encourage you to remember that your own story is worth capturing in perpetuity. James, through his company, Discovering History and Heritage LLC, can offer you a variety of ways to record your history, whether in print, photo books or videos.

History, as I said, is just good gossip. What's your story?

Sue Castaneda
Cheyenne, Wyoming

PREFACE

Throughout Wyoming's history, the weather has affected the lives and resources of those living in the state. Standing strong through tornadoes, severe hail and blizzards, those living in Wyoming have dealt with numerous weather events. The Blizzard of 1949 took Wyoming and several other states across the plains by surprise. Other blizzards had hit Wyoming in the past, causing devastation and financial loss for the state. In 1887, a blizzard recalled by many old-timers during the 1949 blizzard decimated the cattle industry in Wyoming. Wyoming's most substantial commerce was nearly shut down due to the loss of cattle during this blizzard. Historians have estimated ranchers lost one-third of their stock, while others lost everything due to the temperatures and the drifts caused by the blowing snow. Many of the ranchers who faced the blizzard in 1949 claimed it was as dangerous or in some cases worse than the storm in 1887.

There was no immediate concern in Wyoming that a significant weather system was approaching the area as 1948 ended. Snow was on the ground across Wyoming and neighboring states. With a forecast of colder temperatures and small accumulations of snow, Wyoming and outlying states continued with life as usual as the holiday season departed and the New Year rang in 1949. The mention of droughts the summer before mirrored stories of the Blizzard of 1887, as many ranchers recounted tales of a dry summer with no rain and drought-like conditions before the blizzard. The *Moberly Monitor-Index* stated, "The mercury in Wyoming had dipped to 28 below zero."[1] The paper also noted Big Piney, Wyoming, was the coldest area in

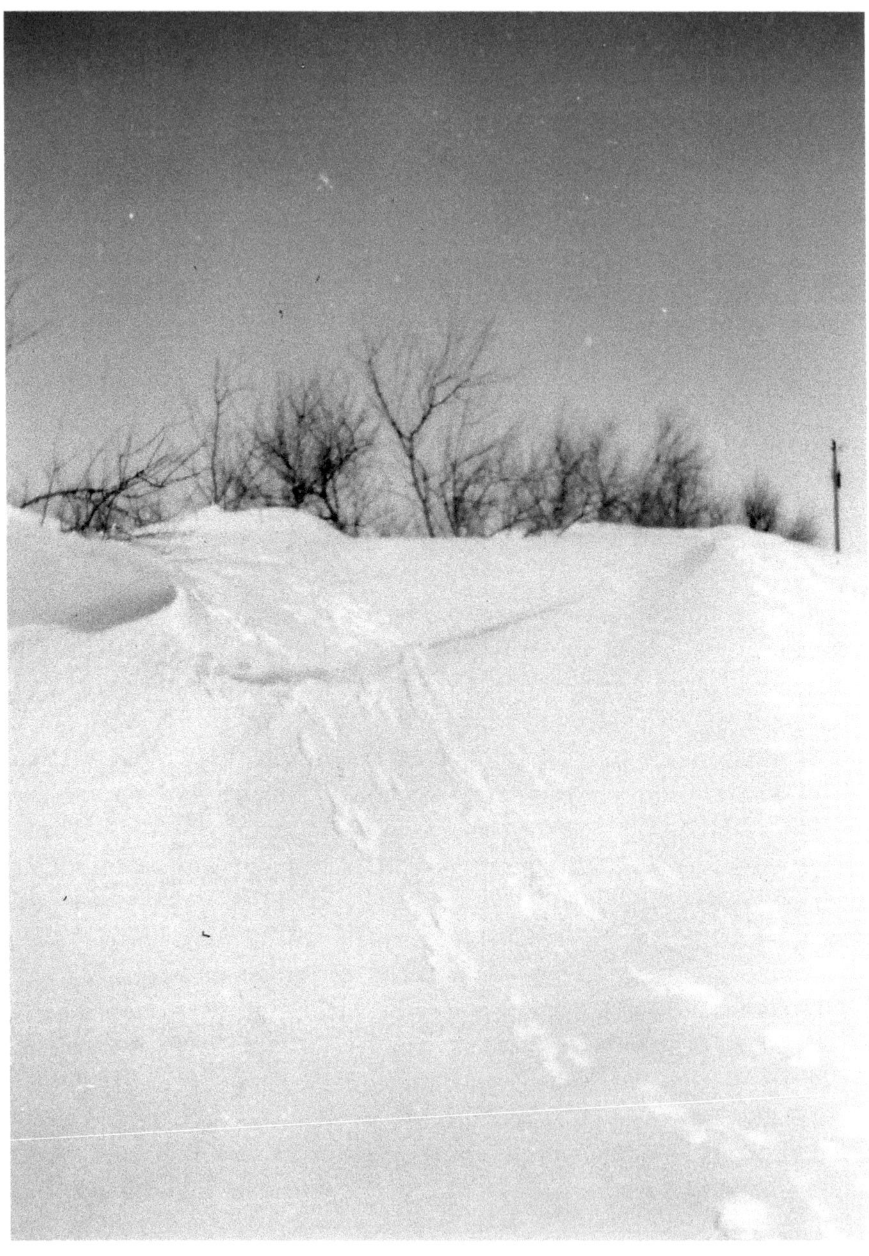

Snowdrifts reach the tops of large trees on the Emerich ranch. *Courtesy of Senator Fred Emerich.*

southeastern Wyoming, as well as in the United States, at that time. From all aspects, this winter did not differ from other winters in times past, and life continued on.

Signs of an approaching storm were seen just days before the blizzard as reports of high winds across Colorado and Wyoming were impeding traffic and wreaked havoc on structures in the city. When wind on the western plains begins to blow, it is a strong indication of a change in the weather. Strong winds across the plains forewarned of a brutal storm approaching. These winds caused a train derailment in Denver, where winds were recorded at ninety miles per hour. In Cheyenne, Wyoming, the roof of a boiler house was torn off due to the excessive winds, according to the *Los Angeles Times*.[2] A change in the weather pattern was moving its way toward the plains, and no one realized its severity. The Wyoming Blizzard of 1949 quickly approached, leaving in its wake accounts of heroism, tragedy and survival. The blizzard, however, left behind a legacy future generations continue to recount. As the seventieth anniversary of the Blizzard of 1949 approaches, many remember the struggles and feats of strength but, more importantly, those who survived the storm.

The events of the Blizzard of 1949 started on January 2, 1949. As snow began to fall, many were unaware of what the next eight weeks held for Wyoming. There was no indication from weather reports that any substantial snowfall was headed for the region. A national forecast in a Pennsylvania paper reported snow flurries and colder temperatures could be expected in Wyoming, as well as Montana, Nebraska, Minnesota, Colorado and the Dakotas, which, ironically, was the intended target for the weather pattern that was forming.[3] However, just days before the fair-weather forecast in Wyoming, the *Mt. Vernon Register-News* reported that the Denver Weather Bureau had issued a severe storm warning. The warning stated, "The southern Wyoming border and eastern Colorado could expect blizzard-like conditions with winds of thirty to forty miles an hour."[4] It is understandable that this information did not travel like it does today, but had this information been passed to those living in Wyoming and neighboring states, the preparation for this monster may have been better.

On January 7, tragedy was reported in Wyoming as two older gentlemen of the community became the first victims of the blizzard. In Torrington, Wyoming, two men succumbed to the heavy snow and frigid temperatures. Joseph Franklin Harris was found dead in his chicken house. It was later discovered that Harris had trudged through the blinding snow and subzero temperatures to turn out a light in the chicken coop. Suffering from an

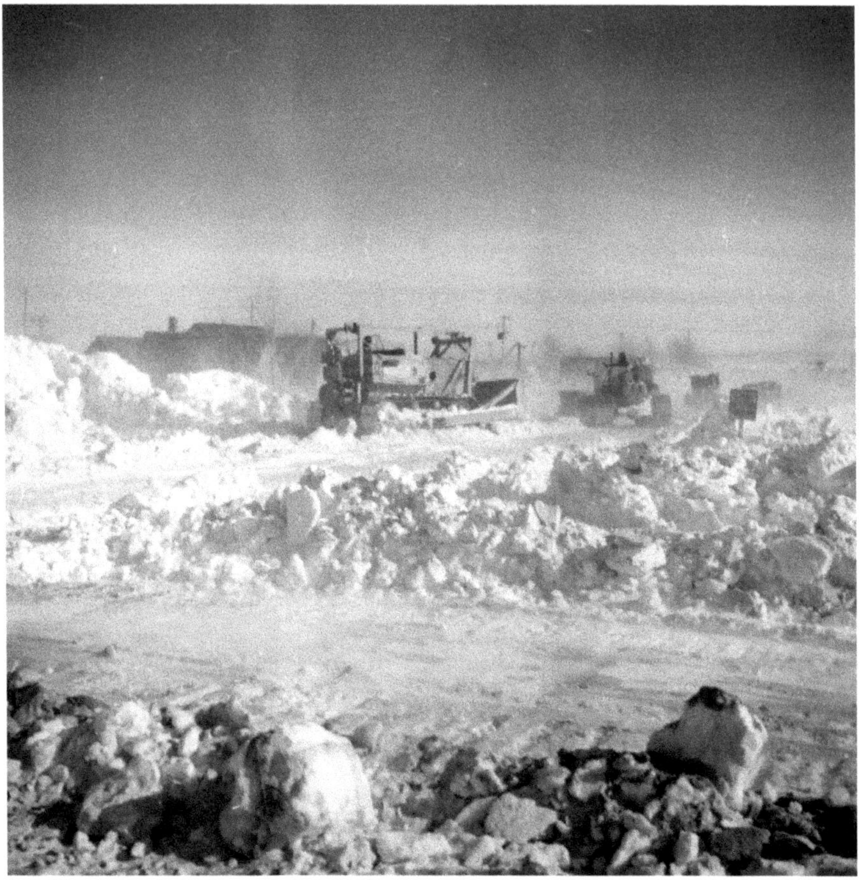

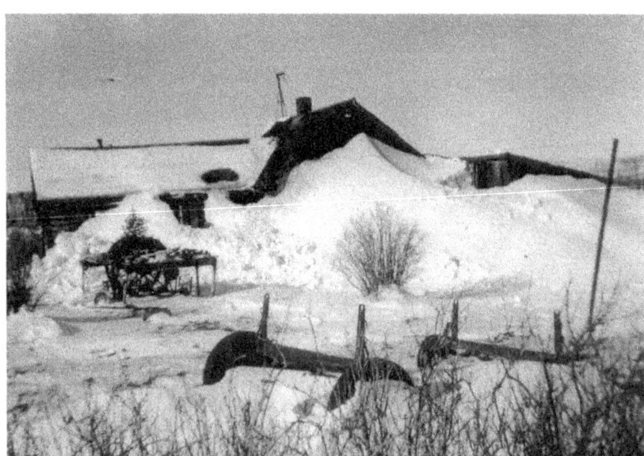

Above: Snowplows clearing the road. *Courtesy of Chuck Morrison, Morrison Collection, Casper College Western History Center.*

Left: Twin Mountain Ranch, home of Maurice and Susan McLoughlin. *Courtesy of Noralee Hoefer.*

already weak heart, Harris was overcome by the cold and froze to death. William Woodrow McHodgkins was taken to a local hospital, as he had succumbed to toxic fumes from his basement furnace, where the venting areas had been sealed off by drifting snow. McHodgkins would not recover from the carbon monoxide poisoning and became the second death caused by the blizzard.

In a quarterly weather report published by the United States Weather Bureau, William H. Klein wrote an article in the April issue titled "The Unusual Weather and Circulation of the 1948–1949 Winter." Klein pointed out the weather patterns were unusual not only in the United States but across the world. The most important issue he saw in this weather pattern was the severe and prolonged droughts, which caused for delays in postwar economic recovery.[5] Klein also noted extreme cold had hit Alaska and Canada. Record amounts of rainfall came to the Hawaiian Islands, and there were storms in Russia, while mild weather fell across much of Europe and Mexico.

Klein continued to analyze the unusual weather pattern during 1948–49, noting that in most of the eastern United States, temperatures were averaging eight degrees above average and many western states were averaging ten degrees below their average temperatures. Klein stated that such sustained cold weather in the West and warm weather in the East had not occurred since 1889–90.[6] He admitted there were storms before 1948–49 more severe and much colder. However, he stated, "Although individual winter months have been more extreme, mean temperatures for this season as a whole were of record in at least one station in every state west of the continental divide and the highest on record in at least one station at Blue Hill[7] (and probably other places) in New England."[8] Klein believed this was not the first time this anomaly had taken place, not only concerning the winter of 1889–90, but now he illustrated this conclusion with weather maps from 1937 when another blizzard had taken place across the plains with similar patterns. Klein continued with statistics, figures and data to validate the fact that changes of weather circulation in one part of the world could, in fact, affect weather circulation in another region of the world. His theories and logic seem plausible with the evidence brought to light after the blizzard. Much of the information he wrote and worked on later would lead the way to the National Weather Service, where he was named the first director of the Meteorological Development Laboratory.

Forecasts in advance of the storm had not given the warning of a storm of this magnitude. In the following weeks, relentless snow, brutal winds, and

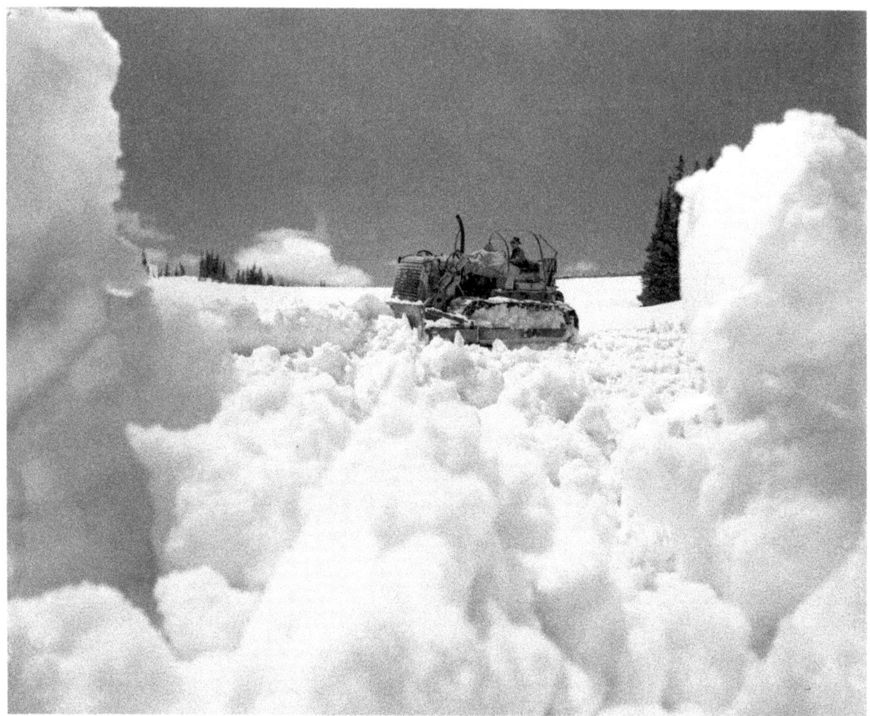

A bulldozer plowing snow off Highway 130, Snowy Range. *Francis Steele Brammar, courtesy of Wyoming State Archives.*

dangerously frigid temperatures cost the lives of cattle and people across the plains and Rocky Mountain region. Although the earlier forecasts were erroneous, the weather quickly changed. What was forecasted as a little snow turned into one of the worst winters of the twentieth century. "Spectacular weather" within the United States centered in the Great Plains and Rocky Mountain region. Klein stated, "Freezes and snow in California, Arizona, and Texas, and ice storms in the Midwest set new records for duration, frequency, and intensity."

Individuals who recalled the storm concurred that local forecasts called for flurries, with little to no accumulation, while across the nation, newspapers foretold of impending weather in Wyoming, Nebraska, and the Dakotas. The *Arizona Republic* noted, "Forecasters warned of winds of 'gale force,' driving a new cold front with heavy snow down through North and South Dakota and Wyoming."[9] The weather system seemed to be changing, with each forecast being different from the last. Some predicted a significant storm, while others forecasted limited accumulation of snow. The state had received snow weeks before the storm, which only added to the problems on January 2. A report from Rock Springs on December 9, 1948, reported that additional snow had fallen. While this was essential for moisture in the region, the article stated the snow in several places was continuing to bury "natural winter feeds for both sheep and cattle."[10] Snow fell across the state at the end of 1948 with a fury. In Jackson, Wyoming, it snowed for fourteen days straight. Newspapers reported drifts were so deep that winter livestock operations had to start earlier than usual. The town of Moran, Wyoming, about thirty miles east of Jackson, received sixteen inches of snow, with temperatures dipping to thirteen below zero. Being pummeled by heavy snow and strong winds, residents "felt the effect of wind gusts reported at one-hundred miles per hour, blowing out windows, knocking down signboards and ripping off roofs in what was branded by many as the 'Big Blow.'"[11]

Not only did stranded passengers, motorists and countless others who were halted by the blizzard give their accounts of the storm, but newspaper editors chimed in as well to offer their perspective. R.F. McPherson, the editor of the *Wyoming Eagle*, gave a short synopsis of the blizzard and the events that took place during the storm. It was "the unusual," McPherson said, that made the news. The Blizzard of 1949, as it became known, was the "unusual" McPherson had spoken of. This event made headlines across the United States and became part of nearly every conversation for the two months following.

McPherson explained that a blizzard in the western states is not unusual, but it was not nearly as frequent of an event as a hurricane in Florida, a typhoon in the Pacific or an earthquake in California. Even the old-timers, McPherson said, referenced blizzards regarding to their severity and temperature. But so many of these men said blizzards were just a part of pioneer life in the West. For nearly sixteen years, Mother Nature had cooperated with rather pleasant weather since the "Siberian Express of 1933."[12] McPherson stated, "This first week of January 1949 proves how deceived we were." He went on to say it had been years since a large majority of Cheyenne businesses were unable to open their doors on a Monday morning. Following the Blizzard of '49, business owners and employees were unable to make it through the large snowdrifts and blinding snow, preventing them from driving or walking the few city blocks to their places of employment. Traffic and public transportation across the city was at a standstill. McPherson said feet and legs were just as important

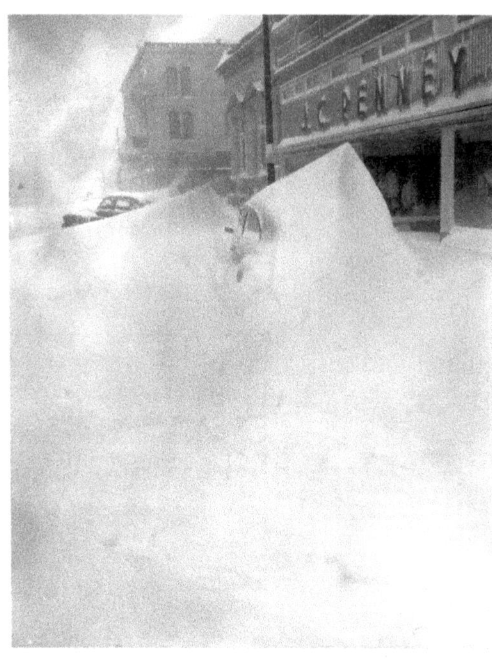

Left: Snowdrifts on Seventeenth Street, Cheyenne, Wyoming, with the JCPenney store in the background. *Francis Steele Brammar, courtesy of Wyoming State Archives.*

Below: Cars in a snowdrift out front of the Plains Hotel, Cheyenne, Wyoming. *Francis Steele Brammar, courtesy of Wyoming State Archives.*

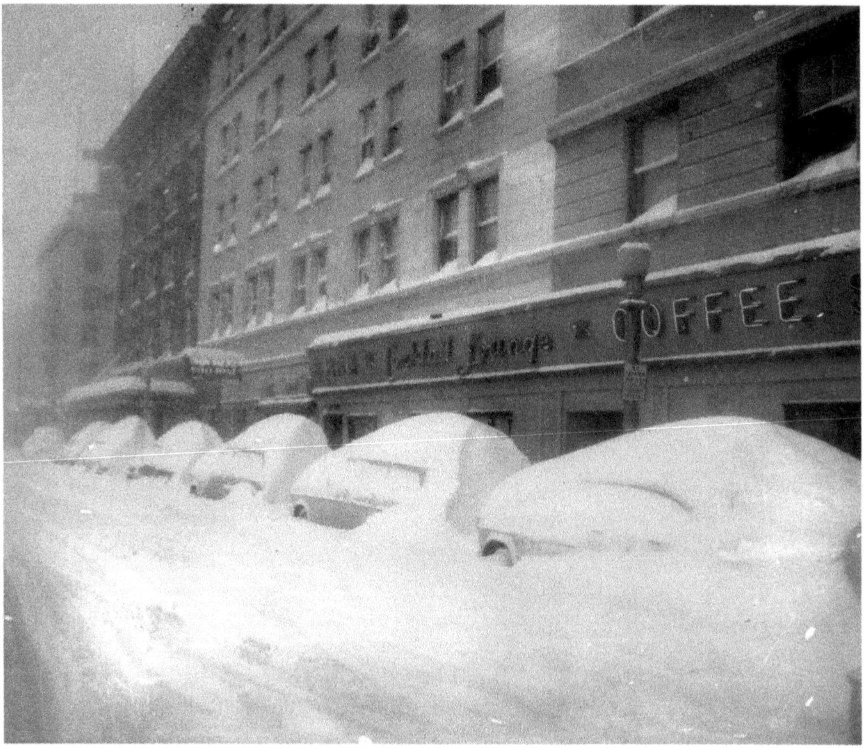

as cars and trucks, regardless of whether a person's trip into town was short or long.

Across Cheyenne, banks, restaurants, hotels and even the hospital were manned by skeleton crews because the snow was steadily coming down, followed by high winds, making travel almost nonexistent. According to McPherson, Wyoming had received a triple dose of what he called "obnoxious weather," with no breaks between storms. He said this type of weather showed just how helpless people are when nature takes the upper hand. In every instance, Mother Nature wins.

Even with "modern" railways and paved highways, transportation across Wyoming came to a screeching halt. McPherson said it was not surprising to think many of those stranded in Cheyenne were probably sleeping in hotel chairs or on railroad or bus station benches, having previously never slept on anything harder than a feather bed. The city's motels were at capacity as hundreds of visitors attempted to make accommodations. McPherson's thoughts on the storm tell the story of how many in Cheyenne were not prepared for such an event, even though many had survived blizzards in the past. He said the blizzard was unlike any storm he had ever seen, and it indeed was a storm the younger generations of Cheyenne would not soon forget. Reflecting on McPherson's final words, it is incredible for this author to experience interviewing the younger generations McPherson alluded to about the Blizzard of 1949. McPherson's prophecy has undoubtedly come true, as numerous people who were young children during the blizzard still have lasting impressions of this incredible storm that hit the plains.[13]

CHAPTER 1

SMALL-TOWN WYOMING

Small towns across Wyoming dealt with the challenges of having thousands of stranded passengers in their towns during the blizzard. These towns all dealt with the influx of people, but it was Green River, Wyoming, that took the brunt of those marooned on trains. Several national newspapers estimated somewhere around 12,000 passengers were stranded in Green River. With a population of just 3,187, the incursion of this many people increased the city by an incredible 376 percent, making it understandable that Green River did not have a plan for such an inundation of people. Aboard the six stalled trains in Green River, the passengers made national news swiftly, as noted athletic teams were aboard. Football teams included the Villanova University Wildcats, Drake University Bulldogs and the East All-Stars football squad, which had just returned from its match-up with the West All-Stars in San Francisco, where the East won a close game by a score of 14–12. Not only were there football teams but the University of Wyoming Cowboys and Hamline University Pipers basketball teams as well. Rounding out these athletic teams was the University of Michigan Wolverines hockey team.

The excitement of having these sports teams in Green River was a treat for many in the small Wyoming town, who had probably not been able to attend college athletic games. Most exciting to those in Green River was the arrival of the University of Wyoming Cowboys basketball team, which had recently participated in the Los Angeles Invitation Basketball Tournament. The Cowboys had taken third place in the tournament,

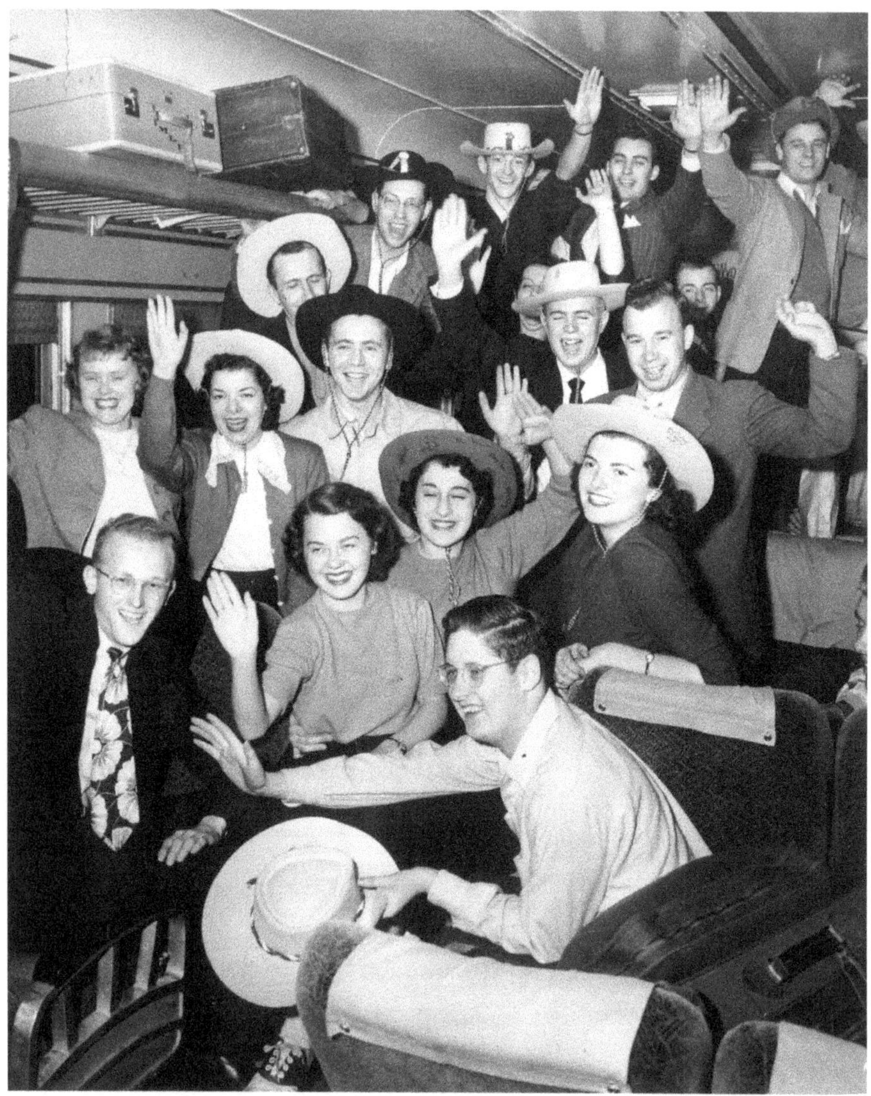

Stranded Northwestern University students on trains in Cheyenne, Wyoming. *Courtesy of Northwestern University Library.*

defeating the University of Montana with the assistance of what the newspapers called the "bright star of the game Ron Livingstone, the Cowboys towering center, at 6'10", who racked up seventeen of the team's winning points, with the assistance of point guard Len Larson, who scored an additional ten points." The Cowboys boarded the train in Los Angeles along with the Hamline University Pipers basketball team, which had won first place in the tournament, defeating the Wyoming Cowboys, 37–35, in what the *Missoulian* called "one of the wildest finishes of the tourney before a roaring crowd of 4,424."[14] With both teams in town, a game between the two squads was a possibility and the hope of many Cowboy fans. Coach Joe Hutton of the Pipers remarked in an article to the *Star Tribune*, "We tried to get a game with Wyoming at the high school, but their coach Ev Shelton had gone ahead to Laramie."[15] Over the years, many have claimed a game did take place in Green River. However, a game between the two squads never took place. In an interview, former team member Kerwin Engelhart recalled that during his time in Green River, the Wyoming squad wanted to play a game against Hamline. Engelhart stated that his coach said since they had just defeated Wyoming in Los Angeles a few days earlier, there was no reason to play them again: "There was nothing to be gained by our team." Although Hamline had handed Wyoming a devastating loss in Los Angeles, Engelhart noted the relationship was very cordial among all the teams, including the Cowboys and the Pipers.

Hamline's perspective of being stranded in Wyoming was different than might have been expected. Engelhart said that upon finding out more about their situation, his fellow teammates were excited since they had never experienced anything like this in Minnesota. He went on to say this excitement quickly declined, as frustration set in. The members of the basketball team had been on the road for quite some time and were anxious to get home. Engelhart said he remembered Coach Hutton contacting the school and informing them of what was going on.[16] A newspaper article confirmed Engelhart's statement, as the paper noted Hutton made a long-distance phone call to assure fellow Minnesotans that the Pipers were hale and hearty and all were anxious to get home, perhaps by Saturday. Hutton also mentioned in the article that the team worked out at the high school gym in Green River to occupy the time. Engelhart said he recalled the workouts with his team but emphatically stated that there was no game between the two squads. Coach Hutton praised the residents of Green River and how they accommodated so many people. He stated, "The people here are treating us swell, they are putting on special matinees at the theater for the people on the trains, and they threw a dance at the gym last night." He went on to say, "There is plenty to eat, we all eat and sleep on the train, but we have to take turns eating. I guess they're serving someone all day long." Hutton continued as he told about his team and the obsession with their new trophy. "The players weren't letting the huge trophy they won at Los

Angeles out of their sight. Vern Mikkelson, had been named the keeper of the cup because he's got one of his own to look after."[17] Finally, like any great father and coach, Hutton asked those on the phone with him to first call his daughter Barbara and let her know the team was all right. He also asked that his daughter call the wives of players Jim McDonald and Bob Lundsten, since according to the coach they had been married less than a year and he guessed their marriages were getting the supreme test.[18]

Two other passengers facing similar situations as the college students were Stacey Green and his colleague Theodore Pratt, who were both staff members of the University of Oregon. Green was part of the music faculty, and fellow university colleague Theodore Pratt was a dean on campus. They shared their Wyoming adventures with their local Rotary Club members after their return to Eugene, Oregon. Green and Pratt, who were returning from a trip east, found themselves stranded in Egbert, Wyoming. Green went into detail of what he saw in this small Wyoming town. He described "the thriving metropolis of Egbert, as a community where the railroad station was the last word in architecture when the Union Pacific first pushed its tracks across the country." He went on to explain that downtown Egbert consisted of the tiny train station, a single country store and an old schoolhouse. He further stated that the residential area was made up of five or six houses, and the town was devoid of trees. He went on to say the town "was surrounded by the horizon," which for many even today would make this a great place to live. Green recounted these events to a local Oregon newspaper, the *Eugene Guard*. In Green's account, it appears he was impatient and frustrated with the length of time it was taking to get to his original destination. When he described it to the paper, his initial statement was that it took "three endless days and nights." Although Green seemed impatient, he gave a great account of what was happening and the craziness surrounding his incarceration by the blizzard.

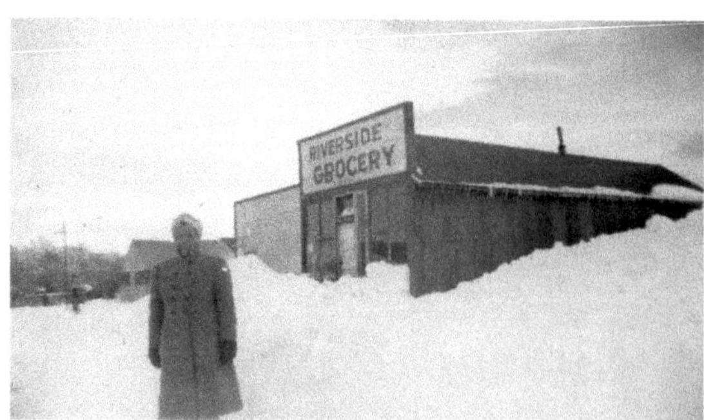

Florence Pantle standing in front of the Riverside Grocery. *Author's photo.*

Recalling the rescue efforts, Green noted the patience of many was growing thin. Arriving in Cheyenne by bus on Tuesday, January 3, many anticipated a train to their final destinations, but this, unfortunately, did not happen. The optimism of many waned as the schedules, according to Pratt, continued to change in the early hours of the following day, with no train pulling into the Cheyenne Depot. As frustrations mounted, tempers flared, and Cheyenne police had to incarcerate several passengers in the city jail, where they stayed into Wednesday, when the railroad company paid their fines. This incident clearly showed not just passengers were beginning to feel the strain of the storm's grasp. Green and his fellow passengers finally boarded a train at two o'clock on Wednesday, afternoon, January 4. There was one positive aspect from all of this, as Green reported the trip back to Portland, where "service to all passengers and all meals [were] on the house." Of course, Green did not let his audience down, as he took the opportunity to leave one final remark regarding his unplanned trip to Wyoming. He stated, "The morale of the passengers was good all through the ordeal, and the Union Pacific employees were to be congratulated on their efforts, with the exception of employees at the Cheyenne station who could learn a lot about handling people." It is apparent that not everyone stranded in Wyoming had the same experience or observation of the efforts taken by those across the state. As many of Egbert's residents were assisting in the entertainment, feeding and lodging of those stranded, other towns across the state were dealing with similar issues.[19]

Twenty-four miles north of Torrington was the small outpost of Burge, Wyoming. The post office was established in 1913, but by 1949, when the blizzard came through, it had already been dissolved. Reports came from those still living in the Burge area as they informed those in Goshen County of the conditions in Burge. Mrs. W.H. Backhaus, who authored the article, started out saying that those there in Burge had been snowed in for thirty-nine days since the blizzard had come through. She reported, just like others across the state, that snowdrifts had buried the corrals, sheds, water tanks, and haystacks.

Mrs. Backhaus praised Mr. Erland "Bud" Anderson, their local Conoco fuel man, who, despite the blowing snow, wind and drifts, ensured that his customers received the fuel they needed during the storm. She said Bud would traverse through the pastures and make his way through the drifts. When he became tired and could no longer continue, he would sleep in the cab of his truck. Bud was resourceful, as in some cases he left fuel in barrels so those in the community could come and get their allotted amounts of fuel.

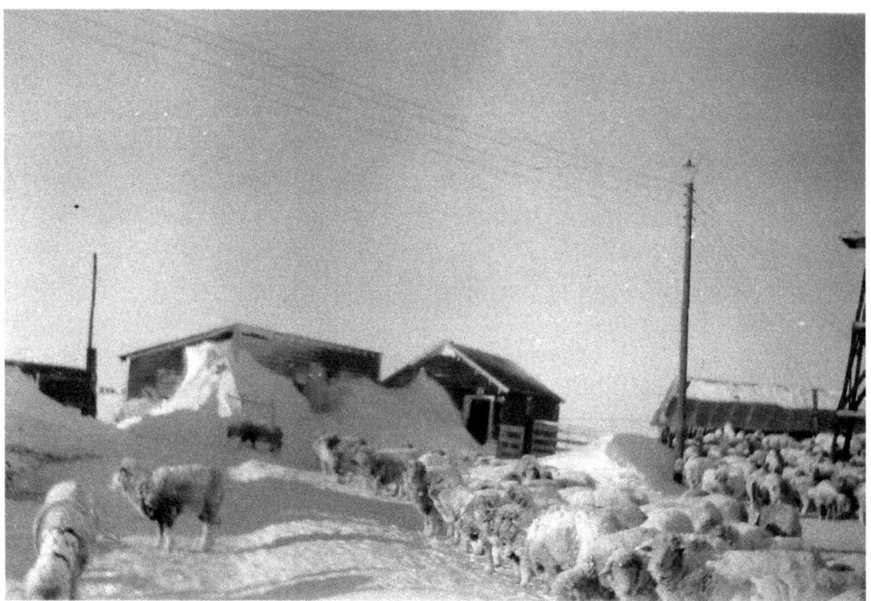

Sheep at the Emerich ranch roam about as they walk over the corral fences with the assistance of snowdrifts. *Courtesy of Senator Fred Emerich.*

Another couple residing in Burge was Wayne and Velda Childers, whose residence was considered by truckers, ranchers and surrounding neighbors to be the halfway point between Torrington and Van Tassell, Wyoming. Mrs. Backhaus said she could not begin to fathom how many cups of coffee and lunches Velda had served to those who were stranded or had stopped during the blizzard. According to Mrs. Backhaus, while Velda was serving up meals, Wayne "could always find a pack of cigarettes for someone who was out, and helped motorists whose cars were giving problems."

Of course, communication was critical to the community, and the local radio station from Scottsbluff, Nebraska, was praised for broadcasting not only the weather but also road conditions there in the community in and around Burge. The telephones were working just fine, according to Mrs. Backhaus, and if a family needed something and another family had enough to spare, they gladly helped those in need. Mrs. Backhaus also mentioned that some of their neighbors were not as fortunate. Mr. Andy C. Grosjean and his wife, Mamie, had been without mail or any other resources for over four weeks. This was because the Grosjeans lived near the state line of Nebraska and were not close enough to neighbors to get assistance. Mrs. Backhaus told of Frank Lewis and Ord Anstey, two other ranchers in the community who,

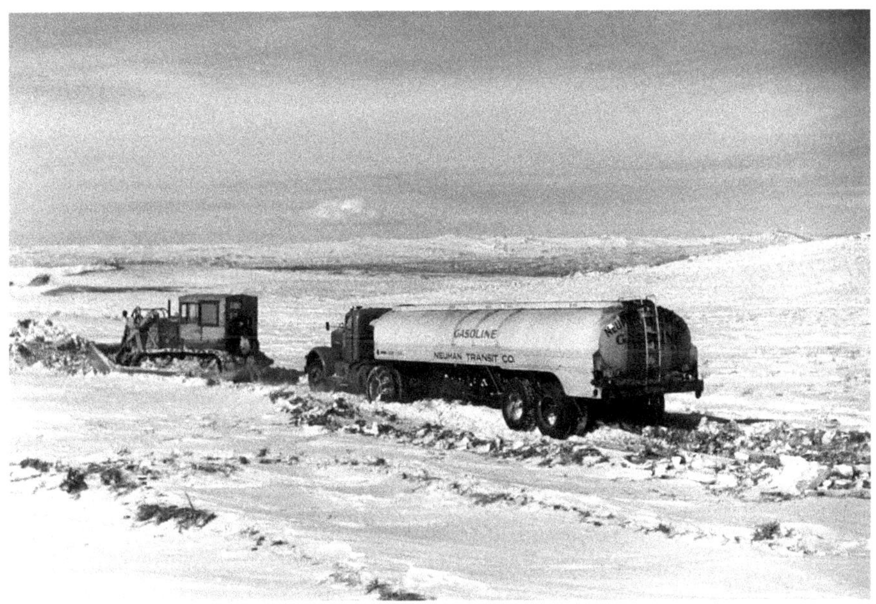

A bulldozer dragging a fuel truck over the hill, trying to get the fuel truck back to town. *Courtesy of John Moyer.*

with their little blue jeep, made it over the Nebraska state line to feed their cattle, but other ranches had more substantial losses regarding their cattle. Of those who lost the heaviest in cattle were Joe McManaman, Frank Lewis, Russel H. Foote and the Backhauses. Frank lost forty of his best calves, while the Backhauses lost twenty-seven cows and one calf. Mrs. Backhaus was unsure of the losses of others in the community but understood they were similar to those she had mentioned.

As always, there was a bit of humor through the trials faced during the storm. Mrs. Backhaus mentioned that Leonard Loxterkamp, Ord Anstey, Frank Lewis and George Backhaus had not shaved for quite some time and now had the look of the old '49ers. Of course, the men made a pact not to shave their beards until the first social occasion when they would have the opportunity to "show the ladies what good looking beards they have to protect their faces." The children in the community, of course, worried whether they might have to attend summer school since there had been no attendance at the school since December 20, 1948. Per Mrs. Backhaus, the schoolteacher, Mrs. Hirch, had been there waiting for school to open, which probably wasn't what the students wanted to hear. Finally, Mrs. Backhaus ended her article stating that women in the area had picked back up the art

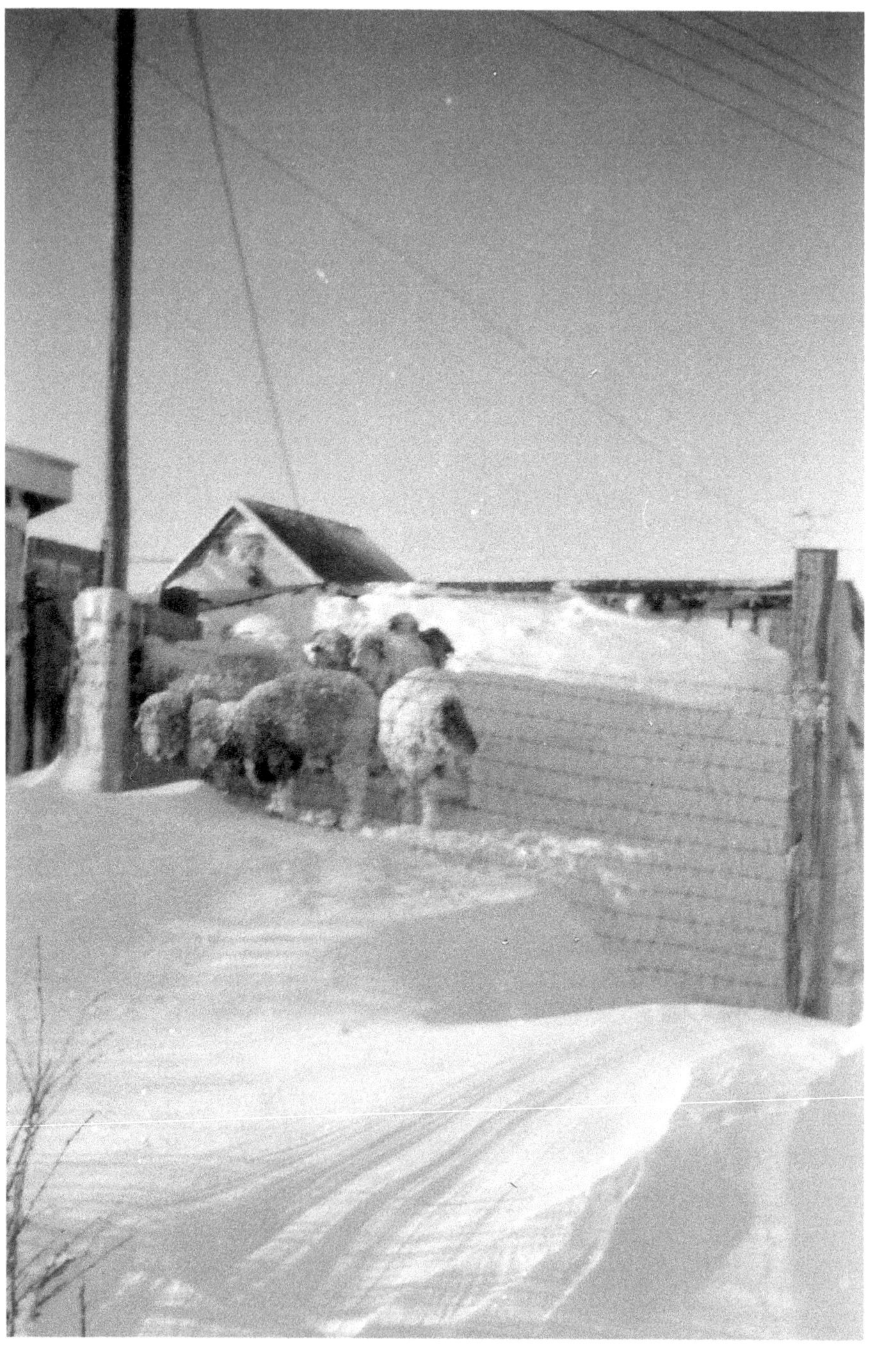

Sheep boxed in by heavy drifts. *Courtesy of Senator Fred Emerich.*

of bread making since the bakeries were too far to travel to purchase bread. She was grateful there had been no accidents in Burge.[20]

With nearly any disaster, government officials of the town or state are willing to lend a hand of assistance to those in need. However, Torrington's mayor, F. C. Calhoun, took it a step further when he loaned the city's wrecker car from his Valley Pontiac dealership. The vehicle was equipped with four-wheel drive and had a high clearance, enabling it to maneuver through the snow easier than other vehicles. The vehicle was used to assist many who were in remote areas or stranded because of the storm. The wrecker was vital in the birth of a baby girl to a family traveling on West Highway.[21] With the use of the wrecker, Mrs. Melvin Hetzel and her husband were assisted from their car and transported to the Platte Valley Hospital, where Mrs. Hetzel gave birth to their daughter.

That same afternoon, the wrecker was sent out to take fuel to George Herman, whose place was two miles west of the Torrington Sugar Factory.[22] Fighting deep drifts to get to their destination, the rescuers finally arrived

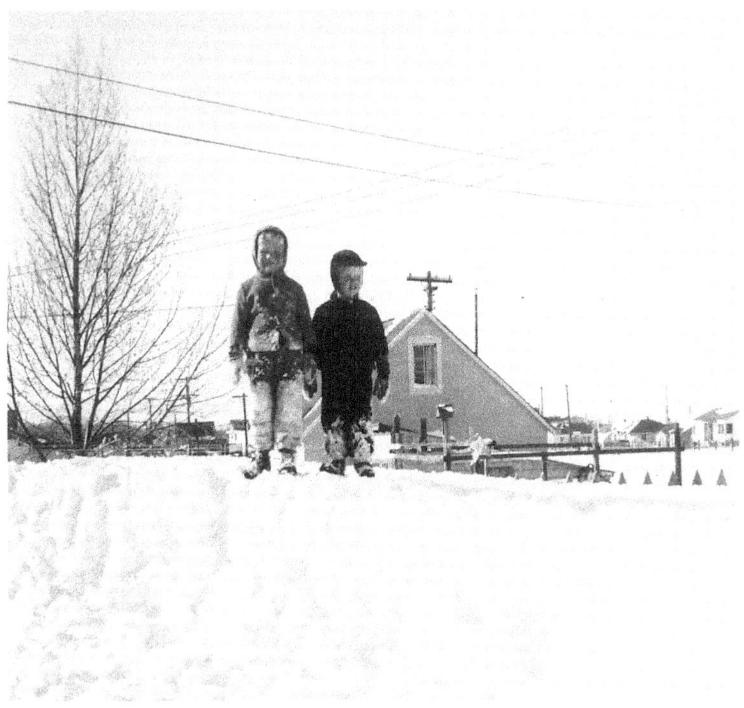

David and Bruce Dudley atop a drift at their home in Laramie, Wyoming. *Courtesy of Richard Felter.*

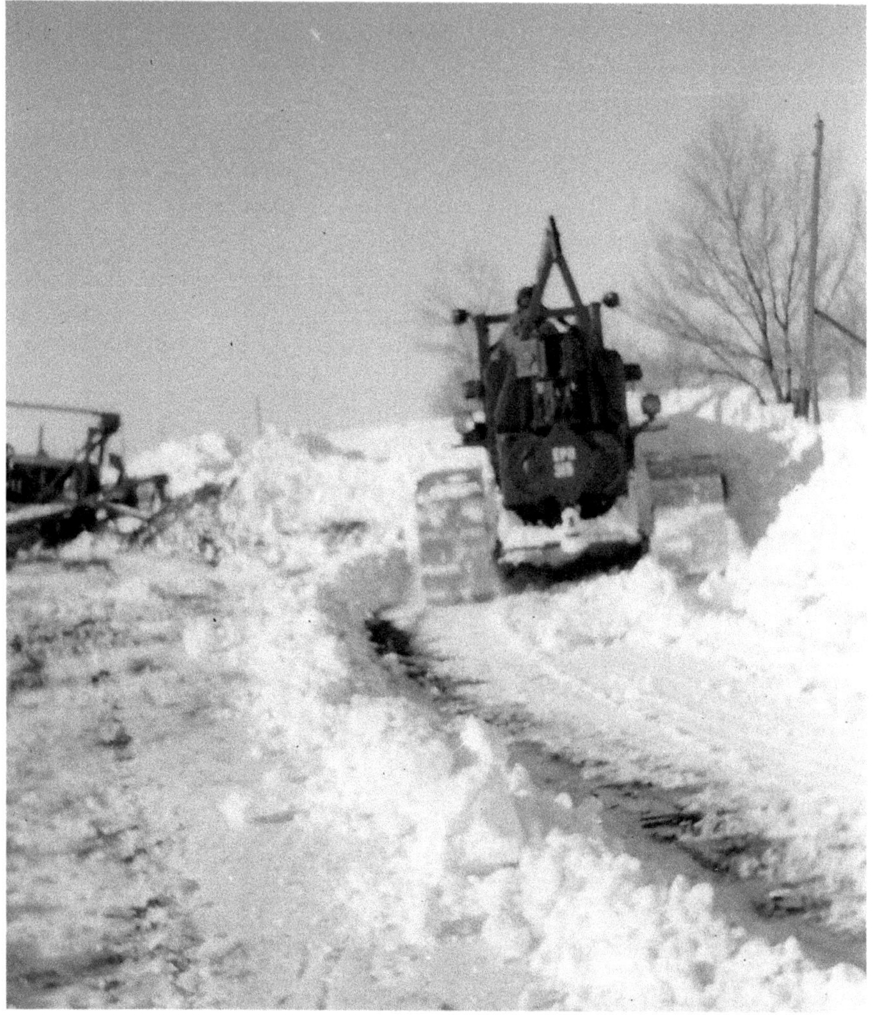

Wyoming National Guard members work to clear Railroad Road. *Courtesy of Senator Fred Emerich.*

with the fuel. Upon their arrival, they found at Herman's place three women and five children in dire straits. Several were crying because of how cold they were; those stranded explained to their rescuers that they had been without fuel oil since the night before. Later that afternoon, the wrecker was sent back out to bring the women and children to Torrington. They were elated to be back in town and not in the rural setting they had been for the last few days.[23]

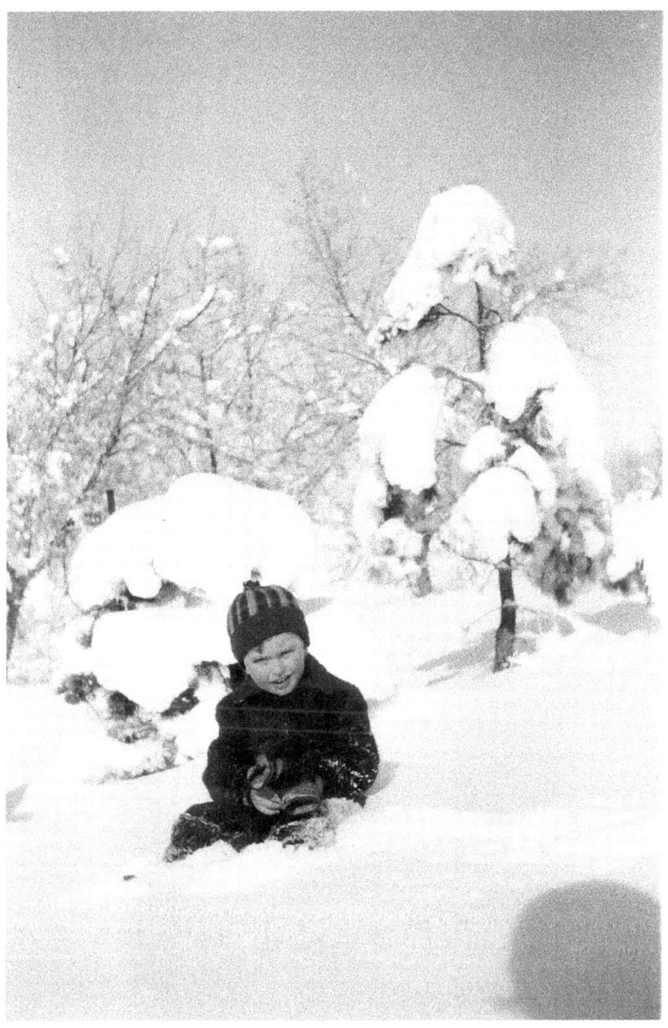

Young Fred Emerich sitting on a drift covering the tops of trees. *Courtesy of Senator Fred Emerich.*

Determination proved to be a deciding factor much of the time when it came to seeking assistance for those in need of medical attention. In Prairie Center, Wyoming, a small town north of Torrington, Rufus Scott was unwavering in getting his wife to the hospital. Snowed in since Sunday, January 2, the Scotts were now in their forty-fifth day marooned on the farm. The road to the farm had been opened by the county late one night after the storm on January 2, but that same evening, fierce winds once again blocked the roads, and they had not been able to leave the farm since. Mrs. Scott's health continued to wane, and soon she became bedfast for ten days. This prompted Scott to act in getting his wife the medical attention she so desperately needed. Leaving his wife and the safety of his home, Scott trudged through three miles of drifts and wind to get to his closest neighbor, Lewis Sherer, who let him borrow a jeep. Using the jeep, Scott drove to Torrington to seek assistance from anyone who would help. That evening, the county plow was dispatched out to the area where the Scotts lived. Plowing a stretch of twelve miles of road enabled Scott to transport his wife to the hospital in Lusk for treatment. Those who assisted in rescuing Mrs. Scott were George Deahl and F.C. Calhoun.[24]

A mercy mission to assist a family just over the border in Nebraska would not have taken place had it not been for the efforts of Jesse Lee Clark. Clark was one of four men who had recently taken ownership of a Nebraska mine in August 1948. Clark went to Louis Groh at the Carbon County Welfare office and explained that he was concerned about the safety of the Landis family, who were stuck at the mine where Landis was employed. Clark told Groh that since December 27, the Sulphur Springs road had been blocked by substantial amounts of snow. He and his brother Charles V. Clark had made a trip through the deep snow to the Landis place to check on them and to see if they were indeed all right. Landis informed Clark and his brother they had enough food to last a week and fuel was no problem since they lived at a coal mine. Satisfied that the Landises were in decent shape for a little while longer, the Clark brothers headed back to Rawlins the next day. Upon their arrival, they spoke with highway department officials regarding opening the road leading to the Landises' home. They were told that snowplows were working to open that area as soon as possible. On January 18, a day before Jesse and Charles Clark were told snowplows would clear the roads soon, crews had battled ground blizzards as well as additional fresh snow. The day of the article, January 19, was the eighth day since the Clarks had visited the Landises and Jesse Clark had taken the problem to Louis Groh.

Groh decided to take money from the county relief fund to purchase groceries for the Landis family. This solved part of the problem. However, the other issue was how they were going to get the food to the family. This was when Clark decided to take the matter to Rawlins mayor Sam Tully for his recommendation on how to resolve this crisis. Mayor Tully felt the best option was to approach the owner of Continental Divide Aviation, "Bud" Rhoadarmer. Rhoadarmer donated the services of Continental Aviation pilot Dick Schumacher, while Joseph Rasmusson donated the use of a ski-equipped plane.

That afternoon, Schumacher, W.N. Schneep and Mayor Sam Tully flew two weeks' worth of food out to the Landis family. As a treat for the young

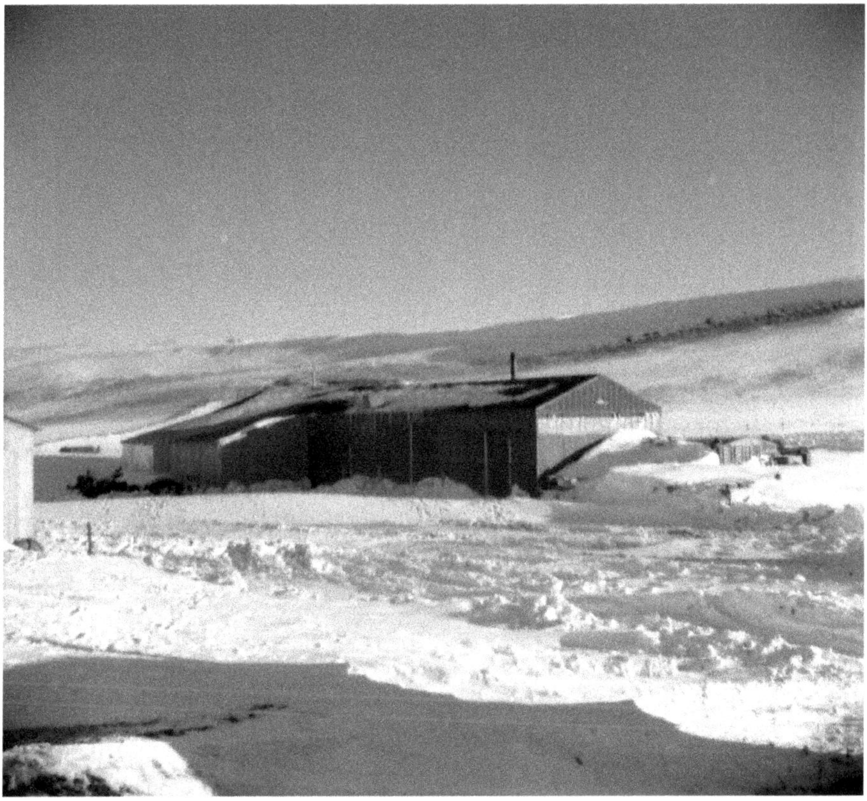

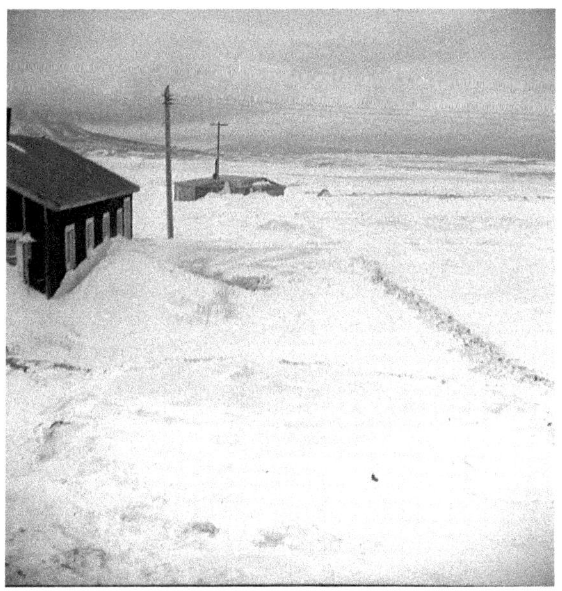

Above: Equipment shed at the mining camp. *Courtesy of John Moyer.*

Left: Another view of the cook shack with Elk Mountain in the background. *Courtesy of John Moyer.*

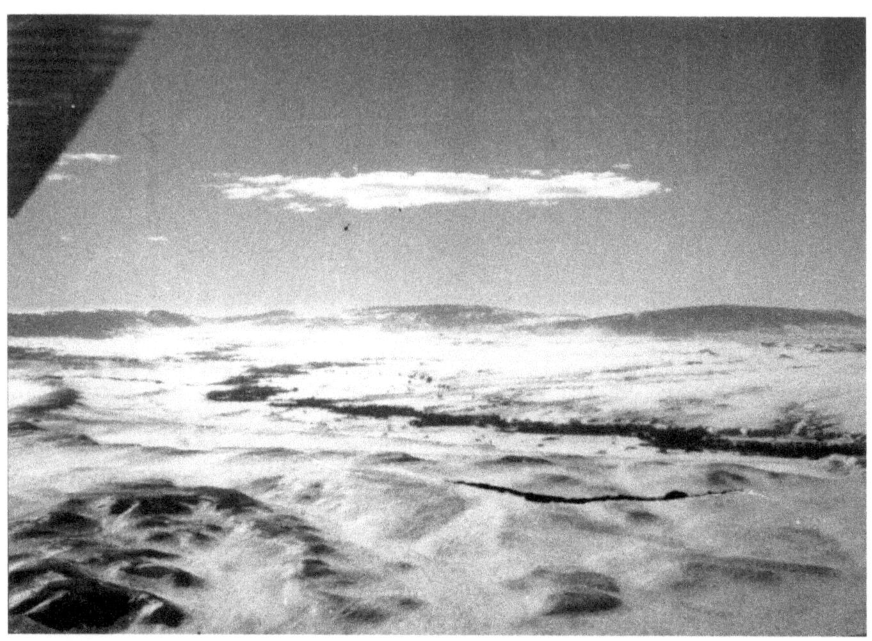

View of a ground blizzard, looking southeast, Deer Creek Range, Muddy Mountain, Casper Mountain. *Courtesy of Chuck Morrison, Morrison Collection, Casper College Western History Center.*

girls, along with the supplies and food there was candy. According to the *Rawlins Daily Times*, Schumacher executed "a perfect power-stall landing on a 45-degree slope covered in three to four feet of snow, taxing within 100 feet of the Landis home."[25] The party was greeted by an excited Landis family, who ran out to meet the plane. The Landis family was overjoyed with the relief they received from the City of Rawlins, which they told those who came was unexpected but very much appreciated. Before the group headed back to Rawlins, Landis told the mayor that his daughters—Rosemarie, eleven; Catherine, nine; and Christine, six—had watched excitedly as the plane circled over the house. One of his daughters said, "I wish they would land here." When Mayor Tully and his party took off back to Rawlins, it was an uphill takeoff with nothing to spare. Their mission of mercy was complete, and the Landis family could survive until roads were opened.

Louis Groh wrapped up the article with a final story of mercy his department assisted in. He stated that on Monday, January 17, crews "were forced" to clear two and a half city blocks in Encampment, Wyoming, for a Mr. and Mrs. William Garoutte, a disabled couple living in town whose coal supply was depleted. Groh hired a blade operator in town to cut through the drifts to clear a path for a coal truck to get to the Garouttes so they would be able to have fuel for heat, as the temperatures were plummeting into the negative digits during the night. Mayor Tully and Groh were aware the blizzard was causing emergency situations across the region. They wanted to ensure those in the city and surrounding areas that the city and the welfare department would continue to work together to assist those in need.[26]

When snowstorms come, many complain about how long it takes to clear the streets, enabling them to get to their places of business or shops. In Rawlins during the blizzard, the reaction was much different. Rather than complain about snow removal not getting done quickly, residents were praising the crews for a job well done. To show their appreciation, money was collected for those who had worked so many late nights and early mornings to get the job done. Thirteen dollars was raised by Rawlins citizens to show their gratefulness to the city for the excellent job of clearing the streets of snow. The contributions came from several individuals, including Charles Earner, five dollars; Mr. and Mrs. J.P. Noonan, three dollars; and the Subway Garage, three dollars. Mr. Reid L. Lowrance started things moving when he donated thirty-five cents for each member of his family after reading an article from the *Rawlins Daily Times* that said the cost of emergency services regarding snow removal averaged roughly thirty-five cents for every man, woman and child in the city. He felt it was his civic

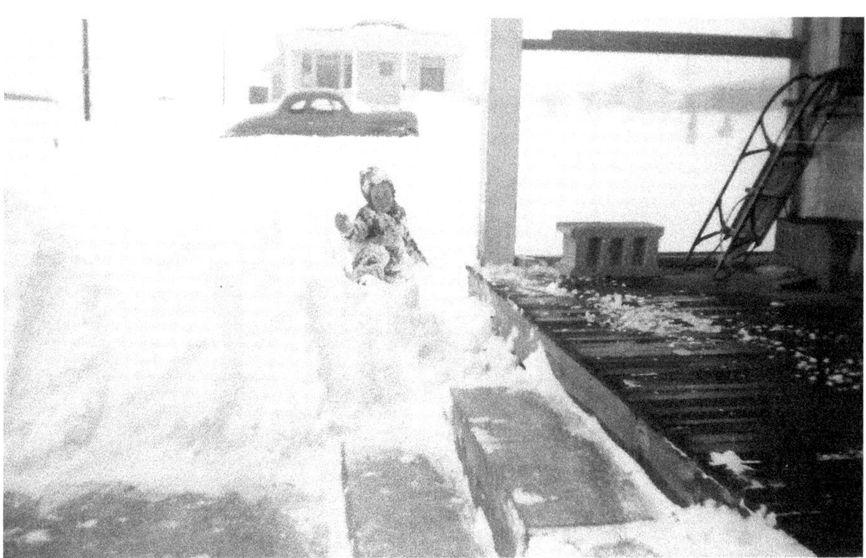

An unidentified child playing in the snow. *Author's photo.*

duty to pay for his family and the cost they had caused the city. Ivan Everett, the Rawlins street commissioner, made one of the most significant single contributions when he deducted from his own pay eight hours, representing an hour for each man who had worked with him during the unremitting blizzard for the last few days attempting to keep the streets clean.

Those street workers who kept the streets clean during the blizzard for the city of Rawlins included Leonard Ferguson and Joe Martinez, who during the subzero-temperature storm, operated the open Caterpillar bulldozer moving the snow, enduring the worst of the jobs required of keeping the streets clear of snow. Other workers included Paul Lawler, Joe Trujillo, Joe Daniels, George Gilbert, Roy Deffenbaugh and Jim Arnold. The citizens of Rawlins wanted to ensure the city could continue its efforts even though it was apparent that thirteen dollars was not going to make even a small dent in the budget required to ensure manpower and equipment was able to make this possible.[27]

The blizzard wreaked havoc with extreme cold and deep drifts, but a dangerous situation occurred when the wind picked up. The combination of wind and snow caused ground blizzards across Wyoming. These ground blizzards made visibility near zero, causing people to become disoriented and lost, whether on foot or in a vehicle.

On Thursday, January 20, Bill West, who lived at 1010 West Pine Street in Rawlins, was shaken up as he narrowly missed personal demise when his truck was struck by a westbound Union Pacific streamliner. The vehicle West was driving was loaded with 116 bales of hay when it was hit by the streamliner, sending the truck end-over-end across the tracks and strewing the hay bales out onto the snowbanks adjacent to the train tracks. Headed southbound from Creston Junction on Highway 33 with a truckload of hay, West was en route to a sheep camp. Sometime around noon on Thursday, West sat patiently as a freight train came through the intersection. As the tracks cleared, West assumed no other trains were headed his direction. As he slowly pulled the truck over the tracks, he instantly heard the train and looked to his left to see a streamliner bearing down on him. Reacting quickly, West jumped from his truck to safety as the train slammed into his truck, sending the hay in every direction. The train stopped after the accident, and passengers of the train exited and assisted in removing the bales of hay before the train proceeded on down the track. Although West came away from the accident with minor injuries, he was treated for shock and was reported to be feeling better at the time of the article.

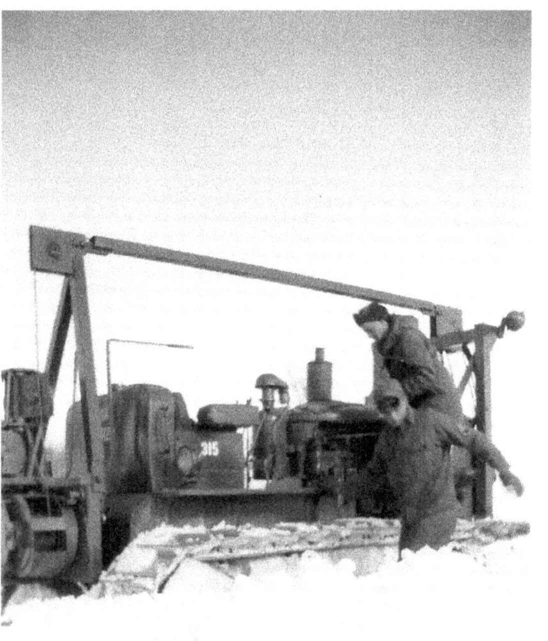

Right: Wyoming National Guard members making repairs to the cable blade of a Caterpillar bulldozer. *Courtesy of Senator Fred Emerich.*

Below: A steam engine frozen to the tracks. *Courtesy of Mike Kampa.*

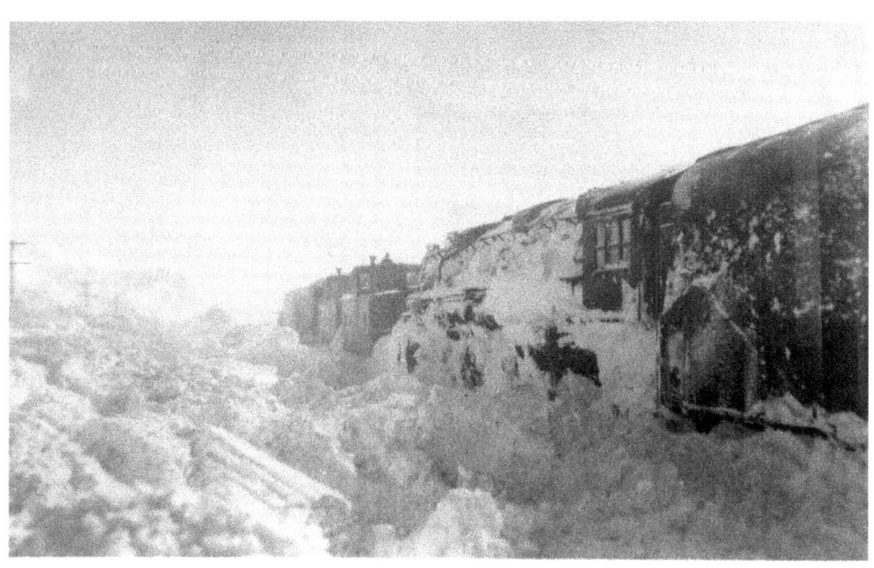

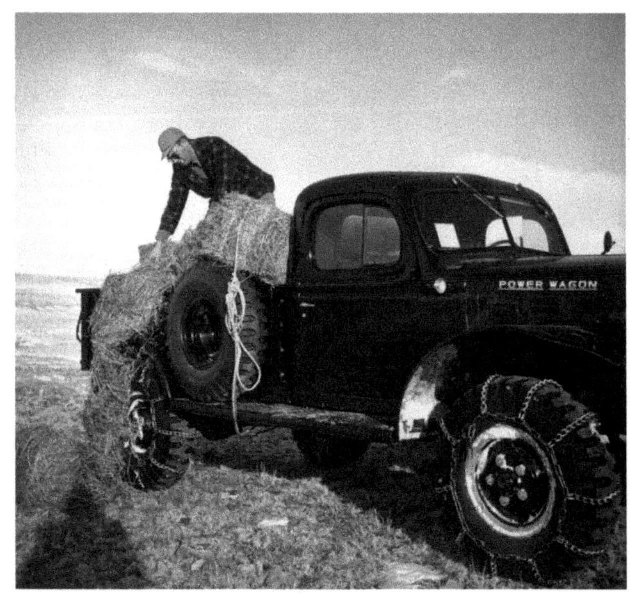

Right: Orville Mayer, deputy game warden, drops off hay to deer herds east of Casper Mountain. *Courtesy of Chuck Morrison, Morrison Collection, Casper College Western History Center.*

Below: Bulldozers clearing snow around the shed at the mining camp. *Courtesy of John Moyer.*

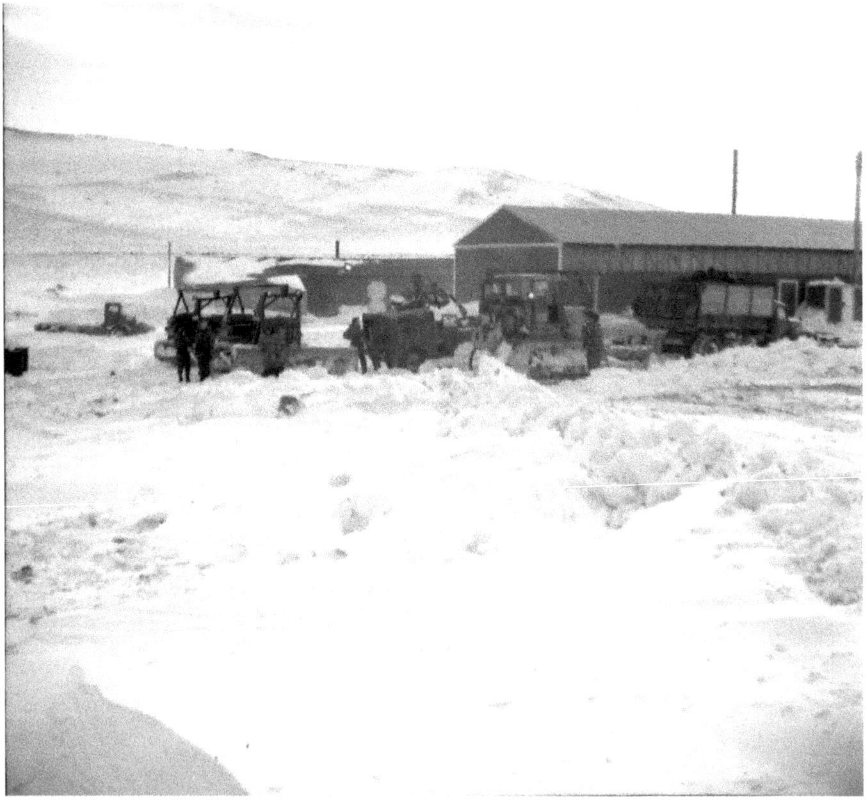

As officials and people were assisting West, another accident took place within a few minutes of the first accident. R.J. Carlson of Oklahoma City, Oklahoma, collided with another vehicle driven by Frank Cullen, who had stopped after seeing West and the problematic situation he was in. Neither Carlson nor Cullen was injured in the accident, which happened just south of West's accident. A third wreck had taken place at this same rail crossing on Tuesday, January 18, when Salom Rizk of Los Angeles drove his automobile into a moving train he could not see because of a ground blizzard.[28] Miraculously, Rizk walked away with no injuries from the accident. Those in these small towns took care of motorists stranded or caught up in the blizzard. The effects of the blizzard continued to pound these towns and cities for weeks to come.

CHAPTER 2

MAROONED ON WYOMING'S ROADS AND RAILS

As the storm approached, warnings were disseminated to the public as many who had thought this would be just flurries now realized a significant snowstorm was approaching. For many, the radio was the only communication they would have for days and sometimes weeks as the wind and snow continued. Jack Babcock of Moran, Wyoming, recalls the events prior to the storm as news came over the radio. "My girlfriend, Beverly Jones of Huntley, Wyoming, and I decided to go to a movie to celebrate our one-year anniversary in Torrington that Sunday, January 2, at the Mitchell Fairgrounds Pavilion. It was a beautiful day, but by the time we left the movie, we noticed the weather was changing. As we headed down the road, we decided to stop and say hello to my folks. My father, always the weather 'worrier,' had been listening to the weather forecasts on the radio and said the weather was going to be severe." As a child, Jack's father had lived ten miles north of Torrington on a ranch, and he knew about blizzard conditions. He advised Jack to "get that girl home," as there was a terrible storm coming. Usually, Jack played down his dad's weather concerns, but in this case, he listened and headed out in his Pontiac for Huntley, which was eight miles south of Torrington. The couple was about halfway to the Jones farm when the storm hit. It was snowing and blowing so severely that visibility became zero. Jack continued to drive but with his head out the window all the way to the farm, where he was snowed in for five days.

In January 1949, eight radio stations covered the state of Wyoming. This included two stations in Cody and one each in Cheyenne, Laramie, Powell,

Drifts rolling along the Emerich ranch appear to be small knolls. *Courtesy of Senator Fred Emerich.*

Rawlins, Rock Springs and Sheridan.[29] On the eve of January 2, 1949, these radio stations attempted to communicate to residents across Wyoming that a substantial winter storm was approaching. There were families like Jack Babcock's who heard and quickly made their way to their own homes or those of relatives or friends. Others, however, had either not been informed of the warnings or attempted to make the trip to friends' or families' houses after the holiday festivities of 1948.

One family found themselves on the road during the blizzard, which ultimately resulted in tragedy. Anastacia Archuletta, known by others as Andy, became a victim of the blizzard, along with his wife, Margaret, and daughter, Nancy. Andy and his family had made the four-hour trip from their home in Blende, Colorado, to Burns, Wyoming, to visit family. From reports, it appears that Andy and his family left after the New Year holiday and decided to beat the storm. Regrettably, the Archulettas never made it back home, becoming stranded in the snow. Only nine miles away from Burns, Andy and his family were stranded near Hillsdale, Wyoming. It is not clear whether their car stalled or was stuck in a drift or whether the blinding snow made it impossible for Andy to see the road. According to reports, the family of three was found frozen in their snow-covered vehicle on the side of the highway. In a desperate attempt to keep his family alive, Andy made an irreversible decision that ultimately caused the death of his family. To keep his family warm, Andy removed one of the hubcaps from his vehicle, and using flammable materials from the car, he started a fire inside the vehicle for warmth. It is likely that asphyxiation took the lives of the family. The papers noted that the vehicle was filled with snow, indicating Andy possibly rolled down the windows to lessen the amount of smoke filling the car. Andy, Margaret and Nancy finally succumbed to the noxious fumes. Today, they lie at rest in the Riverside Cemetery in Fort Morgan, Colorado.

The Archulettas was not the only family who had ventured out in an effort to beat the storm. Phillip Roman; his wife, Elizabeth Ione; and children Peggy and Tony were stranded right at the Wyoming-Colorado line. Although the Romans lived in Rockport, Colorado, they had close ties to Cheyenne, Wyoming, through Phillip's brother Donald Joe Roman and his sister Margaret (Roman) Andrikopolous.[30] The Roman family was visiting Harold G'feller and his family in Wellington, Colorado, before heading back to their ranch near Rockport. The paper noted that when the storm started, Phillip decided it was time to head back to the ranch. As they started out, the snow already had begun to drift and visibility was near white-out conditions. Not more than a mile away from the Hortons' residence, their truck became

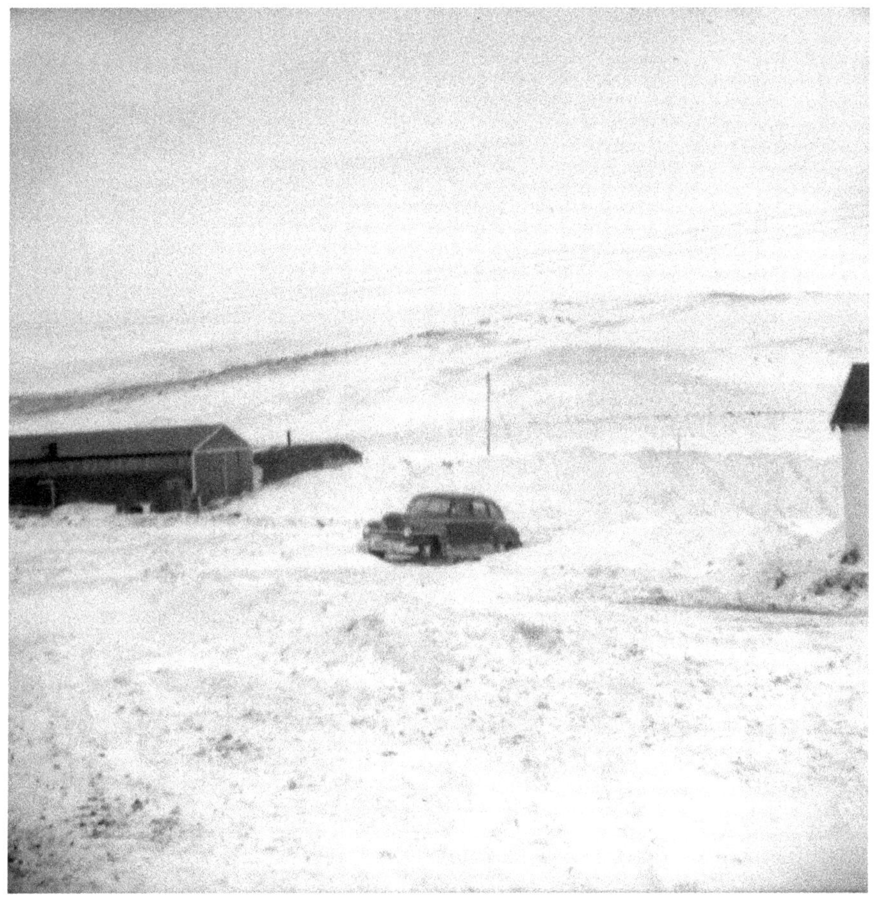

Nowhere to go! *Courtesy of John Moyer.*

stuck in a snowdrift. Roman left his wife and two children in the truck as he made his way back to the Hortons' home. With the assistance of Dave and Frank Horton, the three attempted to dislodge the truck from the drift. Unable to free the truck, the decision was made for the Roman family and Dave and Frank Horton to stay in the vehicle overnight to prevent the party losing their way in the snow. The following morning, they realized staying in the vehicle was not a good idea, so they decided to leave the truck and start back to the Hortons'. With weakened bodies, the Romans attempted to follow the Hortons back to their home. As they made their way through the blinding snow and cold, the Romans begin to fall behind the pace of Frank and Dave. The Hortons continued to assist the Romans, but their efforts were in vain against the prevailing wind and snow. Frank stated, "I can't remember exactly how deep the snow was, but you couldn't carry ten pounds in that wind, and the snow blinded us. The Romans got about one hundred yards [from the truck] and fell down." Dave and Frank both went back to assist them and continued to move through the storm, but Frank said, "Dad and I tried to help them, but it seemed there wasn't anything we could do in the wind." The Hortons made it back to their house but without the Roman family in tow. When he was interviewed at a local hospital, a Denver paper noted that Dave Horton credited his son with saving their lives. Dave stated, "I wanted to stop, but he [Frank] refused to leave and said, 'No Dad I am staying with you,' and that enabled me to make it." For Frank and his father, it was a relief to be home with family and friends. As for the Roman family, the blizzard took their lives, changing the dynamics of the small Colorado town they called home. The First Presbyterian Church of Fort Collins conducted the funeral services for this family of four. One can only imagine the heartbreaking sight of what the newspaper noted: "Four flower-covered caskets occupied the front part of the church." The paper also noted that both family and friends filled the church to pay their last respects to the Romans. The warnings were given, and many heeded; however, there were those who felt they could make it if they left quickly enough. The Blizzard of 1949 was fast, fierce and ferocious, with no one predicting the intensity that this storm would lash out.

Stories of significant events are passed down from generation to generation. The Blizzard of 1949 was no exception. This storm made a great impression not only on the older people who worked to survive but even on the children who may not have realized just how bad it was regarding the safety of their own families. One such story comes from Mary Carroll (Rahm) Johnson, the daughter of Mary Ruth and Carroll Rahm, who recalled the story of how her parents survived the Blizzard of 1949. Mary Carroll quickly explained in her recollection of the storm, "Let's just say this is the kind of story that would be deemed 'fake' if it weren't for the fact some photos of it still exist." Many who hear these stories often have a difficult time truly understanding the storm and just how bad it got during January and February 1949. Just after World War II, Mary Ruth and Carroll Rahm said their vows and became husband and wife, never realizing that "for better or worse" would result in one of the worst blizzards to hit Wyoming shortly after their marriage. In 1949, Carroll and his wife were living at the University of Wyoming as Carroll was working to finish his bachelor's and master's in education. Since Carroll had served in the

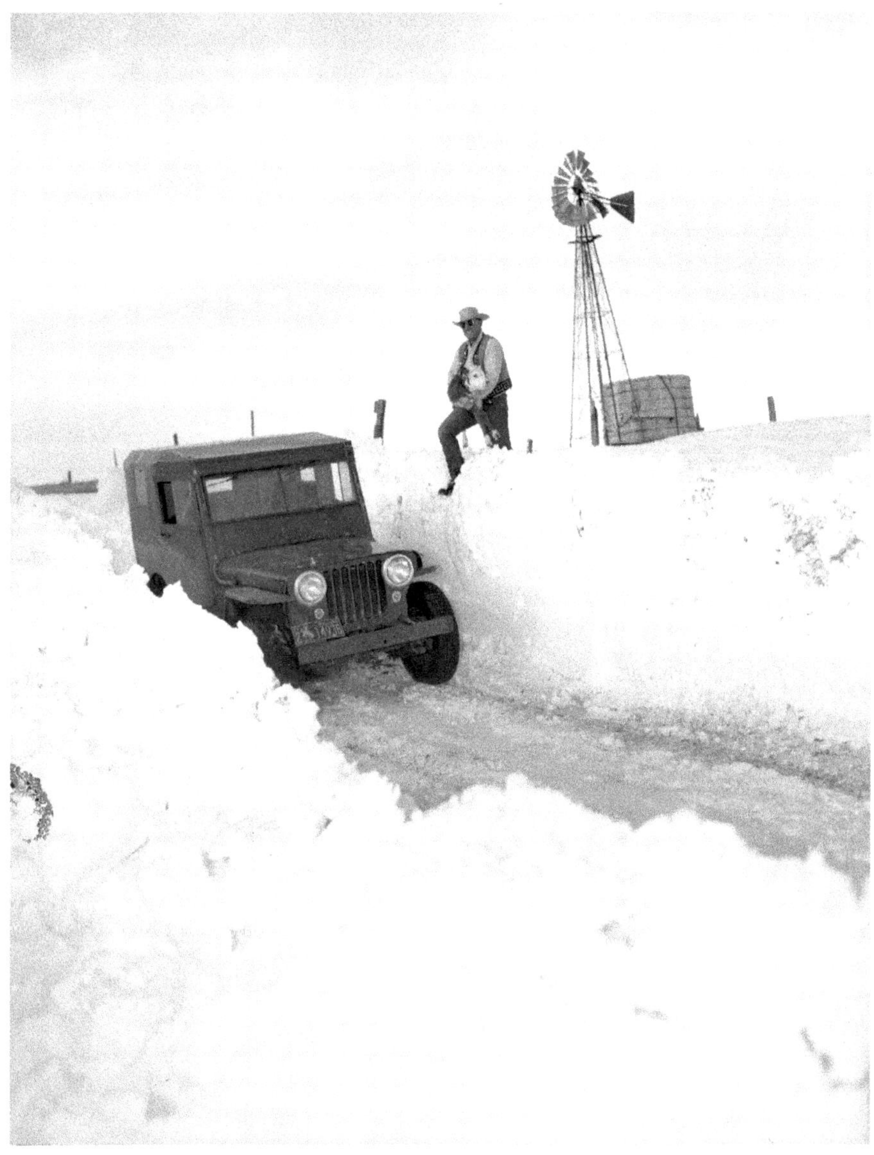

Jack Welch with a small calf on top of a snowbank, with a jeep and windmill visible. *Francis Steele Brammar, courtesy of Wyoming State Archives.*

military, he took full advantage of the Montgomery GI Bill to achieve his academic goals. Mary was not a student at the university but worked as the head secretary under Les Crawford in the Veterans' Office in Old Main there on campus, where she was able to meet and get to know thousands of veterans who had come to the university to earn their degrees. The Blizzard of 1949 became a legend in their family of three as the years passed. As a child, Mary Carroll would make a fuss that the current storm occurring was the biggest she had seen, especially if the school closed due to the storm. Of course, Mary Carroll's mother would quickly chime in with a personal excerpt from the Blizzard of '49. Most of her mother's stories started with "Mary, this is nothing."

When Mary's parents wanted to get away from campus life for a couple of days, they would head out to see Carroll's father, Gottfried Rahm, who was a rancher and trapper from Switzerland now living in the Cora Valley, which was about ten miles northwest of the city of Pinedale, Wyoming. With the drive being just over 350 miles from campus, the family made sure they dressed warmly. At the time, many were saying this was going to be a very cold winter for the region. Mary Carroll's parents heeded the warning and donned heavy winter jackets, rubber boots and any other clothing that would keep them protected from the elements. As the family prepared for the trip,

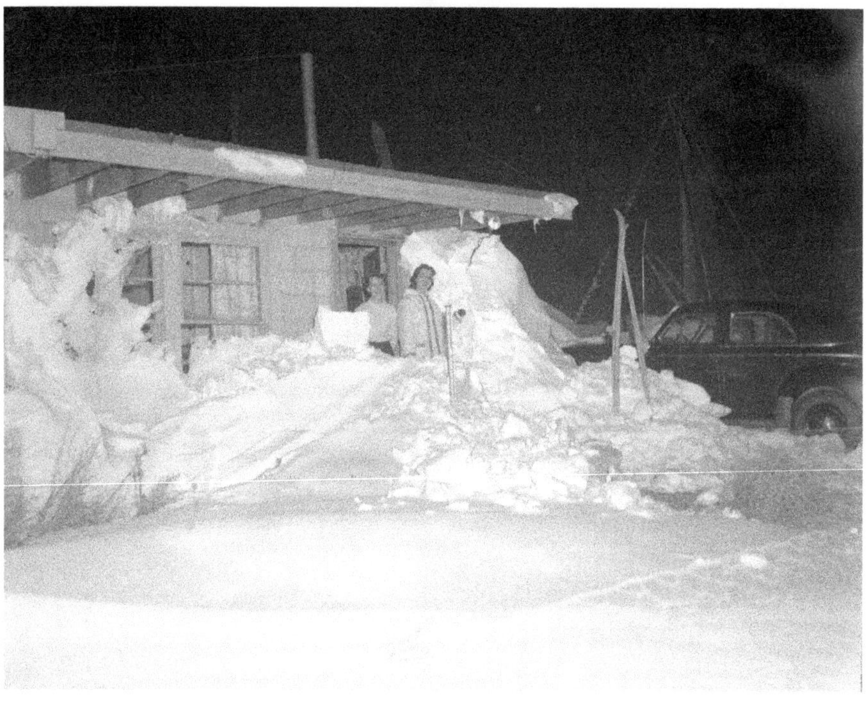

Two young women in the doorway of a house with a path cleared between tall snowdrifts. *Francis Steele Brammar, courtesy of Wyoming State Archives.*

Mary Carroll's father gave the appearance that he was heading out on a hunting trip. Dressed in all of his hunting clothes and Army boots, he looked the part, but he was keeping in mind how cold it might get if perchance they were stranded along the road to Pinedale. Living on a college student salary, Mary's parents did not have the luxury of eating along the highway as they drove. Instead, Mary Ruth packed two tuna fish sandwiches, two Baby Ruth candy bars and two Cokes to drink, and they headed off to Pinedale. That particular trip to Pinedale, the Rahms arrived late in the evening. They made their way through the city and out to the valley. Parking their four-cylinder car, the family made their way to the cabin. As always, the elder Rahm was waiting for the family with a lighted lantern, and they made their way in the dark toward the cabin. In her story, Mary Carroll's mother recalled how she loved to see her father-in-law in his overall bibs that he wore nearly every day.

That night after arriving at the cabin, the Rahms stayed up talking with Gottfried. They loved hearing his updates on the ranch and other things happening in Pinedale. After the family's lengthy evening, they all went to bed as the snow began to fall. Not worrying about the cold and snow outside the cabin, they all snuggled up in comfortable beds with big down quilts, along with the wood fireplace going nearby their beds. These winter nights were a great memory as Mary Carroll's mother recalled sinking into the feathery down and falling quickly asleep. When morning came, Carroll's father would start out these cold days with a shot of 100-proof whiskey (Mary's father brought him a case of whiskey every year). Mary's mother would cook dinner on the old cook stove there in the cabin and end the evening with a chocolate cake made from scratch. Being with their older father was so much fun, but even with his broken English, his warning to his daughter-in-law, or "Roody," as he called her, was very serious in its delivery. He said, "Roody, you two better get goin'. Ets gonna be a bad vun."

On Sunday, January 2, the Rahms did as they had done many times to get ready to leave the cabin and get back on the road to Laramie. The snow was coming down hard, but they had to get back to the university. They both had to be back to school and work on Monday, and they could not forecast if Laramie was getting the same type of snowfall and if the university would be closed. Packing some leftovers for their lunch on the road, they said their goodbyes, which seemed long this time. As he always did, Carroll's father waved as they left and would continue waving until they were completely out of sight. As the Rahms headed out on the road, the snow was coming down heavily. Utilizing the vehicle's windshield wipers, they were still no match for

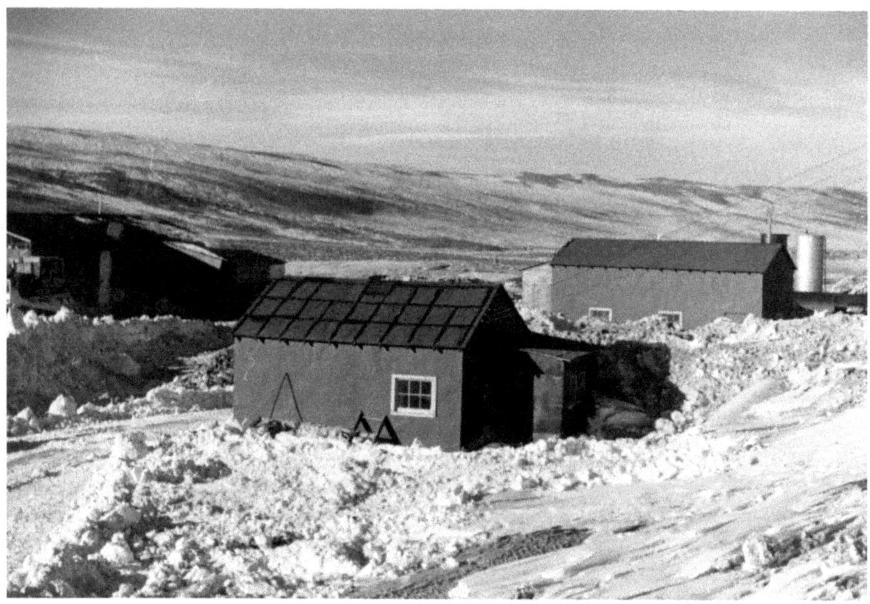

Large snowdrifts throughout the mining camp. *Courtesy of John Moyer.*

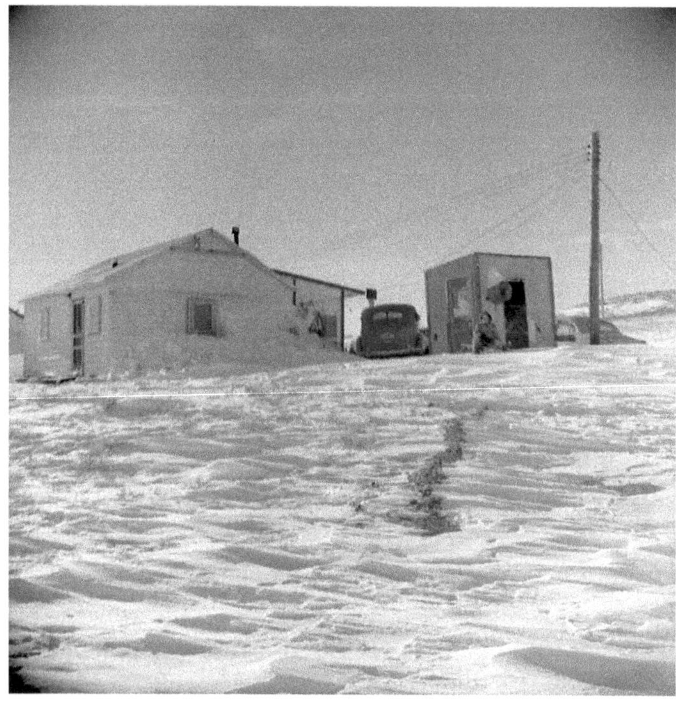

The house of the superintendent, a role filled by John Moyer's father, John L. Moyer. *Courtesy of John Moyer.*

the amount of snow falling. Carroll was having a very difficult time seeing the road as they continued. Unlike today, with markers for the edge of the road, these thoroughfares were narrow and extremely dangerous.

As Carroll headed down the road, the snow was coming down at an amazing rate, causing slick roads and near zero visibility. Mary Carroll's mother recalled, "Your dad had to rev the engine to work his way on the road." The snow began to build on the side of the roads, and the farther down the road they went, the higher these drifts became. After looking at all of their options, the decision was made to stop in a pull-off area near the highway. Due to poor visibility, they did not realize how many other cars were following behind them in the storm. At this point, the Rahms were not sure what to do other than wait out the storm. As they waited in the storm, an unexpected guardian angel approached in the form of flashing yellow lights: a snowplow. As the snowplow made its way down the road, it slowed to a stop beside Mary and Carroll's jeep. The man operating the snowplow exited the vehicle and approached the jeep. Carroll opened the door to speak with the driver. As the driver peered inside the jeep, he said, "You young people are not going to make it out of here if you don't get going and follow right behind me. The roads behind you are closing, and the roads ahead are about to do the same. I'm the last plow headed in this direction, and you are to follow me close and don't stop for anything. Once we arrive in Rock River, another plow will meet you, and you are to follow that plow until you get to Laramie. Do you understand? This storm is a killer!"

As Mary's mother recalled the story, it was obvious those last words of the plow driver were ingrained in her mind as she attempted to convey the same fear she had on the day she heard those words. As they drove toward Laramie, the snow continued to fall, and the drifts lining the road appeared to be growing in size as they got closer to Laramie, traveling at only ten to fifteen miles per hour.

Finally, after what seemed to be the longest trip they had been on, Mary and Carroll arrived in Laramie to their campus trailer. Now they were able to listen to the local radio station to get reports of how the snow was affecting Laramie. Not only was the University of Wyoming campus closed for students, but Mary Carroll's mother did not have to report to work. Radio announcers warned listeners the chances of freezing to death were high if anyone tried to move around outside at night. As reports came over the radio about the storm and how it was affecting the region, Mary's parents quickly realized the peril Wyoming was facing. The trains couldn't run because the tracks were covered over, and grocery stores were fast becoming

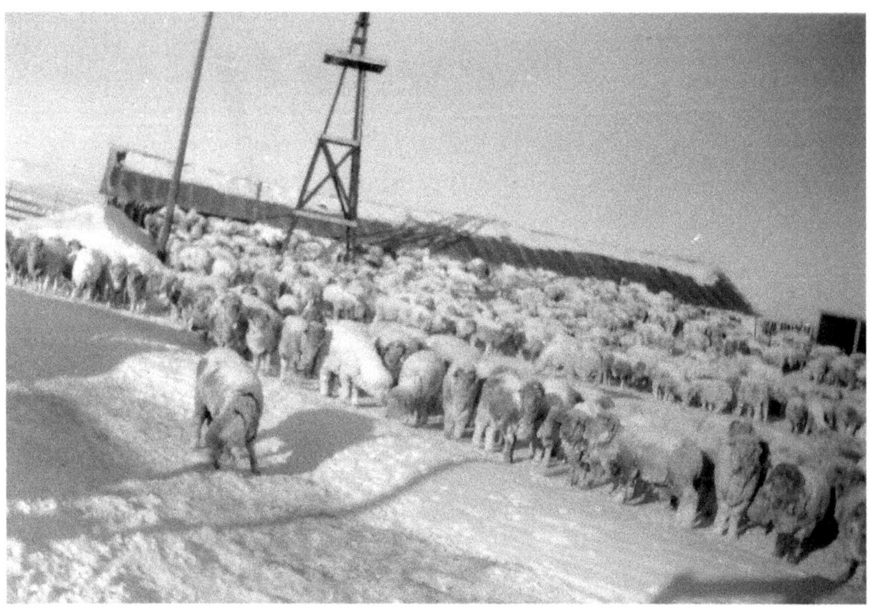

Hundreds of sheep move about the ranch freely as drifts cover up fences. *Courtesy of Senator Fred Emerich.*

empty. Carroll and Mary realized they needed to move to action if they were going to survive in the trailer. They quickly got their jeep dug out from a drift, which at this point had not been completely covered over with snow. Carroll was able to get the jeep running and made his way into town for provisions. Snowplows in Laramie did their best to keep the roads clear, but it was a losing battle, with the wind pushing snow right back where they had previously plowed. The first place the Rahms made their way to was a local grocery to buy what necessities they needed. Mary Carroll's mother recalled she still had the rubber boots on that covered her shoes, but her feet were nearly frozen with such little protection from the frigid temperatures. After buying food and other supplies, they made their way back to their trailer. Now they could bundle up and wait out the storm. However, that is not what happened. Mary Carroll's father unloaded their groceries and supplies and then started going to other couples' homes and driving them to and from the grocery store so they could stock up as well on resources to survive the blizzard. Mary Carroll's mother continued to convey her story to her daughter, stating, "It was an awful weather experience of our young lives. Mary Carroll, you have never experienced anything that bad, nor have you had to walk to school in anything that high [referring to the snowdrifts]. The

Blizzard of '49 was something that will be a story you should remember to tell others, and I bet it will be on record as the worst ever." Of course, Mary Carroll, seeking verification, looked to her dad with disbelief, and he would simply say, "You better believe it." Although her parents have passed, which is certainly sad, Mary Carroll says, "I still have their stories to cheer me up because they were so real."[31]

The blizzard affected not only the populated areas but also many of the rural areas and ranches just miles from many Wyoming towns. Pearl Platt, a resident of Cheyenne living at 1202 East Twenty-Third Street, informed reporters that she and her husband, Jack, were stranded two miles north of the highway junction between Cheyenne and Chugwater on Sunday night, January 2. Pearl stated there were forty-two others stranded along the highway in their vehicles. That evening, many of the travelers sought refuge in their cars, while others waited in the stalled Trailways bus intended to pick up passengers of another bus that was in an accident that same afternoon. Among those who decided to take shelter on the bus that night were the Platts. Pearl conveyed the story of how cold the temperature became on the bus. She stated that the passengers cut up toolboxes from a Gallagher truck, burning them in a bucket to warm the fifteen passengers enduring the bitter cold.[32]

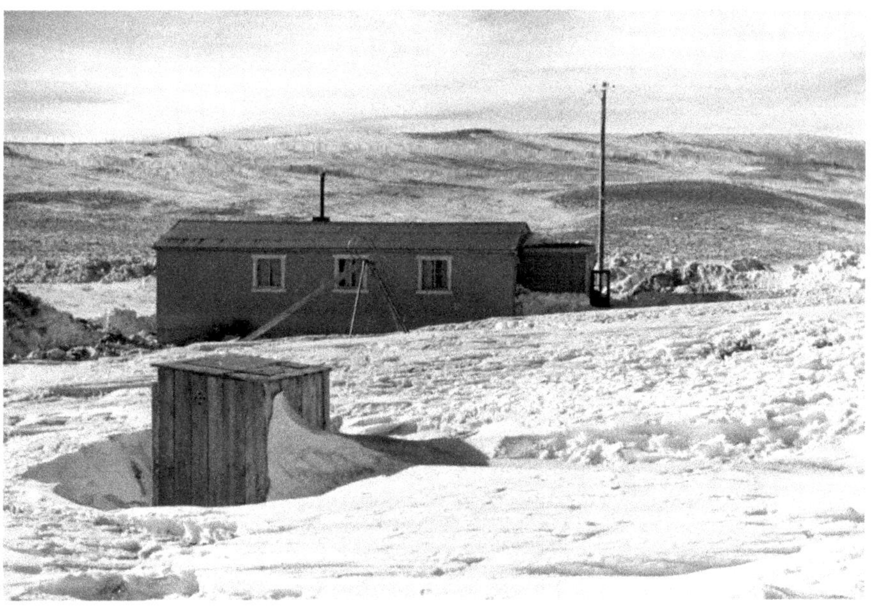

The school and outhouse for children living at the mining camp. *Courtesy of John Moyer.*

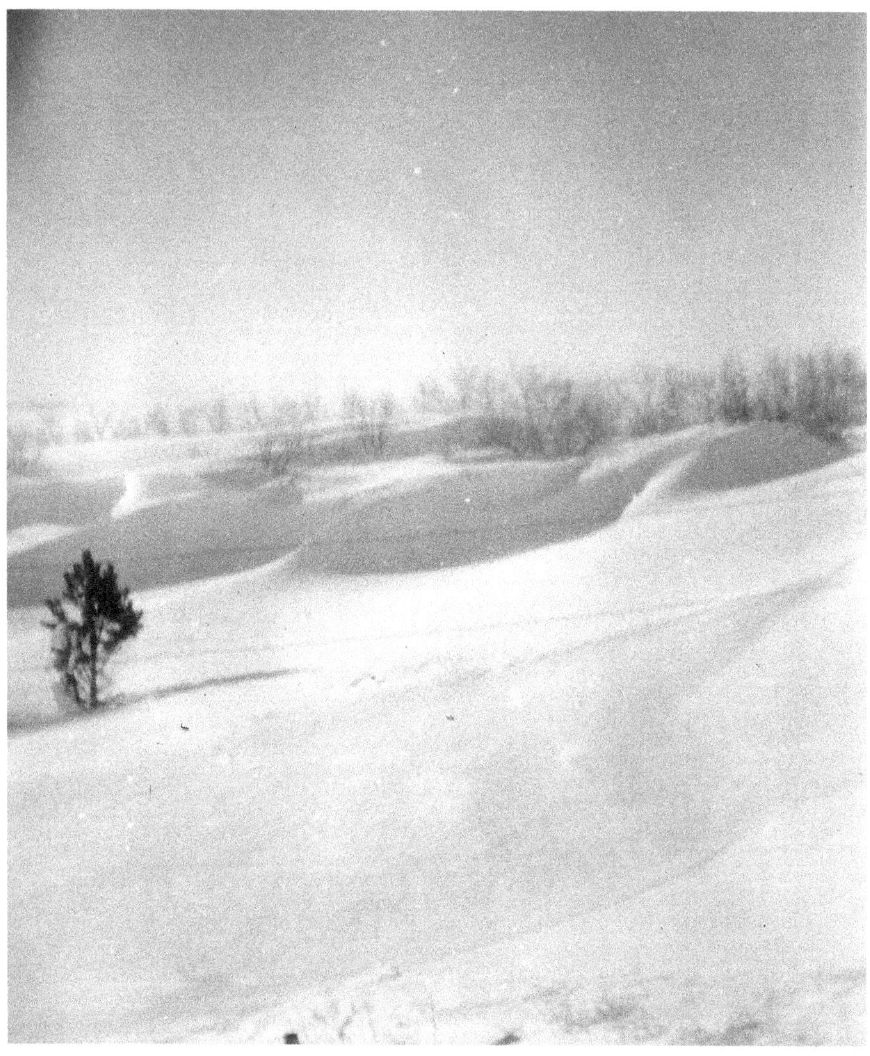

A line of trees on the Emerich ranch nearly buried beneath snowdrifts. *Courtesy of Senator Fred Emerich.*

On Monday afternoon, Grieg Thompson, one of the stranded motorists with the Platt family, remembered that before his vehicle stalled, he had seen a dairy farm in the near vicinity. Thompson set out through the drifts to find what was the Reymore Dairy Ranch, owned and operated by Mr. and Mrs. Clyde Karish. Once Thompson discovered the location of the ranch, he quickly returned to his fellow travelers. With the help of Ernest Robinson, an employee at the Reymore Dairy Ranch, they assisted the stranded motorists

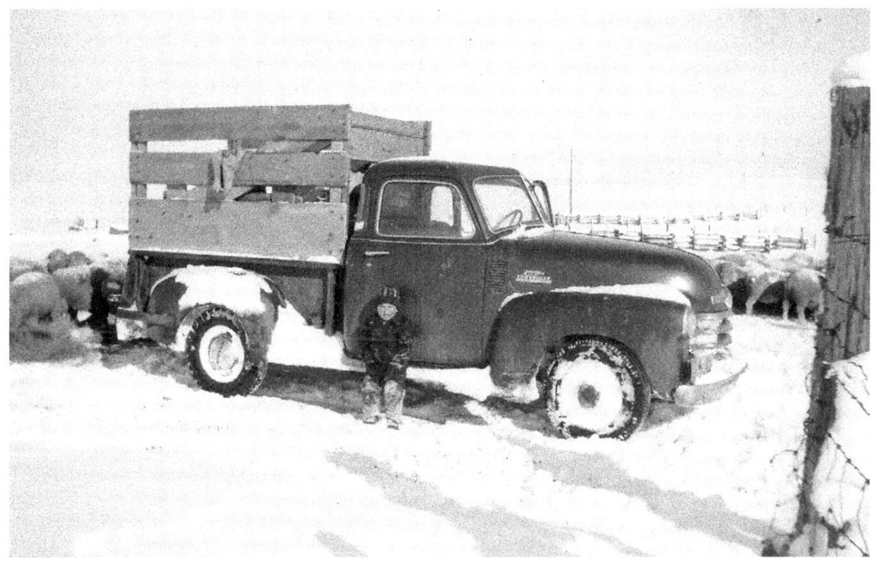

Fred Emerich stands beside a three-quarter-ton truck. Notice the advertisement for local Cheyenne car dealership Tyrell Doyle. *Courtesy of Senator Fred Emerich.*

to the ranch, which was about a quarter mile from where they were stranded. All but one carload of passengers preferred the shelter of the ranch to their cars. One of the stranded motorists, Goldy Fox, mother of Charles Fox of Cheyenne, had to be carried to the ranch. Of the forty-two passengers, she was one of eight who had to be removed to the hospital due to frostbite and frozen extremities. Those who decided to stay in their vehicles had sleeping bags, and when the others left for the ranch, they seemed comfortable with their accommodations. However, they soon realized that staying in their vehicles was not a great idea, and the following day, they made their way to the ranch with the other motorists.

Platt stated that everyone fared quite well at the ranch and was comfortable. She noted, "We were plenty warm, and some of the men chopped wood and kept the fires going while others milked the cows and did the chores." By Tuesday, Platt said, "we were out of food except for milk."[33] Attempting to lodge forty-two people in a four-bedroom house had to be quite an undertaking on the part of the Karishes, but Platt once again seemed upbeat about the accommodations. She stated, "We had sanitary facilities, but the electricity had failed the first night of the storm." There was a gas lantern and kerosene lamp they were able to use to provide light in the dark house. Pearl said, "We spread blankets on the floor of the living room and adjoining bedroom, and we slept in shifts."[34] It is hard to imagine a group this size working together in such close quarters without food, electricity or bedding. These conditions show how disaster brings out the good in so many people.

Several men in the party understood assistance was needed and left the safety of the ranch to find help in the blinding storm. The men found access to a telephone and called for help. Later on that same day, members of the Wyoming National Guard flew in food and medical supplies due in part to distress signals devised by the stranded passengers that could be seen from the air by pilots and crew members. Along with providing the medical supplies, the National Guard was able to alert the authorities that ambulances were needed to move certain individuals to hospitals due to their conditions. The first eight passengers requiring medical attention were taken by the first ambulances that arrived. Platt went on to tell reporters that an ambulance returned the following day for the remainder of the group, taking them back to Cheyenne. These passengers, however, were not in need of medical attention.

After nearly four days at the Reymore Dairy Ranch, Platt said the passengers who were still waiting for assistance in digging out their vehicles

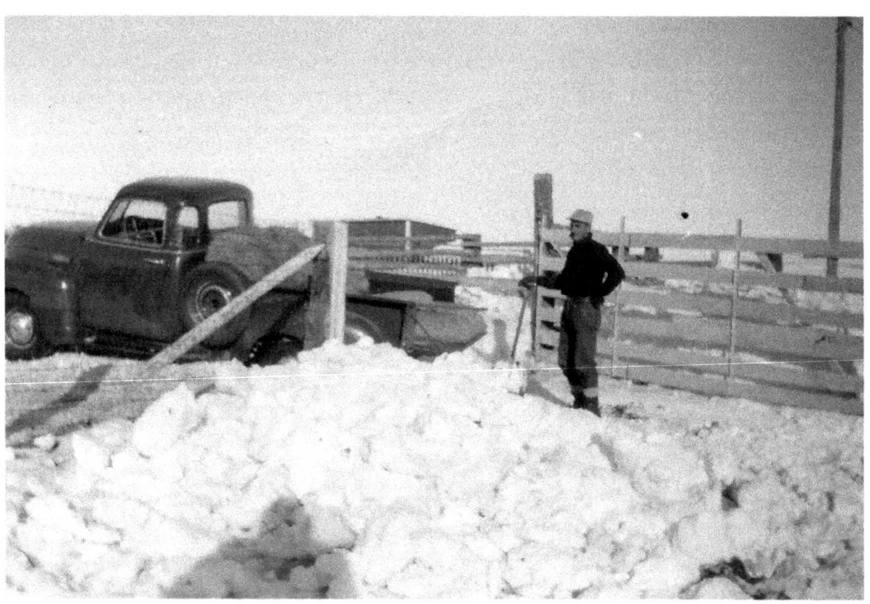

Carl Emerich moving hay to sheep on the family ranch. *Courtesy of Senator Fred Emerich.*

helped the Karishes clean up their home and dig out their barn and other outbuildings. She also stated that she was hopeful she would have her car out of the snow the following day. Among the stranded were several college students, and per Platt, five were going to stay with the Karish family there at the ranch until their vehicles were dug out of the drifts on the highway. Platt continued her story with one final note. Historians would often like to thank those who go to such detail, as she named each of those who were stranded with her at the Reymore Dairy Ranch. Those who spent four long days there in Chugwater were Mr. and Mrs. W.D. Tredwey; Charles, Evelyn, Bill and

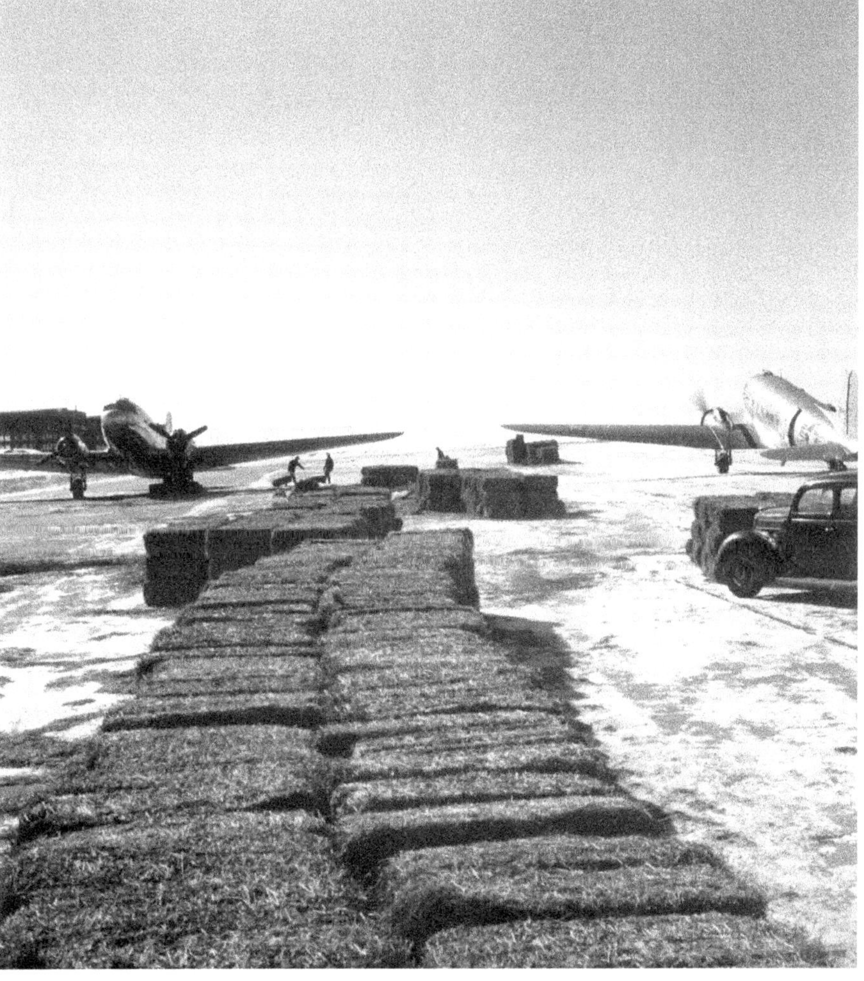

Operation Haylift, which brought in hay from La Junta, Colorado, for starving animals. *Courtesy of Chuck Morrison, Morrison Collection, Casper College Western History Center.*

Goldy Fox; Evelyn McClane; Bob and Kay Powell; Peggy Powell; Bob and Kay Brubaker; Mr. and Mrs. Ernest Robinson; Stan Davis; Dale Mackey; Marvin Jageler; Morris Goeman; Gladys Greenlee; Hugh Bird; Brad Spear; Bob Ross; James Carson; Ike Hackenberger; D.C. Hicks; Duane and Jean Cole; Andrea Malcomb; Grieg Thompson; Barbara Scott; Bert and Edna Peters; Helen Vogt; and Dick Marcotte.

Helen Vogt was one of the forty-two passengers who spent a vast majority of the first week of January 1949 in a four-room ranch house with the Platts and others stranded near Chugwater. Helen stated to the paper that she had left Wheatland on Sunday, headed to Cheyenne to pick up her two children, Eddie and Louise, who had been visiting with family there in town during the recent holidays. As Helen headed toward Cheyenne, her vehicle became stuck in a drift near Pole Creek, but through the kindness of a passing motorist, she was assisted in removing her car. Sometime around eleven o'clock on Sunday evening, as the storm continued, Helen again found herself and her vehicle in a drift. This time, neither she nor anyone else could help get the car removed from the drift. Following close behind Vogt in another vehicle were three young students from northern Wyoming. The three took shelter with Vogt in her car, where they stayed until Monday afternoon. Just as Platt mentioned, several were suffering from frostbite, including Vogt, who said her hands and feet were nearly frozen from the frigid temperatures. She said most people were comfortable and did well, but by Tuesday they were out of food, with the exception of milk. Vogt described the condition of the food delivered by the Wyoming National Guard, who had seen the makeshift distress signals in the snow. She said the crate of potatoes dropped was smashed, causing several ladies to stay up late that evening peeling the potatoes so they did not go to waste. The container storing the bags of spaghetti, beans and rice also broke, tearing open the bags and mixing all the contents. According to Vogt, quite a lot of time was spent in sorting out each of the contents into some type of organized manner. Once they were all taken to Cheyenne on Wednesday, she stayed with her sister and children until Saturday and then headed back home to Wheatland, Wyoming.

While families like the Platts and Vogts found safety in homes of strangers in ranches spread across parts of Wyoming, others found safety in the fate of those who happened to be in the right place at the right time. One such individual was Dr. Allen M. Boyden, a physician from Portland, Oregon. Dr. Allen and his son Frank were en route from Chicago when their train, the City of Portland, was delayed by massive snowdrifts in Egbert,

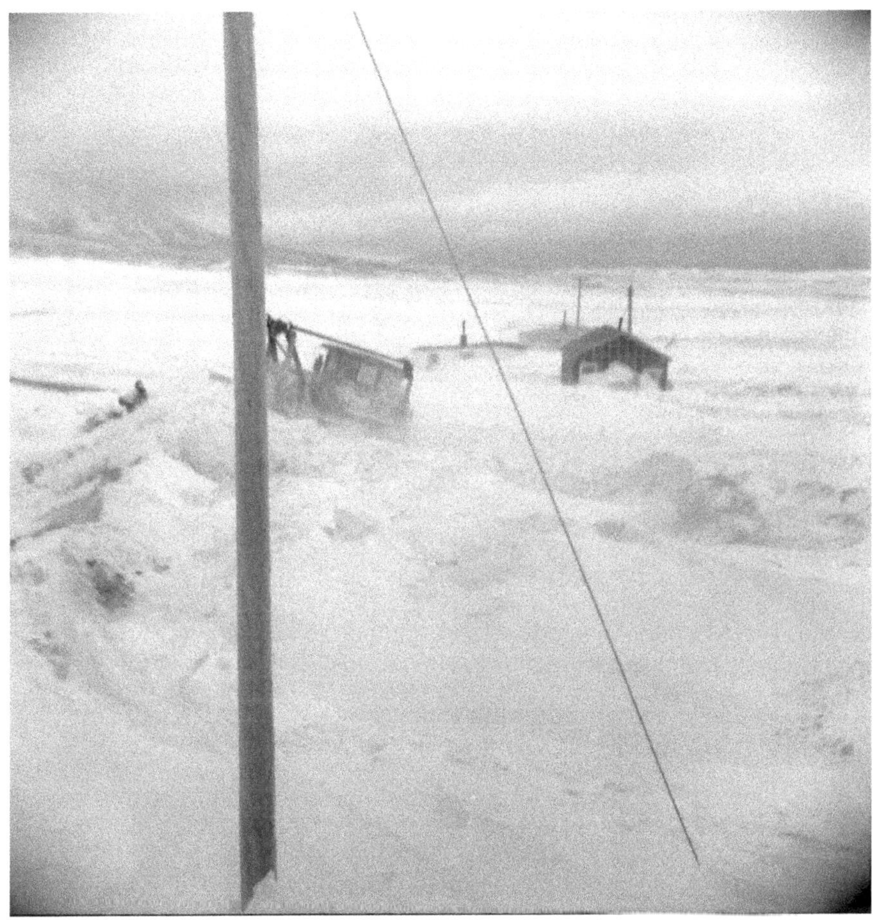

A Caterpillar bulldozer attempting to clear large drifts. *Courtesy of John Moyer.*

Wyoming. John Snyder, a Denver staff writer, interviewed Dr. Boyden upon his arrival in Cheyenne after the passengers were rescued from their snowy encampment in the small town. Dr. Boyden described how a child was born while they were stranded and stated that the delivery of the baby was "little trouble." Charles M. Rohrbaugh, the father of the baby, approached the doctor soon after the City of Portland was stranded. Rohrbaugh knew that all roads leading into Egbert were impassable from the heavy drifts and Dr. Boyden was the only physician available to assist his wife in the delivery. Dr. Boyden recalled during the interview, "Everything went smoothly until Wednesday afternoon, and then the labor pains started, and we knew it would not be long." Two hours later, Mr. and Mrs. Rohrbaugh were

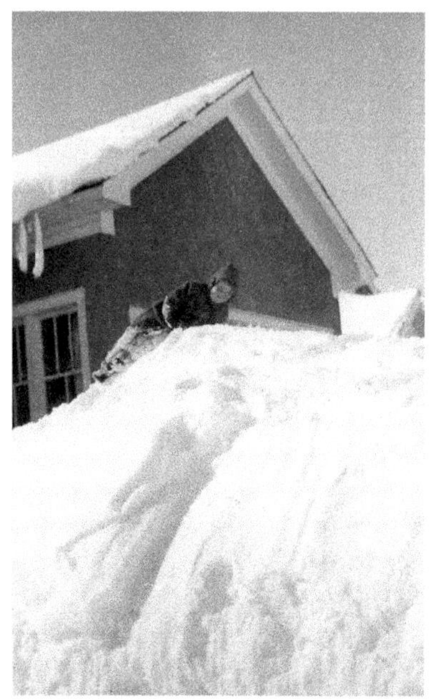

Left: One of the Dudley children sledding down a steep drift near their home in Laramie, Wyoming. *Courtesy of Richard Felter.*

Below: Homes buried in snowdrifts. *Courtesy of John Moyer.*

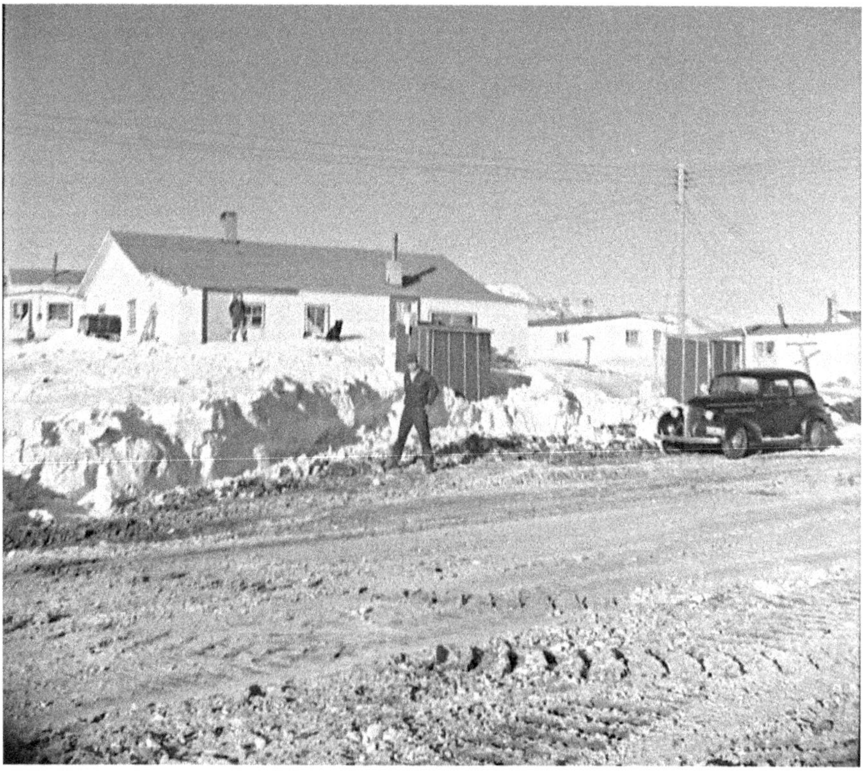

the parents of a five-pound, six-ounce girl, promptly named Anita Jean. Dr. Boyden was assisted by two nurses, Beverly Anderson of Omaha, Nebraska, and Shirley Detlefson of Hastings, Nebraska, who were also stranded passengers aboard the City of Portland. Snyder concluded his article by giving his readers a better understanding of why Dr. Boyden did not hesitate in assisting in delivering the baby and also assisting where he could on the train. Snyder reported, "Dr. Boyden left his Astoria practice in 1942 to enter the United States Army. Boyden served in Africa, Sicily, and the European continent during the war, leaving the service in 1945 with the rank of major. A graduate of the University of Michigan medical school, Dr. Boyden located in Portland after the war. He joined the staff of the Portland clinic in July 1948 and currently lived at 4091 S.W. Greenleaf Drive there in Portland." Snyder highlighted Dr. Boyden's service to the country during World War II, which had just recently ended, and made him a hometown hero not only to those living in Portland but also to so many throughout Wyoming and abroad.

Bill Mill, the owner of the Silver Tip Refinery, was driving home with his wife and daughter when they became marooned in Torrington. They had gotten as far as the Y at the Huntley-Cheyenne highway when the storm intensified, forcing them to turn back to Torrington to seek shelter. There they joined another group for the night at the Trail Hotel as they settled in for the evening.

Another motorist stranded near Torrington that evening was Doug Essert, the son of Mr. and Mrs. Bill Essert of Yoder, Wyoming. Doug, who attended Denver University, had started out to Denver from Torrington on Sunday night. He had managed to get eleven miles south of the Silver Tip Refinery when, as Doug stated, he had to "give up the battle."[35] Realizing he could go no farther, Doug pulled his vehicle into a garage there at the refinery and stayed the night. He realized there was no one there but discovered there was sufficient fuel oil for heat and food. The following morning when Doug awoke, he found his car inaccessible since the snow had drifted and created a blockade, preventing him from moving his vehicle. He made a telephone call to his parents in Yoder to explain his quandary and his delayed arrival to school. The Mills called from Torrington to Doug there at the refinery, informing him it was best to stay there and "hold down the fort."[36] Oral Yates, who was an employee at the refinery, made a heroic two-mile trek from Yoder to the refinery. There, he and Doug waited out the storm until they could make their way home.

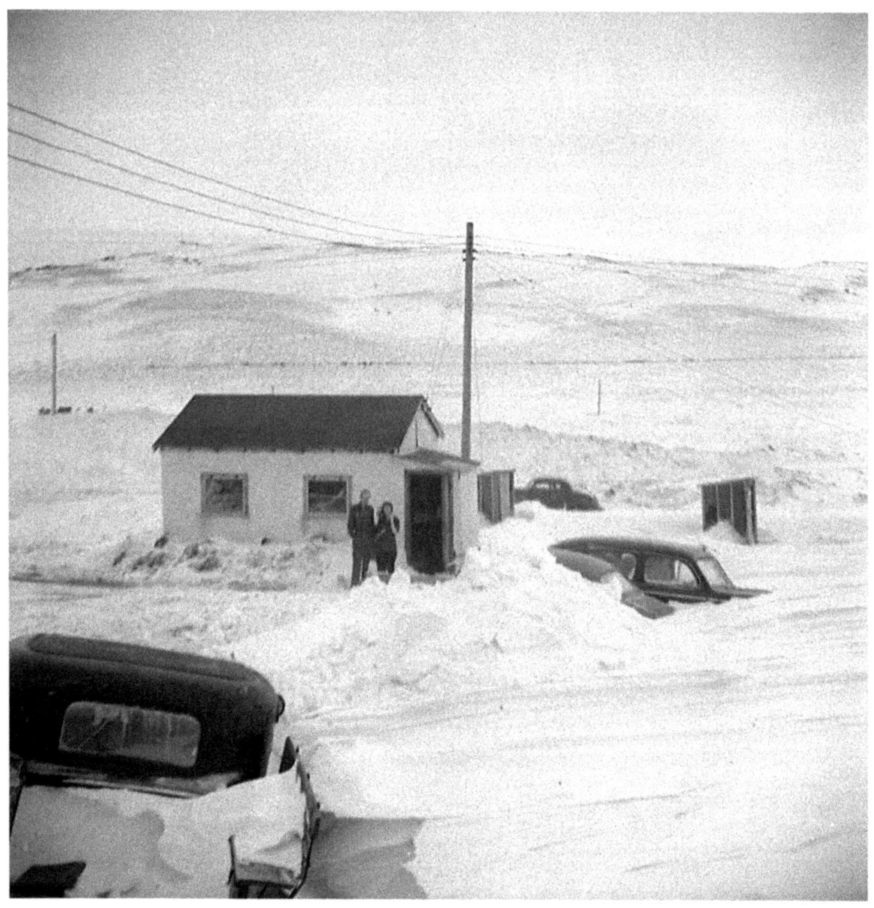

Automobiles stuck in snowdrifts in the mining camp. *Courtesy of John Moyer.*

Throughout the storm, many had to improvise ways to keep warm, go to the bathroom and look for food and water. Vaughn Burgess from Niobrara County, Wyoming, spent some forty-plus hours in his vehicle along with a Mr. Winter just south of Cheyenne on Highway 80. Burgess and Winter were leaving Torrington for Fort Collins, Colorado, on a business trip. Burgess's account indicates they were about seven miles outside Torrington when they were overcome by the storm. Hoping to reach Cheyenne before the storm intensified, Burgess and his companion forged ahead. They continued toward Cheyenne, but the blizzard continued to grow stronger as the snow and wind became a critical factor and the storm decreased the visibility not only for Burgess but also for other motorists along the same route. As the

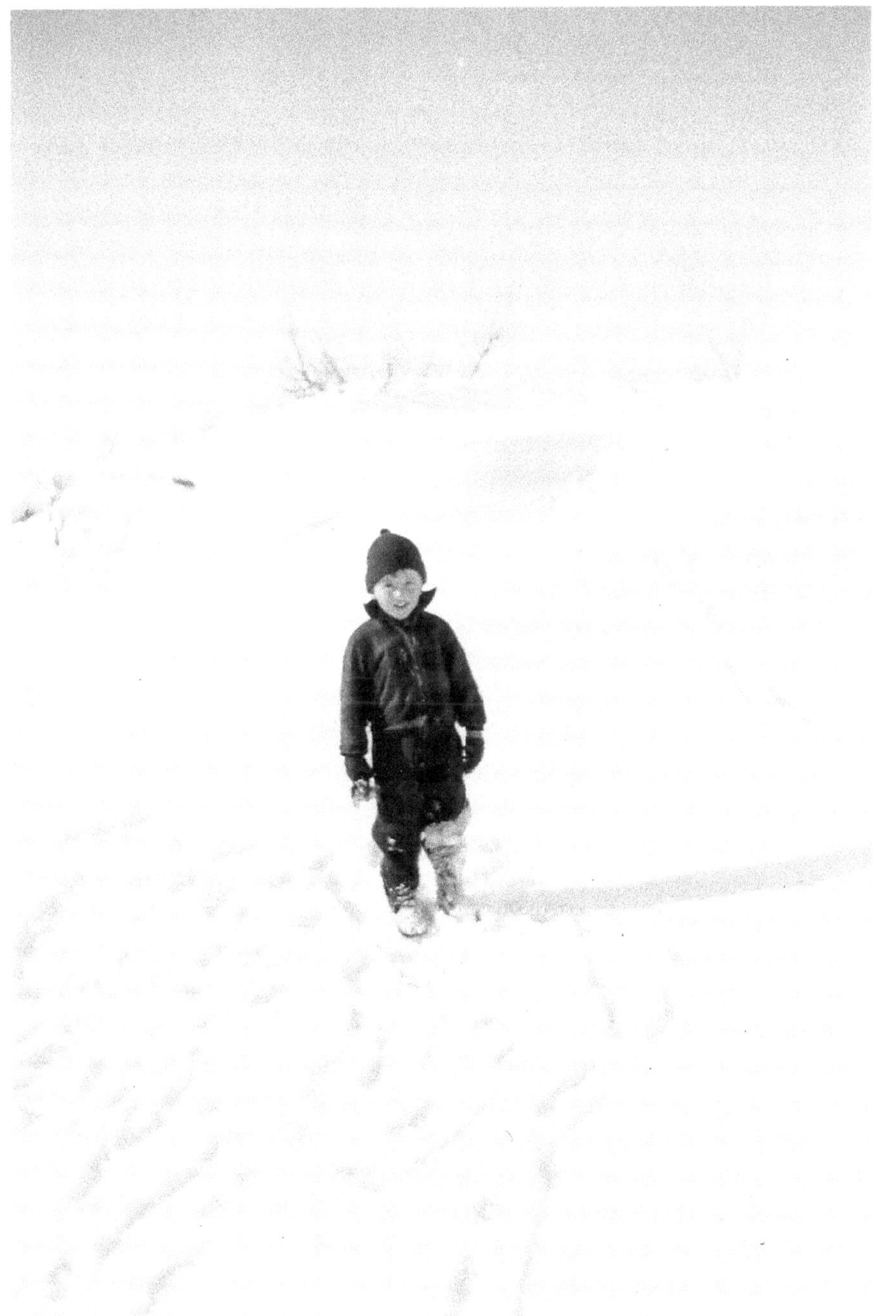

Fred Emerich walking on another monstrous drift near his home; notice the treetops just behind Fred. *Courtesy of Senator Fred Emerich.*

two men continued down the road, they began to see other cars that had stalled and whose passengers could not navigate through the blinding snow. Vaughn made the decision to pick up two men and a woman with a small child they found sitting in their stalled vehicles waiting for rescue. Burgess and his group made their way down the road, but soon the car stalled in the heavy drifts, leaving the party stranded on a highway. Their only hope was that someone traveling down the road could assist them.

Burgess and those in the vehicle began their long wait, but as the hours turned into days, fear of not being rescued began to enter their minds. With no heat in the car, the group grew weary as the hours passed. The snow found its way through the cracks of the windows in the car, and soon their clothes became wet from the snow that had blown in. They managed with no food, but the lack of water was difficult. However, someone in the group thought of an idea with the snow that was coming in the vehicle. Although the snow was cold, it was a perfect way to stay hydrated. Everyone continued to eat the snow to quench their thirst and attempt to quell their appetites. They had been on the road for nearly two days when Dave Cook, a foreman at the Warren Livestock Company ranch just north of Cheyenne, and six ranch employees reached the highway to assist Burgess and his group, along with twenty-six other stranded motorists. Cook and his men assisted the motorists and guided them back to the ranch through the continued blinding snow.

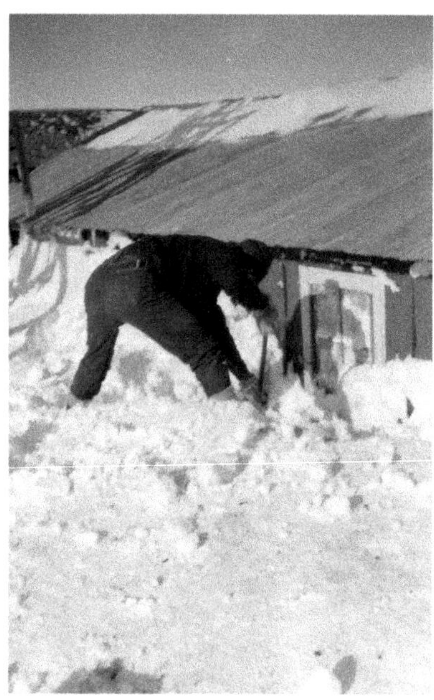

Fred's father, Carl Emerich, digging out the door to the barn. *Courtesy of Senator Fred Emerich.*

As Burgess, stated, "Without the aid and care of the men at the Warren ranch, many people would have died." He continued by saying, "We received food, warm blankets, medicine and cigarettes free of charge!" It was not until later on the next day that employees on the ranch were able to repair broken phone lines on the ranch and those who were taking shelter there were able to call out to family and friends to report their safety. There were several in the group who required medical attention and were taken to Cheyenne the next day on Thursday, January 6. Although isolated at times, several ranches across Wyoming came to the aid of stranded victims of the blizzard.[37]

In today's world of smartphones, tablets and other forms of communication, it is difficult to understand not being able to reach someone during a weather disaster. However, during the Blizzard of 1949, the telephone was the only means of reaching someone to find out his or her plight. Many times, during the snowstorm, friends and families did not know where individuals were and if they were stranded somewhere and needed assistance or were safe and warm in their own homes or that of a good Samaritan. This exact scenario took place in Torrington, Wyoming, on January 9–12. For seventy-two hours, Forest and Grace McIntosh were unaware of the whereabouts of their twenty-two-year-old son Marv McIntosh, a University of Wyoming student. With the blizzard raging, their worst fears as a parent were made real. However, they did not know that twenty-five miles north of Cheyenne, Marv was safe and warm from the elements in a farmhouse he had reached. With no telephone there at the farmhouse, Marv was unable to contact his parents and put them at ease regarding his whereabouts and that he was safely out of the blizzard. Marv had left Torrington sometime around two o'clock in the afternoon on Sunday, January 2, on his way to Cheyenne the day of the blizzard. During his journey, the storm came up, and before he arrived, he was unable to see the road to drive. At some point, Marv's car began to stall, and eventually he had to pull over because his vehicle could go no farther as the snow started to build up. Fortunately for Marv, when he stopped, he saw the light of a farmhouse in the distance just beyond the road. He made the decision rather than wait out the storm in his vehicle to take his chances to head toward the farmhouse and take refuge there. His quick thinking paid off, as he made it to the farmhouse just as the storm picked up intensity.

On Wednesday morning, just after the storm passed, Forest McIntosh was aboard a plane to search for Marv. The pilot flew the aircraft low along the highway, which was now only a snowbank rather than a route for transportation. As they flew along the path, Forest spotted Marv's car buried in the snow. There are no indications of what Mr. McIntosh did upon detecting Marv's car, but it is not hard to imagine the emotions and thoughts that flooded his mind. Marv caught a ride from the ranch into Cheyenne, where he phoned his parents and let them know of his adventure and that

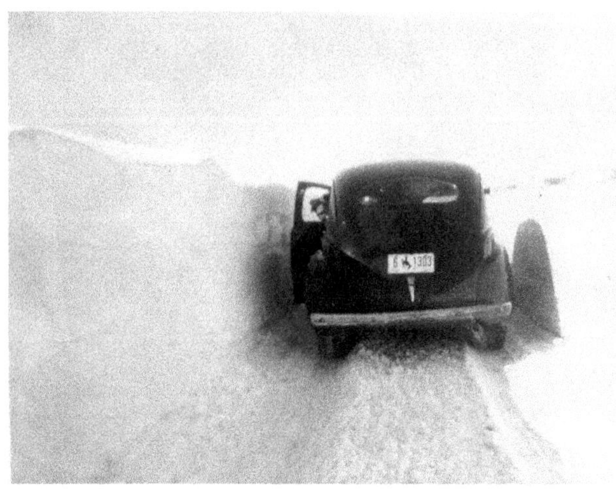

Driving down cleared roads beside large snowdrifts. *Courtesy of Karen Kruel.*

he was safe from any harm. That phone call was something they had been anticipating for many days, and the relief they felt to know their son was safe in Cheyenne must have been overwhelming.[38]

Wayne Yohe a twenty-five-year-old man from Glen, Nebraska, froze to death during the blizzard. Yohe's name and the picture of his frozen body appeared in papers across Wyoming and other media sources throughout the United States. The Yohes, who had been driving a load of hogs to Denver on Sunday, January 2, hit a stalled vehicle as they headed down the highway. Yohe's would-be savior's name was not as widespread. The efforts of Merl Peters, who had been driving on the Cheyenne highway on January 3, saved not only his own life but three others and nearly that of Wayne Yohe. Peters was coming from Torrington in his Melton Oil transport truck and was nineteen miles north of Cheyenne when he came upon Yohe and his family in their stalled vehicle. Peters placed the Yohe family and a young college student by the name of Melvin Carlson from Boulder, Colorado, in the cab of his truck. Young Carlson had accepted his fate, believing death would come soon. Peters reassured Carlson, telling him there was hope and he would save him from dying. After just one night in the close quarters of the truck cab, Yohe became frantic. He exited the vehicle into the blizzard without any apprehension for his safety. Peters stated that he restrained Yohe on two separate attempts to leave the truck, but to no avail; Yohe abandoned the group. Peters assumed Yohe was seeking temporary shelter or was fearful of the current conditions he and his family were in. According to an interview with Peters's daughter, Merl made every effort to keep Yohe from leaving

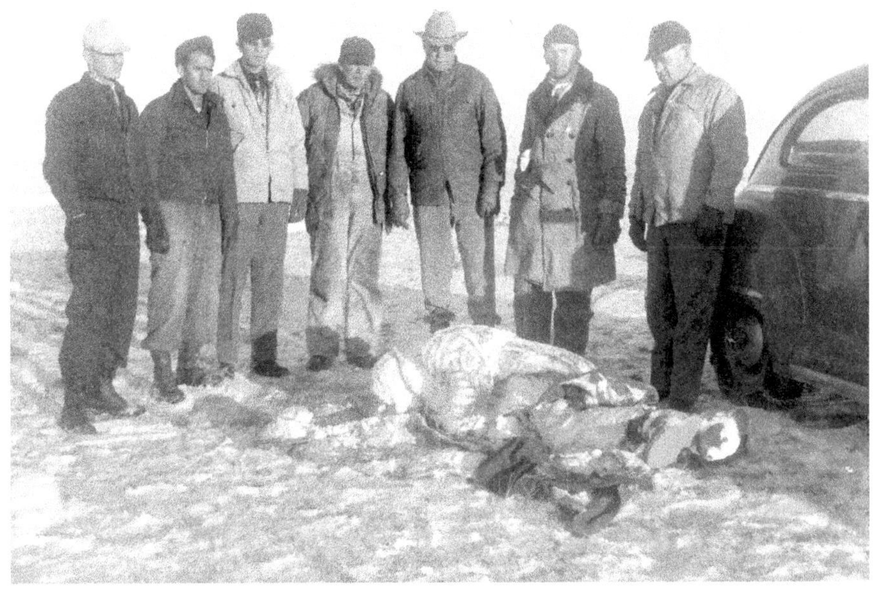

The frozen body of Wayne Yohe was found in snowdrifts. *Francis Steele Brammar, courtesy of Wyoming State Archives.*

the safety of the truck. Merl's efforts were to no avail, as Yohe insisted he had to go for help.

Yohe left behind in the vehicle his wife, Rosetta; four-year-old daughter, Theresa Ann; Carlson; and Peters, who were attempting to stay warm under heavy quilts. By Wednesday afternoon when the storm subsided, the motley crew had survived the cold and hunger they had endured the last few days. Merl, according to his daughter, always carried a box of food in his truck. Merl relayed to his daughter years after the blizzard that he had gotten out of the truck to retrieve the box of food from the tool compartment on the side of the truck. Merl said that he had pulled the box out of the compartment and had set it on the ground to close the door where the food had been stored. However, the wind and snow were blowing so hard that Merl was unable to locate the box on the ground and had to return to the truck without it. Thinking quickly regarding the survival of the group, Merl utilized the truck's heater to melt the snow in order to help keep everyone hydrated. The snow, however, did not relieve the hunger pains of those stranded in the truck, and Merl told of how young Theresa cried because she was hungry. Merl, in an effort to ease the child's hunger, was able to find a candy bar and some gum in the truck's glove box. Reports revealed that Yohe had made his way to the ranch house of an elderly couple. When Yohe realized the couple had no phone, he became hysterical, as he insisted he needed to get to a phone so he could reach someone to assist his family and other members of the party. Yohe, desperate to find help, headed out to yet another location; however, this time he did not reach his final destination. Yohe's body was discovered on Tuesday afternoon the following week in a ten-foot drift near the Warren Pole Creek ranch. The fate of Yohe was tragic, but the determination of the other four was noteworthy. Even when starved and fatigued from the bitter cold and lack of food, they survived on eating frost scraped from the windows until their rescue. As the years passed, Merl's daughter said that every Christmas after the blizzard, Rosetta would send a card to the Peterses that included a letter letting them know how she and Theresa were getting along since that fateful week in 1949.[39]

Heroism abounded during the blizzard, coming from all directions. A local rancher took the spotlight with his efforts to save a family stranded on the highway nearly a half mile from his ranch. Forn Marlatt, a well-known rancher in Goshen County, owned a ranch sixteen miles north of Fort Laramie, Wyoming. The *Goshen County News* stated, "Mr. Marlatt at the risk of physical injury and possible life went to stalled vehicle outside his ranch to rescue a mother and her three little children." According to the article, few could have battled the storm and made such painful and tedious effort in his mission as did Marlatt. No sooner had Marlatt brought the family back to his ranch than he had the woman back on a horse and subsequently led them through another precarious set of routes of blowing snow and frigid temperatures to Guernsey, Wyoming, for medical treatment. The trip, of course, could not be taken over the normal route but through "ridge country" to avoid the unsurmountable snowdrifts that blocked the route typically taken. The paper proudly credited Marlatt with saving four lives during the Blizzard of 1949.[40]

Stories of stranded motorists in Wyoming were reported across the United States. A Windsor, Colorado paper told of the Reisig family, who were returning from Scottsbluff, Nebraska, after the funeral of Mrs. Reisig's mother and became stranded in Wyoming. The Reisigs had decided to stay after the funeral for the family's New Year's Day family reunion. The day after the party, those relatives living out of town headed to their homes. According to Mrs. Reisig, there were fourteen cars in the motorcade.

The Reisigs made it as far as the small town of Meridian, Wyoming, some forty-five miles northeast of Cheyenne. The family was able to find shelter with fourteen other stranded motorists in a small cabin. The group kept themselves sustained on potato chips, canned meat, fish and milk. The Reisigs' eighteen-month-old child's diet consisted of just canned milk while they were stranded in the cabin. During the time the group was stranded, several of the men made their way to a nearby creek to get water for the group. Upon their return to the cabin, they said they had witnessed the horrific sight of at least forty head of cattle frozen solid in the creek.

By Wednesday, the food supply and the fuel for heat were nearly expended, but the group heard the sounds of a plane engine as it approached their location. When the plane was heard, several of the men quickly rushed out of the cabin and formed a line in an attempt to signal the plane. Seeing the stranded families, the pilot dropped a list of code signals to the group. Once the men received the list, they quickly rearranged the vehicles in the

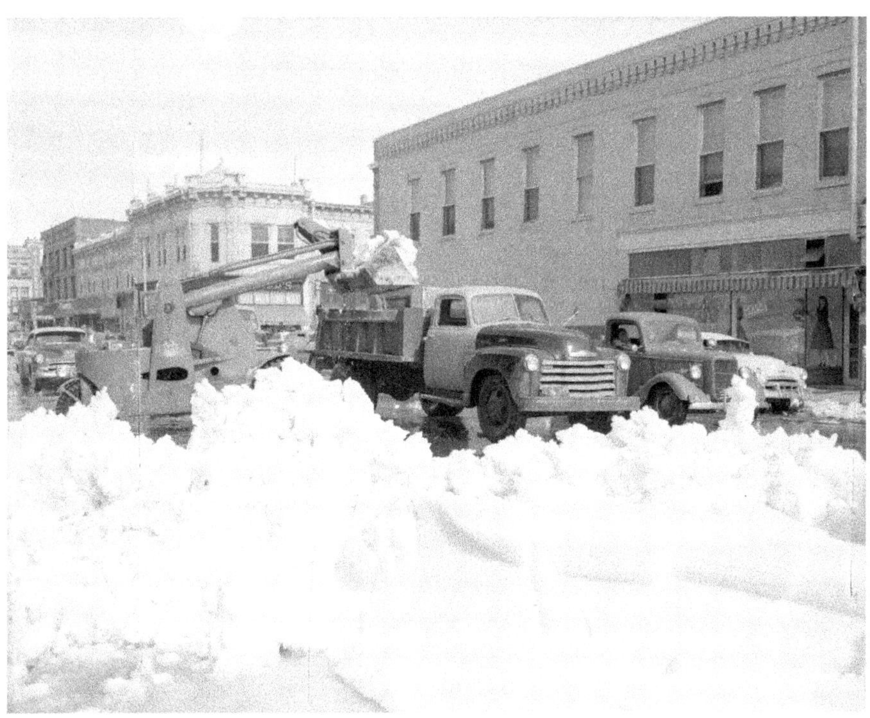

Hauling away snow, downtown Cheyenne. *Francis Steele Brammar, courtesy of Wyoming State Archives.*

shape of the letter L, which indicated they were in desperate need of fuel. The following day, the wonderful sound of a convoy of snowplows was heard as they cleared the path, making their way to the marooned group. Although the Reisigs were held up in Cheyenne for an additional night due to the storm, the following day they headed out, arriving safely home in Nebraska.[41]

Mistakes are not what most would consider a blessing, but that was the case for John Anderson, an employee of the Gulf Exploration Company. Fortunately for John, when he came to the Y intersection just south of Gillette, Wyoming, on Wednesday, January 5, 1949, he inadvertently turned onto the Douglas highway and not Casper road, as he had intended. An article in the *Torrington Telegraph* states that Anderson may not have been discovered had he taken the highway to Casper.

After spending fifty hours in his car, Anderson was hungry and very chilled, to say the least. A crew with Peter Kiewit Son's company was working with bulldozers to clear the roads and spotted Anderson's car nearly buried in snow, which held Anderson captive. However, this was a blessing because it kept the vehicle warm. During the long duration inside his car, Anderson huddled under a blanket and quilt waiting for aid to come. When relief finally arrived, the engine was dead and snow had filled the exhaust. Anderson's rescuers said if he had taken the Casper road, he would have indeed frozen to death, since the route to Casper was "securely snowbound." This is another fantastic story of survival by someone who defied the odds during the blizzard.[42]

Other residents of sister states also found themselves stranded in Wyoming as a result of the blizzard. On January 6, three young people from Miles City, Montana, were stranded eight miles north of Cheyenne. The individuals in the vehicle were Jim Frisbie, Louis Gordy and Walter Magnuson. According to Walter's son Erik, the group was heading back after Christmas vacation to Boulder, Colorado, where they attended the University of Colorado–Boulder. Magnuson, who was born in Miles City, graduated from Custer County High School in 1942 and continued his education at St. Olaf College in Northfield, Minnesota. He earned a degree in chemistry and pursued a medical degree, which sent him to Columbia University Medical School in New York. There Walter met his bride-to-be, Sarah Elizabeth Sykes, who at the time was attending Women's Medical College of Pennsylvania in Philadelphia.[43] After Walter's short stay at Columbia, he was placed in a military technical school, where he learned diesel engineering and shipped out just after VJ Day.[44] After Walter's

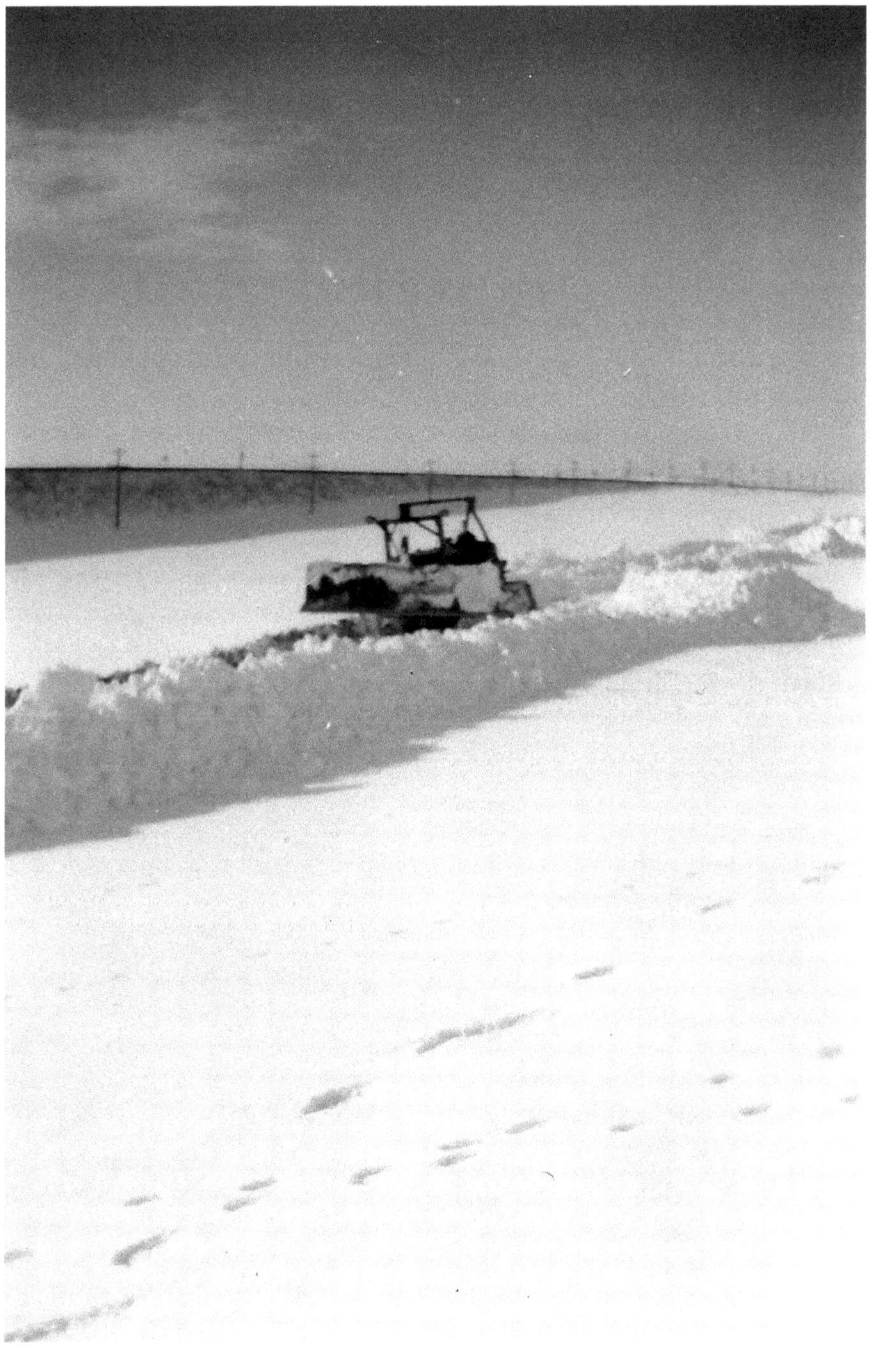

Clearing snow at the Emerich ranch. *Courtesy of Senator Fred Emerich.*

discharge from the Navy, he headed back to Miles City, where he became a high school teacher and made the decision to enroll at the University of Colorado–Boulder to pursue his doctorate.

Walter and his college peers coming off their Christmas break were headed back from Montana with plans to return to Boulder in time for classes, but this was not to be. The students left early on Sunday morning heading to Boulder, but that night, their vehicle stalled, and they were stuck just north of Cheyenne. Jim Frisbie, the driver, said they were traveling between two trucks as they made their way through Wyoming. As the storm increased in intensity, they lost sight of the truck following them. About the same time, they realized they could not see the front truck either. Within a matter of minutes, they came upon the leading truck to find it was stalled on the road. Realizing they could go no farther, they stayed in the vehicle until around three o'clock in the morning on Monday. By this time, their engine was frozen and could not be started. They decided not to stay in their vehicle and instead make their way by foot to the truck that had pulled over the evening before. When they got to the truck, they discovered the driver was not in the vehicle, apparently having set out on foot to look for shelter. The three took refuge in the cab of the truck as they waited for snowplows to clear the roads. All three were dressed warmly enough that staying warm was not an issue, as stated by Walter's son. Erik recalled his father had mentioned the paper embellished their story, making it a bit more dramatic than the reality of what happened. The real problem Walter relayed to his son was fighting boredom and figuring out how to "answer the call of nature," stating that one of the men stranded with Walter left the car to take care of his business and nearly did not make it back. Walter said he and his friends were certainly much more bored than scared of their situation.[45]

The blizzard was not without its fun and exciting times, as shown by an incident in Rawlins on February 1, 1949. Due to the storm and the heavy snow, transportation out of the city was stalled. Not only were just ordinary everyday individuals being held up because of the weather but famous people as well. One of the favorite personalities of the time happened to be in transit through Wyoming when the storm hit, stranding him and his wife in Rawlins. His name was Billy Bishop, aka "Bish the Magish" Bishop, who was known by name in the 1940s as a great master of magic. The storm had stalled Billy and his new bride, Ann, in their vehicle at Warriner's service station in town, where they met Harlan A. Warriner, owner of the gas station and president of the Rawlins Rotary Club. Bishop and his wife were en

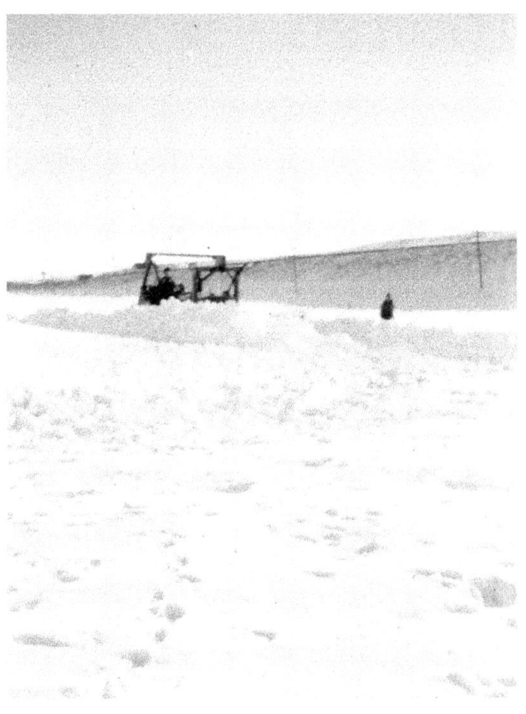

Left: A Wyoming National Guard soldier walks in front of a bulldozer. *Courtesy of Senator Fred Emerich.*

Below: A woman standing in a boat and waving on top of a large snowdrift. *Francis Steele Brammar, courtesy of Wyoming State Archives.*

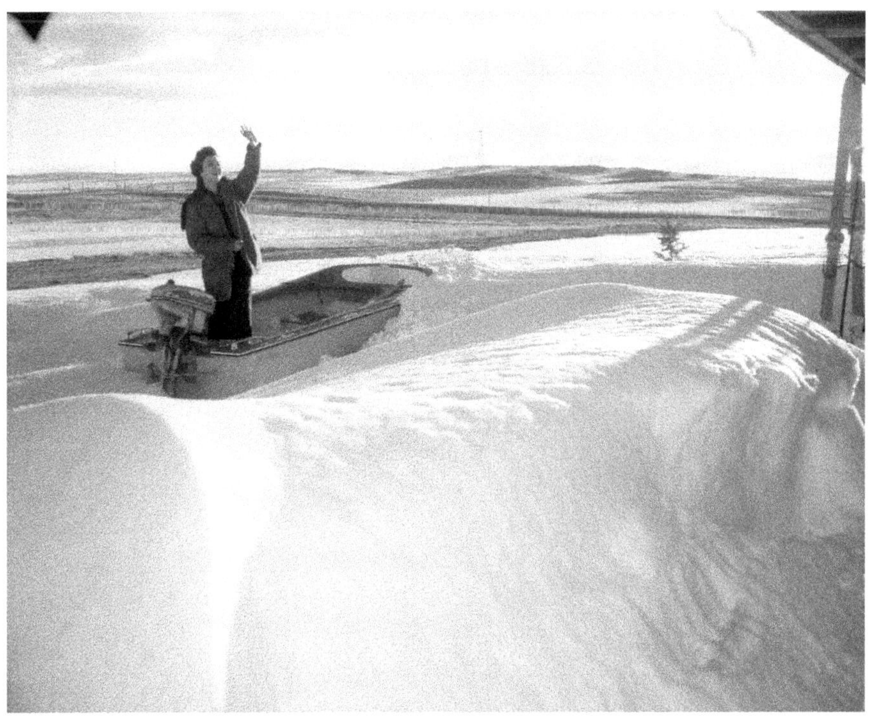

route from Portland, Oregon, to Denver, Colorado, when they were caught up in the storm and had to seek shelter.

Billy and Ann had met in Portland sometime back through their mutual manager, Earl Mossman. Earl had bumped into Ann on the streets of Portland one afternoon and informed her that he was headed to see a new show at the Capital Theater, a vaudeville theater. Earl invited Ann along to come see the show. Ann accepted the invitation and went to watch (unbeknownst to her) the man who would become her future husband, Billy Bishop. Ann and Billy were a perfect match; she was a dancer and singer, while Billy was a magician. Soon they were married and crossed the United States from one nightclub to another with Billy's show. Ann, who had not been part of the act, was learning the ropes and would soon be part of the stage act of "Billy Bishop and Ann." Leaving Portland, they made a stopover in Reno, Nevada, where the couple was robbed at gunpoint. After they survived this horrific incident, the thought may have crossed their minds that nothing else bad could possibly happen on this trip. As fate would have it, they found themselves in the middle of one of Wyoming's worst blizzards.

Warriner took the couple "under his wing" and ensured they were comfortable during their stay in Rawlins. Bishop was impressed with the assistance and hospitality shown to himself and his wife. The kindness made such an impact on Bishop that he called his manager, Jack Blue, in Denver, to tell him that the folks in Rawlins had been so hospitable. He wondered whether it would be a good idea to give the Rotary Club and their families a small magic show. Blue loved the idea.

The Rotarians and approximately twenty-five girls and boys enjoyed a $3.50 program free of charge. The *Rawlins Daily Times* stated, "Bish has a hat-full of good tricks too. His deceptions are quick, entertaining, and different from the 'old-lines' of magic." The paper indicated that Bishop's trickery was shy and boyish but still clever and entertaining. The Rotarians and their families enjoyed the magic performed by Bishop during his short stay. As the storm subsided and the roads cleared, the magician and his wife continued their trip to Denver. A handful of citizens in Rawlins had a chance to see the performance of "Bish the Magish" and passed this on to future generations as part of the Blizzard of 1949 legacy. Billy and Ann traveled on after the blizzard to Denver and eventually to New York City, and they also performed in the Catskills. Their act would premiere in some of the top nightspots of their day, including Billy Rose's Diamond Horseshoe Club in New York, the Palace Theater on Broadway and the Silver Cloud Room, eventually making its way onto television's *Toast of the Town*, which was the precursor to *The Ed Sullivan Show*. The state of Wyoming also hosted several other noted talents during the blizzard.

In Morgan, Utah, the local paper, the *Morgan County News*, was owned and operated by Albert W. Epperson, who had bought it only a few years earlier in 1947. In February 1949, he wrote an article about those who were stranded on the trains in Laramie, Wyoming. Epperson looked at the humorous side of what these passengers were dealing with rather than the problems that were receiving most of the coverage in papers across the nation. Albert Epperson found himself, along with 1,225 of his closest friends, stranded in Laramie on Sunday, February 6, 1949, due to the second wave of the blizzard that took place. Epperson stated that the trains stopped in Laramie at approximately 2:30 p.m. that Sunday for a delay, for what he and the other passengers assumed would only be a few hours at the most. He would later learn three other trains were stranded in Rawlins, Hannah and Sherman, Wyoming, just west of his location.

Epperson was returning from a Wyoming Press Association meeting in Cheyenne and was headed back home on what started out as an eight-hour trip to Utah. He pointed out to his readers that he had purchased a coach seat because of the short duration, not expecting any chance of overnight stay along the route. After several hours of waiting and no movement from the train, Epperson realized he should make some sleeping arrangements or his coach seat would be his bed for the evening. In his search for sleeping accommodations, he met a good friend of his from Salt Lake, Utah, Royal Chamberlain, who happened to be a traveling passenger agent, and explained his dilemma to his friend. Later on, as Epperson continued his search, Cy Forsythe, a Pullman conductor, informed him that Chamberlain had signed him up for the last train berth available on the train, which happened to be an upper berth, making Epperson very happy to have a place to lay his head for the night.

It was soon understood by the passengers that they were stranded indefinitely or at least until snowplows and train rotaries could reach the area. When the realization of this became apparent, many passengers, as Epperson stated, had to reach the "outside world." The Western Union telegraph station in Laramie became inundated with people sending out telegrams to friends, family and businesses, informing them of their current situation. In the first evening alone, $200 was paid in fees to send out telegrams by the stranded passengers.

That evening, word was posted by Union Pacific that the train would not be moving anytime before eight o'clock the next morning and the passengers

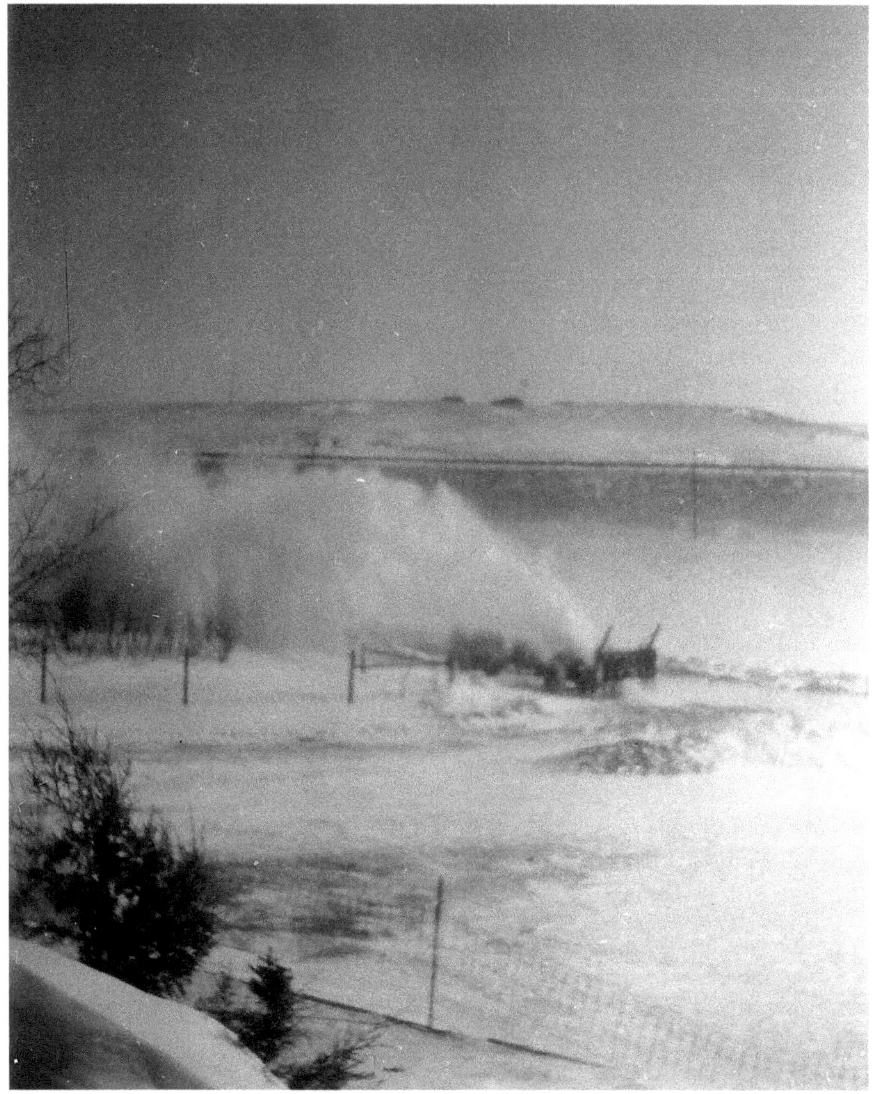

A Caterpillar bulldozer clearing Railroad Road just across from the Emerich residence. *Courtesy of Senator Fred Emerich.*

were on their own. They were informed they could attend movies or, as the bulletin communicated, any other "spots" in the city. Epperson said most of the passengers gradually came around to the idea of being stranded. As with most situations when in the proximity of a stranger, conversation is hard, but after hours of silence, Epperson said all of that changed as passengers

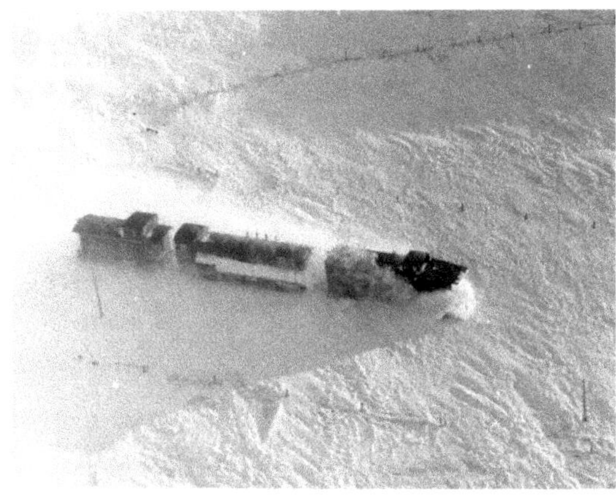

A train pushing through heavy drifts. *Courtesy of Mike Kampa.*

began to learn of fellow passengers' businesses, families and even hobbies rather than sit in awkward silence. Sadly, Epperson mentioned that aboard the train, his friend Royal Chamberlain and Harry Engleson from Denver were escorting the body and family of G.O. Jackson, the president of the Washington State Wool Growers Association. Jackson had attended an association meeting in Texas and was on his way back through Denver when he fell from a train in the Denver yards and was killed.

Nevertheless, Chamberlain and Engleson received praise for their arduous work for the duration of the delay in Laramie. Epperson said both men were "working their hearts outs" as they tended the needs of some 1,200 Union Pacific passengers who were sending wires; making cancellations for hotels, trains and boats; and making phone calls to Cheyenne United Air Lines in hopes to make reservations upon their arrival to Cheyenne. Epperson also observed the agents attending to the "hundred and one" other things required by the passengers and noted how Union Pacific should be grateful for such efficient men on its staff. They worked hard to meet emergency needs and care for the passengers to ensure that the untimely delay in Wyoming would not be too inconvenient.

Although Epperson was quick to applaud the work of the men of the Union Pacific, he did not forget the citizens in Laramie. As soon as the delay of the trains was learned of by those in the city, they quickly extended hours of businesses across town as owners began to organize for the massive influx of people. The Laramie Chamber of Commerce and Elks Lodge 582, along with the University of Wyoming, organized events. By the second evening, the passengers were entertained at the train station by a local group, the Laramie Society for the Preservation of Barber Shop Harmonies Inc., directed by Roger Frisby. After the forty-five-minute show, the Chamber of Commerce hosted a show at the Conner Hotel in town with celebrities stranded on the train. One celebrity on the trains was Little Jack Little, a famous bandleader and singer headed to Las Vegas for an event who was gracious enough to entertain the stranded passengers, which was enjoyed by all. Another noted celebrity who was marooned was Lee Trent, a famous actor on the silver screen, stage and radio famous for his portrayal of the Lone Ranger. Laramie attempted to keep everyone happy even though many had not planned on an extended stay in Wyoming. The party moved from the Conner Hotel, Epperson told the paper. Lee Trent joined his party on the train, which included Jimmy Armour and C. Buckner, who were dining car stewards. Cy Forsythe, John Palmer, a Minneapolis attorney and a couple of others joined in the late-night excursion. Epperson said they were treated like royalty by Joe Kalinay, the manager of the club, and O.N. "Chalky" Peterson, the secretary of the Elks Club and assistant cashier at the First National Bank. Chalky co-hosted the event with Kalinay with a late-night snack at the Diamond Horseshoe located on the outskirts of town, one of the only all-night spots in Laramie.

By Tuesday, Epperson said, "We're still sittin' in front of the station in Laramie. The first question we ask as do 1,200 other stranded is, 'What's the latest?' It's still the same as it was two days ago, 'we can't dig out until the wind dies down.' One-hundred miles of snow-drift track with eighty miles per hour winds is too much of task for 'snow' fighters. At points, it is being reported; the drifts were fifty feet in depth. As fast as the rotary plows made a clearing, the wind would fill in behind." Many of the passengers being from the East had a hard time understanding how this was happening. With this information coming from the tracks only a few miles up the rail and the sun shining in Laramie, it was hard to comprehend. However, for those who lived in the West, this was something that happened quite often.

With transportation coming to a halt, many passengers were looking for alternate routes to their final destinations. Tuesday began day four of what many thought was an endless delay in Wyoming. Passengers paced, circled and sauntered around the depot. The bulletin board—which had one sign posted: "No Trains Will Move Before 6 P.M."—was perused numerous times by passengers hoping for a new post indicating movement of trains. Epperson said some passengers walked downtown to pass the time during the delay, while others stayed in the depot drinking scotch and soda and playing cards. At this point, approximately one hundred passengers had found transportation to Cheyenne to catch planes to their destinations. However, one lady stated to Epperson that she had

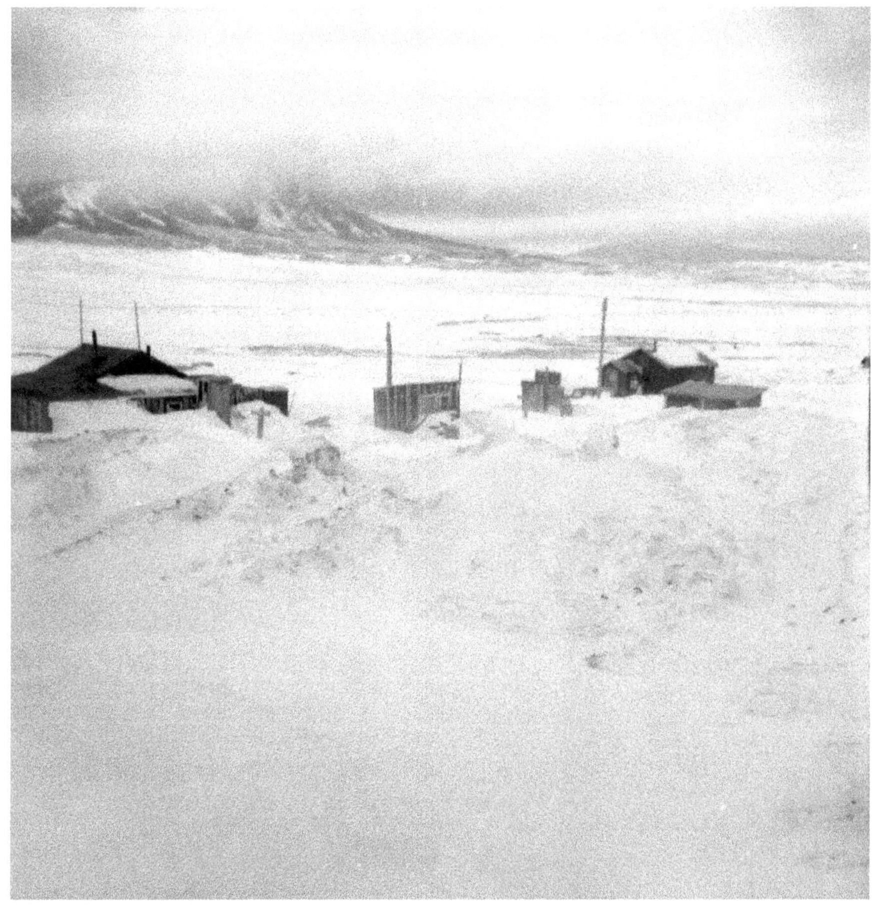

A view of Elk Mountain from the mining camp with snow piled up. *Courtesy of John Moyer.*

not even gotten off the train. She and her husband were heading to San Francisco for a convention. They decided if they made it to California by Friday, they would consider it a wonderful trip. It was not surprising when Epperson stated that he was able to observe nearly every human characteristic during his time in Laramie. He said that by Tuesday, there were two types of attitudes from most: "'I am going to stick with 'er' or 'I'd like to stick around, but I just have to catch a plane to make my connection.'" As anxious passengers continued to look for ways in which to leave, arrangements were made to transport those passengers with urgent needs by plane to the West Coast.

Railroad officials soon realized the trains were not going to be moving at 6:00 p.m., and the announcement came informing passengers the trains now would not run before 8:00 a.m. on Wednesday morning. When this announcement was found out by members of the Elks Club, another open house was organized, and Epperson said the gang from the evening before once again enjoyed the Elks' hospitality and a night filled with dancing and other forms of entertainment. After a great party on Wednesday, many were prepared to head west the following morning but were quickly disappointed as they arrived back to the train station to the same answer as the days before: "We can't move till the wind quits!" Passengers continued to book flights to make connecting trains or meet in other cities. Epperson told of a family who he felt showed a great example of cooperation during the craziness. Mr. and Mrs. L.L Kvam and their two daughters had planned a family vacation to Hawaii. They took each event in stride, but by Wednesday, when they realized they would not be able to reach San Francisco by Friday by train, they decided to book a flight.

Food was not an issue for those passengers stranded in Laramie. Epperson and his fellow passengers were made as comfortable as possible. After breakfast on Monday, passengers reported that meals "were on the house." The steward on Epperson's dining car stated he had purchased 475 pounds of steak since leaving Chicago. However, the four-dollar steak dinner on the train's menu soon became the meal to eat as, of course, it was free. Those marooned on the train stated the stewards did not skimp on the meals, and from reports, the meals were even better than before. While in Laramie, the train had to replenish the food supply three times to keep up with the demand. Epperson said that fresh linens, toilet tissue and paper towels were brought in by truck from Cheyenne. In the spirit of keeping business local, a Laramie laundry was given a rush order on table linens, and waiters' coats were ready just before the trains were to pull out on Wednesday.

Finally, the announcement came: "Call all passengers for a 1:00 p.m. departure." With this proclamation, things began to move at a fast pace. Everyone was ready to head to Cheyenne. From Cheyenne, they would head out to Denver, traveling over the Rio Grande. Union Pacific set up loudspeakers in town to issue reports, ensuring everyone made their trains. Everyone was headed back home or to the destination they had planned nearly a week earlier.

With the trip of a lifetime finally over, Epperson was happy to be back home in Salt Lake City, Utah. He had made plans to spend the weekend in Cheyenne and be back in Salt Lake on Sunday, but this trip lasted for what Epperson stated was "six long days, but an experience that will not soon be forgotten." As he reflected on the time spent in Laramie, Epperson said there were a few individuals who topped his list of new friends. These included Union Pacific's two traveling passenger agents, Royal Chamberlain and Harry Engleson, who took great care of the passengers when it came to sleeping arrangements; Miss Ruth Person, a stewardess on the train; Jimmy Armour and C. Buckner, who assisted in the dining car as stewards there; Emil G. Stanley, vice president and secretary of the Traffic Service Corporation; Robert J. Bayer, editor of *Traffic World* and other transportation-related publications; J. Frank Carpenter, who worked with Movie Advertising Bureau; Richard Kemp from Susanville, Nevada; John Palmer of Minneapolis; and too many others to mention.[46]

While many on the trains were frustrated and bored, there were two individuals who were showered with gifts while stranded in Rawlins, Wyoming. With nearly four hundred stranded passengers aboard the City of Los Angeles streamliner train, they were the guests to the birthday party of two other passengers, eighty-year-old Grace Braley from Cherokee, Iowa, and one-year-old Janet Kay Voss from Omaha, Nebraska. The merchants in Rawlins gave Braley numerous gifts, which included an orchid shawl, bookends, hose, handkerchiefs, an album of records and jewelry. Little Janet also received several gifts, which were not mentioned in the article. During this party, a young marine, Rtc. Gilbert E. D'Ortiz, who was stranded aboard the troop train headed for Japan, sang "The Lord's Prayer" during the party, and for his participation, the Larking Jewelry company gave him a billfold. There were plenty of treats had by all, as The Ideal and Waltel's bakeries and Vernon "Jiggs" Johnston supplied cakes for the party. Belle Welch, who was the chairman of the Carbon County Chapter of the American Red Cross, brought cookies to the train to add to the treats for the party. Generosity from the small towns across Wyoming was graciously accepted by the stranded passengers and other motorists. Those in Rawlins showed their hospitality by opening up restaurants and facilities for passengers to shower and clean up since for most it had been nearly four days since they had a bath. This western hospitality took a strenuous situation and made it somewhat better for many.

Local Rawlins restaurant proprietor Verne R. Salisbury, owner of Saddle Grill, celebrated his birthday at his establishment and invited forty-five travelers who were living in the motels near his restaurant on West Spruce in Rawlins. Also in town, Mrs. Hoyt Strawberry opened her establishment, hosting passengers who had not had access to bathing facilities for the week. The nurses' home at Memorial Hospital in Rawlins ensured the children on the train were given baths and physical checkups to verify colds and virus were not spreading in such close quarters.

The members of the Young Women's Service Club (YWSC) operated a Red Cross–sponsored canteen under the direction of Mrs. Bud Fisher. The canteen served three meals a day at the Elks Club to the train passengers. For entertainment, the YWSC directed tours in Rawlins and parties for children and adults to assist in passing the time. Groups and organizations throughout the city, including the local radio station, helped those stranded too. KRAL, Rawlins's local radio station, dropped regularly scheduled programming to ensure announcements were running not only for those living in Rawlins but also for those stranded, keeping everyone updated on the storm and the status of the clearing efforts of the roads. The radio station also sent messages to the Red Cross, Mayor Sam Tully, personal messages and urgent messages for assistance from the YWSC while they assembled everything needed for the Red Cross canteen.[47]

Throughout the blizzard, hundreds of motorists were stranded along Wyoming highways in an attempt to reach their planned destination or find shelter somewhere along the route. On the third day of the blizzard, five adults and an eleven-year-old boy found themselves stranded near the Wyoming-Colorado border. The group spent sixty-eight hours in the vehicle without food, water or sleep in what was described as an "ice-encrusted passenger car." Four Army trucks and a party from the Warren Livestock ranch found the stranded group.

The marooned group, who spent three days and nights together, consisted of John T. Doyle, a section foreman for the Colorado and Southern Railroad, along with his stepson and wife, Roberta, from Loveland, Colorado. Also from Loveland was Edward Heintzelman, a candy salesman. From Carr, Colorado, was eleven-year-old Marvin Towe, along with Arden and Mable Glassburn. The stranded group unexpectedly became trapped together some fifteen miles south of Cheyenne en route to Loveland. They came together after the Doyles, who were visiting Ralph Stratton in Cheyenne, became stuck several miles from Loveland. The Doyles, in an attempt to get out of the storm, decided to return to Cheyenne. However, when they were just four miles from the Wyoming border, their vehicle stalled in a snowdrift from which they could not free themselves. Shortly after the Doyles became stranded that afternoon, they were joined by young Martin Towe and the Glassburns, who sought shelter with the group.

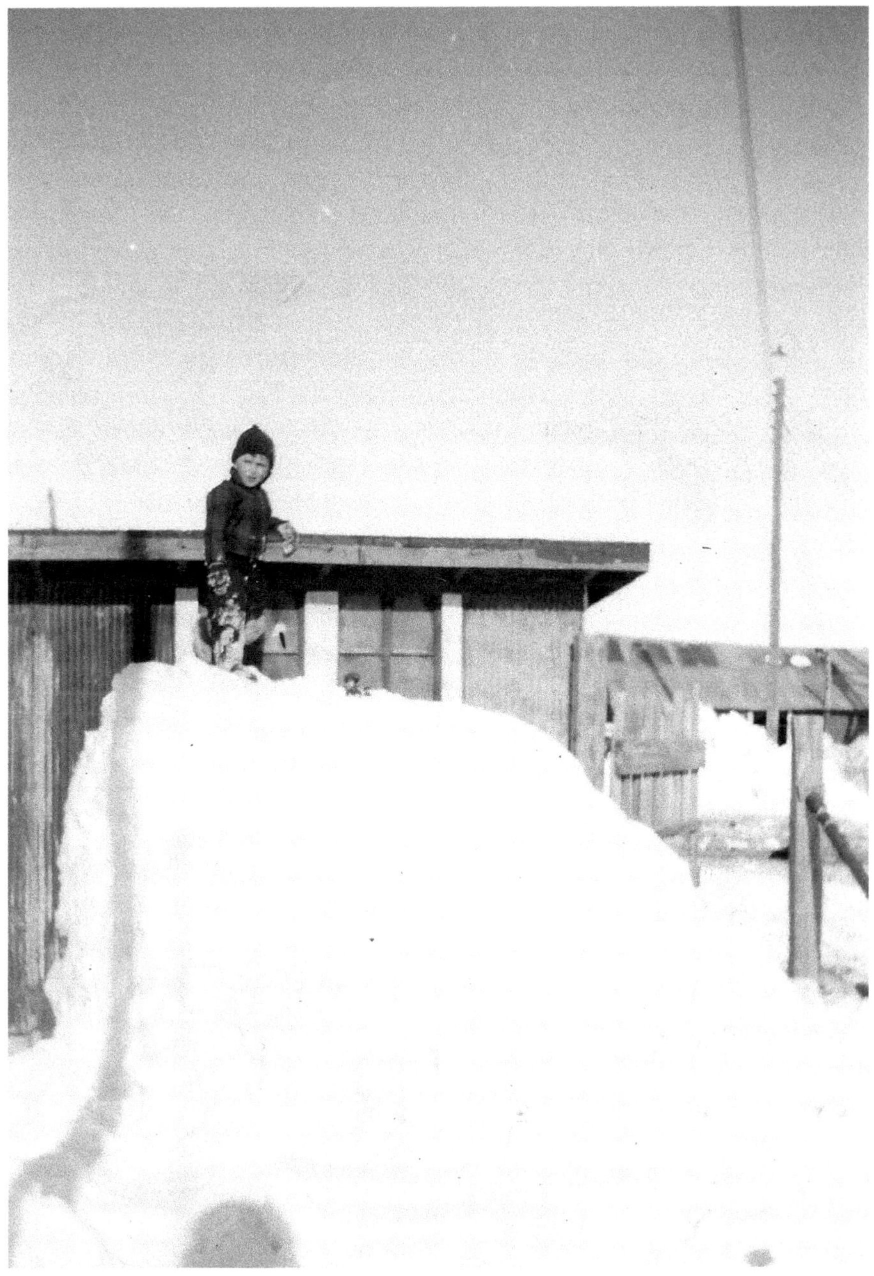

Fred Emerich stands on top of a chicken coop as the drift reaches the top of the coop. *Courtesy of Senator Fred Emerich.*

Edward Heintzelman, one of the stranded motorists, was outspoken on his time confined with the other five passengers. Heintzelman, a veteran of World War II, spent three years in a Japanese prisoner of war camp in the Philippines. He stated, "In the camp, we lived on worms and tree bark after Bataan fell. Those three nights and days were just about as tough as those four years." According to the *Wyoming Eagle*, the inside of the vehicle that now was their temporary shelter was covered in a half inch of ice caused by the breath of the six occupants. There was no food to eat, and the only way they were able to keep hydrated was from melted snow. The motor on the car was dead from the heavy, wet snow, giving the passengers no heat from the car's heater. Without a radio in the car, it was impossible to know what was happening during the storm or hear if rescue efforts were in progress. There were only two blankets in the car; however, with dirty and frozen clothes, the blankets did little good. The only other item they had was cigarettes, and they had burned through those by the first evening.

Heintzelman continued with the exploits of the event, saying, "We couldn't see beyond the radiator cap from the time we stopped until the time of our rescue. One side of the car drifted shut. The wind was blowing at sixty-five miles per hour, and by Monday the temperature had dropped to ten degrees below zero." As most might do in the situation, the people in the group did a lot of praying in hopes they would be rescued or at least spotted by vehicles passing by. Heintzelman said a snowplow passed no more than seventy feet from the vehicle that day. Even with the lights on and blowing their horn, they were not heard by those operating the plow. As those in the car heard the men talking and the roar of the snowplow's engine, they were afraid to leave the safety of the vehicle. After what they assumed was the snowplow getting stuck, they heard no more voices or the plow's engine running.

The paper spotlighted Francis E. Warren's great-grandson, Walter Nelson from Cheyenne, who had organized the search party for the two families.[48] Nelson, along with some ranch hands from the Warren Livestock Ranch, assisted in moving the party back to the ranch. After their arrival at the ranch, a Loveland Highway Patrol officer, John Stramel, drove them all back to a hospital in Loveland. Upon arrival at the hospital, both Mrs. Doyle and Glassburn were treated for swollen feet from being in the below-zero temperatures and lack of circulation, which was caused by not being able to move around freely in the vehicle. No one else in the worn-out group was in serious condition after being checked out at the hospital.

Sixty-eight hours in a vehicle with six others had to be problematic for everyone. However, these marooned individuals pushed through the grueling hours of cold with no water or food and came out with little to no injuries. The fortitude of many who survived events like this prove that quitting was something that never crossed their minds. Many people who went through the blizzard have stories that intrigue readers, giving them a glance at what so many endured during this particular storm. One eyewitness who gave her story was not from Wyoming but a stranded passenger on one of the frozen Union Pacific trains. The marooned person was Barbara Allason, who served as a delegate to the United Nations Educational Scientific and Cultural Organization (UNESCO). Allason was also the author of *Memorie di un'Antifascista, 1919–1940* (*Memoirs of an Anti-Fascist*). She was returning by the Union Pacific's streamliner the Overland Limited from California, where she was visiting her son, Professor Samuel K. Allason, who was a physics professor at the University of Chicago but was at the University of California as a visiting professor. She planned to take the train to New York and there catch her ship, the *Queen Mary*, back to Italy.[49]

Allison told the papers, "Yes, everything I see in the United States is the biggest. In New York, I saw the buildings and they were the biggest in the world. In California, I saw the atom-smashing machine [partial accelerator], and that is the biggest in the world." Her description of Wyoming was just about the same: "Then in Wyoming, I see the blizzard that is the biggest in the world." She said she had never seen a blizzard in Italy but was amazed by the storm that was making its way by the Pullman car window where she sat.

Sharing this weather spectacle with Allison were other passengers on the Overland Limited and the Portland Rose. The Portland Rose was host to a large number of passengers, many of them returning from the Christmas holidays with family and friends. Other passengers included GIs and college students who were returning to their duty posts and college classes.[50] Most of the students and soldiers felt they would not have a problem explaining their delays due to the storm. However, one soldier was not so certain. The soldier, in desperation, pleaded with a journalist who was covering the story: "Buddy, please send me a copy of your newspaper. My commanding officer is tough as nails, and he'll never believe that a snowstorm could be bad enough to make me late on my furlough unless he sees it in print."

Many of the passengers on the trains had never visited Wyoming and had pictures in their minds of what it would look like, even during the middle of a blizzard. One of the Pullman porters stated most of his passengers were accepting of what was happening regarding the storm and were in fairly good spirits. One woman on his train took advantage by stepping off the train to do a little sightseeing in Rawlins. Once she got back on the train, she was quite disappointed in what she saw—or what she didn't see. She explained she had plenty of time to take pictures but was unhappy that she was unable to find any cowboys and Indians to photograph.[51]

Humor was just another part of the experiences that many stranded passengers used to take their minds off the blizzard and being stranded in the middle of Wyoming. While passengers did not see any cowboys and Indians, it is clear many were excited to tell their stories to those who would listen, especially local reporters. These stories now are not only part of this story but one that has been passed down from generation to generation.

Towns across the United States spotlighted hometown heroes who had survived the blizzard in rural Wyoming. One such story came from Carroll, Iowa, and told about a young lady named Irene McDonald who was headed home to Carroll when she was halted in Green River, Wyoming. McDonald informed the staff writer she "was having a wonderful time," and this was after being stuck in the small town for three days. The only complaint she had was that there were no lights and candles to be used, but with free food and plenty of entertainment, everything, in her words, was "perfect." Irene told the reporter the town even held a dance at the high school gymnasium for the stranded train passengers, which assisted in passing the time for at least one evening. Along with the dances held in Green River to entertain the guests, there was a special paper printed for those stranded, *The Growler*. This special edition kept the passengers entertained as they learned some of the gossip on their train and others. The train McDonald was traveling on had about 650 passengers aboard. Per McDonald, one of the trains was already stranded when they arrived and was in a snowdrift that completely engulfed the train. She also stated there was very little snow in Green River, so it is evident that the wind was the cause of the massive drifts and delays for the trains. In an attempt to contact her business partner, Agnes Finnegan, in Iowa, McDonald waited in line for five hours to make a call from one of the two available telephone booths in the town of 2,500. Once she made it to the phone to make her call, it did not go through, so she decided to send a wire to Agnes. She explained to the reporter that railroad officials from Los Angeles made their way out to Green River to see that the passengers were doing well and to have an inspection of situation. She said they brought all the latest magazines for everyone to read and writing material so those on the train could keep up with their correspondence. However, the writing material seems a bit ironic, since there was no way mail was leaving Green River.

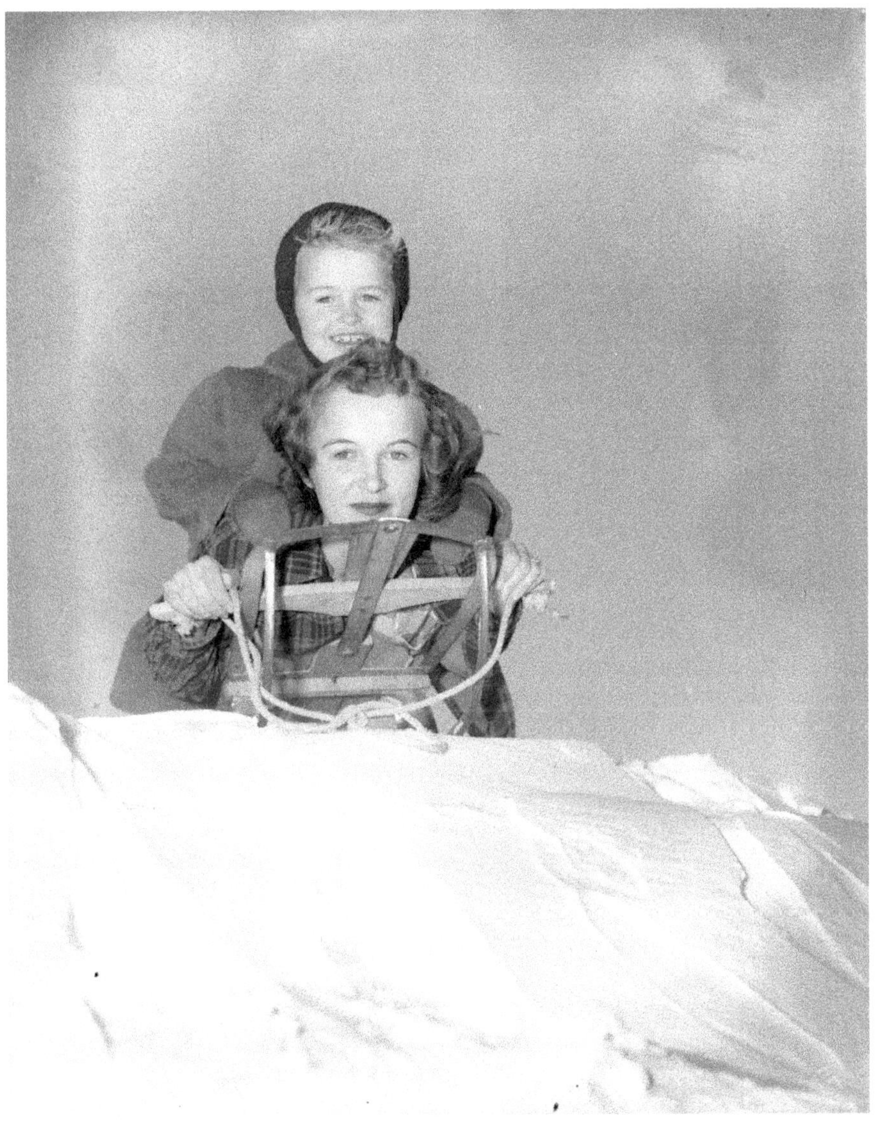

An unidentified young woman and girl on top of a snowbank. *Francis Steele Brammar, courtesy of Wyoming State Archives.*

A depressing note to McDonald's story came to light. According to McDonald, a Magdalena McDonald (no relation to Irene) and her daughter Ava Ruth were traveling from California to Nebraska with the deceased body of their husband and father, taking him to his final resting place. Upon their arrival in Green River, they became aware the body of McDonald was not on the train, and neither the family nor the train employees knew his whereabouts. On a lighter side, a mother on the train was headed to Chicago to her daughter's wedding. The funny anecdote is that the wedding was on Friday, the mother had the wedding dress and it was Saturday! Others experienced their trip much differently than McDonald, from pleasant to frantic.

"Wind a-moanin' past the door, Snow a-flyin' in on the floor. Passengers trompin' to and fro, Wonderin' when the train will go; Life gets teejus, doesn't it?" So began an article in the *Eugene Guard* on January 19. However, in a Wyoming blizzard on a stalled train with the temperature dropping to fifteen below, life was "teejus" (tedious). Lottie Mitchell described her adventures during the Blizzard of 1949 as she and her husband experienced the stresses of being stranded during this major snowstorm. Lottie and her husband did not start out as passengers on one of the many trains stranded across Wyoming. Their journey started by bus in St. Louis, Missouri, as they made their trek back to Lorane, Oregon. The bus they were traveling on made it as far as Sidney, Nebraska, before blizzard conditions kept it from going farther down the road. Lottie noted that upon their arrival, arrangements were made for them to continue by train to Cheyenne the following morning on the 3:48 a.m. since their bus could not make its way through the snow. The Mitchells and their fellow passengers spent the night on their bus as they awaited transportation to Wyoming. Around 7:00 a.m. the following morning, Lottie reported the snow was so intense she and the other bus passengers did not even notice when the westbound City of Portland pulled into the Union Pacific depot. As they anticipated boarding the train, passengers met with disappointment, as they were informed the train was not taking passengers upon arrival. Lottie called these "false alarms," as she and her fellow passengers gathered their belongings several times in anticipation of the streamliners' arrival into Sidney, Nebraska. Of course, the Mitchells and others were overjoyed when they were allowed to board a train headed to Cheyenne. Fortunate enough to secure a coach seat, Lottie recalled how many of the passengers had to use their luggage for seats, while soldiers who had hitched a ride stood in the club car. Expressing her excitement upon boarding, Lottie stated, "Ah! now we have a comfortable seat, and we are really on our way again." According to Lottie, this was about 9:30 a.m. After an hour and a half, the train stopped and could go no farther. They had made it to Egbert, Wyoming, which was only seventy miles from where they had departed. It is obvious Lottie was not overly impressed with the small town of Egbert, as she described it in brief: "It [the train] came to a final stop Egbert, Wyoming—population 55." Lottie and her fellow passengers came together as they made the best of a bad situation in Egbert. Recalling the events as they took place upon their arrival, Lottie remembered how many of the college boys and soldiers on the train put together barbershop quartets to sing to passengers to help pass the time. She recounted a couple of the songs sung, which included "Let Me Call You Sweetheart" and "The Whiffenpoof Song." Although this brought smiles and pleasant memories to those aboard the train, Lottie told about several struggles that were not so pleasurable to recall.

Feeding the passengers was a daunting task, as the first dinner call for passengers started at 6:30 p.m. that first evening, but by 9:30 p.m., there were still people standing up in Mitchell's coach to receive their dinner. Along with the long lines for dinner was the snow that continually blew in the car as people came in to find their place in the dinner line. With each passenger making their way through, the door opened and the snow found its way into the car until at one point the door would not shut. Evening came, and many of the passengers fell into a slumber. Lottie noted that the snow had covered nearly the full length of the passenger car, and people were attempting to sleep as best they could in the freezing conditions. Soldiers who were in transition had their duffle bags, which they utilized as pillows. As the night grew colder, they opened up and began to share the clothes they had inside with passengers around them in an attempt to keep warm. Humorous in her explanation of the next morning's fashions, Lottie stated, "By daylight, some of the costumes were natty! However, with a temperature of fifteen below, a style was easily sacrificed for comfort."

The dangerous temperatures prompted the head conductor to take action in moving the passengers from the ill-fated train to the depot, which was about a block from where the train was encased in snow and ice. The decision to move women and children was made, and Pullman towels and pillowcases were improvised as protection for people's face and in some cases feet. Train crew and soldiers led the departure mission as they assisted in getting the group to the depot. Lottie noted one of the first things she noticed upon entering the depot was the fire-red potbellied stove and the warmth of the building. With such great numbers, the men were moved to the schoolhouse about a quarter mile away from the depot. Cold, tired and hungry, the passengers enjoyed plenty of warmth and, Lottie reports, a feast of chicken, roast pork, green beans, mashed potatoes and bran muffins that was prepared by a local diner in town. The ability to feed 270 passengers and crew was due to the quick thinking of the train stewards, who broke into a freight train that was also stranded in Egbert, securing the meat, potatoes and vegetables needed to feed this famished group.

On Thursday, January 6, what was supposed to be a departure sometime after breakfast turned into a departure just after three o'clock in the afternoon. Relieved at the sight of snowplows and buses, passengers anxiously waited to board. Reports indicate there were two passengers who became ill during the ordeal and were loaded onto the buses first, followed by parents with small children and married couples, who loaded prior to college students and the soldiers who made up the group. Once the Mitchells and the other passengers arrived in Cheyenne, they were informed the trains were still not operating and other forms of transportation west might be operational the following day on Friday, as the anticipation was that Highway 30 would open that day. As Lottie finished up her story about her time in Wyoming during the blizzard, she put a little laughter into all of the craziness she and her husband had endured over the last week. On Friday morning around 7:30 a.m., the Mitchells made their way to the Union Pacific depot in Cheyenne to purchase tickets after what Lottie phrased "an uninterrupted night's sleep in a bed." Not surprised by yet another delay, they were informed they could not purchase tickets until 11:30 a.m. As predicted, Highway 30 opened up, and the Mitchells caught a bus headed west. As they arrived at their Oregon home on Friday evening, they read that the Union Pacific's City of Portland had not departed until late into the evening. Ironically, Lottie said upon their arrival back in Oregon that they came home to snow![52]

One young man, also interviewed after reaching Cheyenne, was a fellow passenger with Dr. Boyden and his son Frank on the Portland in Egbert. Robert S. Reed, from Kansas City, Missouri, quickly told the Cheyenne *Wyoming State Tribune* editor he would not take a million dollars to live through an experience like that again after nearly eighty hours on a frozen train with 240 newfound friends. Reed emerged from the adjacent room at his quarters at the Frontier Hotel, where he had just had his first warm shower and change of clean clothes in three days. He informed the editor that the shower was one of the most refreshing baths he had ever experienced. He stated, "It seemed like a nightmare, first of all, it was cold, and it was a real problem trying to keep warm. Almost as bad was the frustration and boredom of sitting there knowing nothing about the question everybody was asking—'when are we going to get out of here.' Train officials would not tell us anything, even after the snow plows arrived on Wednesday. We played bridge in the morning in the dining car. Then the tables would be set up for lunch, and after lunch we would play bridge again. I got so I couldn't read

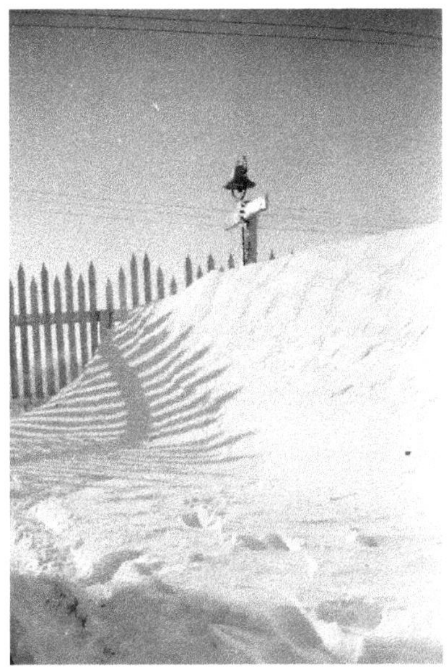

Snowdrifts up to the fence that surrounds the Emerich family's residence. *Courtesy of Senator Fred Emerich.*

the numbers on the cards." Although most aspects were bleak, Reed said the food made up for it. On Tuesday, January 4, train officials were permitted to break into freight trains also trapped in Egbert. Passengers were well fed with an abundant supply of eggs, ham, bacon, sausage and lettuce during their stay. Having breakfast three times a day may not have been a thrill, but it was sustaining nonetheless. Water, however, was not available except the water set aside and saved for the children on board the trains. No one on the train went thirsty, Reed informed the editor. The club car was providing beer, and coffee was being brewed with the use of melted snow in the dining car. Reed pointed out there was no milk for the children; however, there were cigarettes, but they were rationed. It is obvious what was a priority for the young University of Oregon student.

Of course, the absence of water on the train caused additional problems when it came to the water pipes. Without water, toilets could not be flushed, the washing areas were no longer functional and laundry could not be done. Reed stated that mothers started using napkins and towels as diapers for their babies since there was no way to wash diapers. Even with the harsh conditions that passengers faced, Reed and a fellow passenger, J.D. Jesseph, praised dining steward John Draper, the cooks and the kitchen crew not only for the fantastic food they were delivering but also for doing all they could to ensure the passengers were as comfortable as they could be under the current circumstances. Soon, the heating system in the trains could no longer maintain a heating level to keep passengers warm.

To ensure the women and children had a better environment to rest in, they were moved from the train and taken to the train station, where they had sufficient heat both Tuesday and Wednesday night. Other passengers made their way through fifty-mile-per-hour wind and waist-deep drifts to reach the high school/museum, which was four blocks away. Those passengers who remained on the train moved from to the dining car to keep warm. Reed said they were huddled together with blankets attempting to sleep because the boxcars where they should have rested were cold as well. Temperatures inside the sleeping cars were reported at ten degrees below zero.

Reed continued his story as he told of who he believed to be one of the busiest men on the train during those four days in Egbert, Dr. Allen Boyden. Reed stated that even though there was no severe outbreak or sickness on the train, Dr. Boyden had several patients whom he was attending to aboard the City of Portland, including several with colds and two who were seriously ill. Reed mentions one individual who was in a diabetic coma and had to be transported to the hospital in Cheyenne on Thursday, January 6. Reed also told of the delivery of the baby girl, Anita Jean Rohrbaugh, by Dr. Boyden, but while Dr. Boyden stated the delivery was "little trouble," Reed's perspective, or that of the Cheyenne editor, was much more colorful and descriptive: "While death was near at hand in one case, life was emerging in another. Lacking the medical essentials and facilities, Boyden delivered a baby girl, born in a private home Wednesday morning."

When the trains initially were stalled in Egbert, passengers did have radio contact with others outside their new location. However, after the first day and the realization this was not going to be a quick overnight stay, the use of the radios became only for emergencies to assist in saving the little electric power remaining. There were radio stations in the region broadcasting information regarding the storm, updates and development, but the passengers were unable to learn much from these updates. Reed expressed the humor that came over in a Denver radio announcer's broadcast: "If it were not for the discomfort it would have been funny when we heard the Denver announcer who probably assumed the passengers were good, stated the passengers of the City of Portland [Reed's train] was in Cheyenne safe and warm." As the interview ended, Reed said the sun started to finally show, and word came that buses from Cheyenne would be arriving on Thursday morning. A sense of relief permeated as many passengers now seemed to have confidence that assistance was on its way and the end was near. Reed pointed out that one group headed to Sun Valley Ski Resort retrieved their skis and winter togs and practiced on the fifteen-foot drifts that had accumulated over the last three days. The *Wyoming State Tribune* editor concluded with a great perspective on the blizzard and those marooned in Egbert: "At noon today, aboard a train assembled in Cheyenne, most of the passengers were on their way west again, warm and comfortable, and with an unforgettable story of an unscheduled stop-over at a little Wyoming village which is still locked in

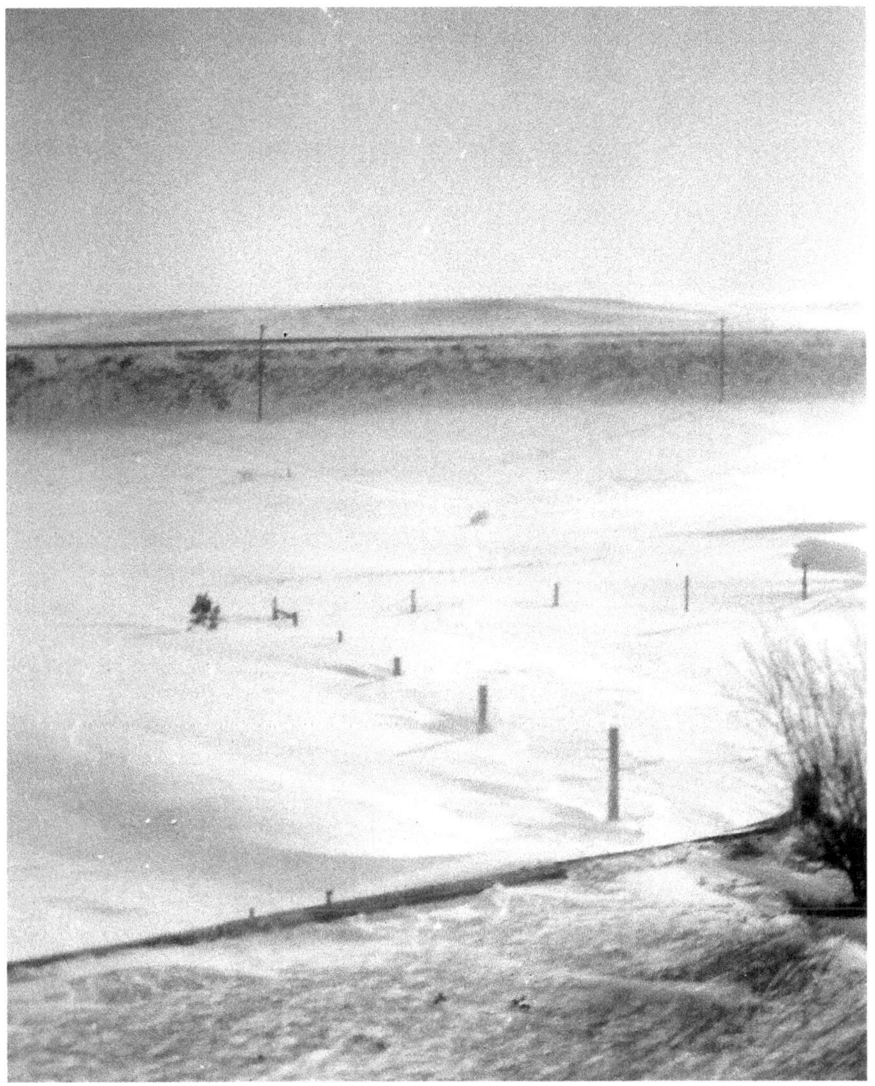

A photo taken from the Emerich residence looking over the sheep corral; notice the Union Pacific line in the background. *Courtesy of Senator Fred Emerich.*

by snow drifts that could completely hide the town's entire population of some three-score citizens." It would be several weeks before Egbert dug out from the drifts, as Wyoming road crews worked their ways from city to town moving mountains of snow out of the way for highways once again to be accessed.

A youthful perspective many times is overlooked when stories are told, but when stories of the blizzard were passed along, age was not a factor. Two young men, Don Uphoff and Albin Johnson, were from Minonk, Illinois, population of just under two thousand. These young men attended the Colorado State College of Agriculture and Mechanic Arts in Fort Collins, Colorado, and were headed back from Peoria, Illinois, by bus. As their hometown newspaper stated, they were two great reporters, as they gave a very detailed recollection of the events as they happened. They left Peoria at 7:45 p.m. on Saturday, January 1, arriving in Omaha, Nebraska, around 7:30 a.m. They continued by bus to Sidney, Nebraska, reaching their destination around 6:30 p.m. on Sunday, January 2, when they stopped for dinner. Snow had started falling in Sidney, and by the time both men had finished eating, the storm was in full swing. The bus company realized the intensity of the storm and quickly transferred all passengers to the train depot for departure by train. As Uphoff and Johnson waited, the storm increased in strength, the temperature plummeted to five below zero and the winds began blowing at seventy miles per hour, resulting in their train not arriving as scheduled. Finally, at 2:00 p.m. on Monday, they boarded a train headed to Colorado. Their train made it as far as Egbert, Wyoming, and this is where they met up with others who had made Egbert their temporary quarters for the last day or so. They reported that the train engine froze up and they, along with other passengers who had accompanied them from Sidney, slept on the train that night in temperatures ten degrees below zero. Per the Minonk boys, they had not slept in three nights, and at this point in their adventure, they were walking around in a daze.

Finally, on Tuesday, Uphoff and Johnson were part of the group taken to the schoolhouse for shelter from the brutal cold and wind. They stated, "Can you imagine two-hundred some people in a schoolhouse?" The boys fell asleep at seven o'clock and did not wake until eight o'clock the next morning." It is obvious both were exhausted from the lack of sleep. On Wednesday, January 5, they woke up to blowing snow, which now inhibited them from seeing across the street, with a temperature of fifteen below. According to Uphoff and Johnson, there were two serious conditions among the passengers: one individual was deathly ill, while another woman, through all the stress of being stranded, had succumbed to a nervous breakdown. The doctor who cared for the people may have been Dr. Boyden, but from what the two men observed, he was about to go crazy himself from all the work he was doing for those on and off the train. The doctor had not slept in nearly four nights as he tended to the needs of those sick on the marooned train, as well as those in the town of Egbert.

By Thursday, January 6, the sounds of airplanes meant needed food, medicine and other supplies were incoming. Uphoff and Johnson were ecstatic when word came from Cheyenne that buses were coming and their stay in Egbert was coming to an end. After watching the road nearly the entire day, they spotted snowplows with three buses in tow. Everyone was excited to see the buses, but this soon ended as the sick were loaded on the first bus, followed by young children and mothers filling up the second and third buses. Although those left behind were disappointed, they knew the wait now would only be about two hours or so. As the paper retold the Minonk boys' story, the Cheyenne buses arrived just before five o'clock, loaded up the remainder of the passengers and headed for Cheyenne. Upon their arrival in Cheyenne around 5:30 p.m., they went to a restaurant in town and ate a big meal, which, according to the two college students, tasted good. They went back to the depot and caught a train to Fort Collins. Arriving in Fort Collins, they played the parts of the young college students quite well, as they stopped and grabbed a hamburger before heading to their house. Per the article, Ron, who presumably was a friend or roommate, said he was surprised to see them both and indicated he had almost given up hope on the two guys after hearing about the intensity of the storm. The article goes on to say the guys later read in a newspaper in Fort Collins that the storm was the worst the region had encountered in the past eighty-four years, which amazed them. The *Minonk News-Dispatch* fact-checked the information the boys sent in their letter. The paper added that when the young men had evacuated the train at Egbert, the temperature in town was, in fact, eighteen below, with winds blowing at seventy miles per hour. The train passengers had to be led by the hand to the schoolhouse because they could not see more than three feet ahead of where they were walking. The trains had run entirely out of food when they were evacuated, and there were only four gallons of water remaining. These young men, as well as their fellow passengers, survived a terrible ordeal and gave many the opportunity to read about what they endured during the blizzard and its aftermath.[53]

Passengers aboard these trains did not realize the journey they would encounter as they headed to destinations across the United States. As the trains pulled out, the idea of being stranded for nearly a week probably did not cross the minds of those who had just boarded. The snow had already started across several states in the plains, including Wyoming, by January 2. Reports of the blizzard did not start coming across the newswire until the following day. One of the first status updates on the delays on trains occurred on January 3. The *Mercury*, a paper out of Pottstown, Pennsylvania, stated that areas in eastern Colorado and Wyoming were where the snowfall was the heaviest, and drifts were slowing down trains and automobile travel.[54] There was also mention of delays at the Denver airport, as well as a report of two hundred motorists stranded in Nunn, Colorado, just twenty miles from the Wyoming border. By the next day, the newspapers were filled with articles relaying the news of stranded trains and vehicles. The first reports stated that eighteen trains were stranded in Wyoming, with three trains in Cheyenne, three in Egbert, one in Pine Bluffs, another five in Rock Springs and six others in Green River.

Stranded passengers throughout the blizzard found ways to entertain themselves and others as they struggled with boredom and hour after hour of just sitting and waiting. In Cheyenne, a large group of students from Northwestern University was headed back from the Rose Bowl, where the Northwestern University Wildcats had defeated the California Golden Bears 20–14. The students did not allow the storm or their temporary quarters to quell their spirits after arriving.

Student George Likeness, who was the editorial chairman of the university's *Daily Northwestern*, took full advantage of the situation, penning the events as they took place. The *Daily Northwestern* staff contacted George to receive the full story from someone who was experiencing the blizzard. With this eyewitness testimony, George informed his classmates and families who were curious to know what was happening in Cheyenne. George said the group was made up of Roland F. McGuigan, the university's men's counselor; the *Wildcat* cheerleaders; and about one hundred additional students who went down California to cheer on the university players on the gridiron. Sometime early Monday morning, January 3, the Wildcat Special left Laramie, heading toward Cheyenne. The duration of the train ride was about an hour but, according to George, a very long hour. As the train made its way to Cheyenne, it moved slowly, covering increments of about a half mile, navigating through drifts that covered the tracks.

Not only was the trip long and frustrating, but the steam pipes that heated the train cars had broken, leaving the coach and lounge cars unbearable in the frigid temperatures. As students moved between the cars to visit with fellow passengers or find a warmer car, they were instructed to wear coats since the temperature was at ten below zero. By late Monday afternoon, the train had arrived in Cheyenne. There, the students waited out the storm with five other trains filled with passengers. At the time

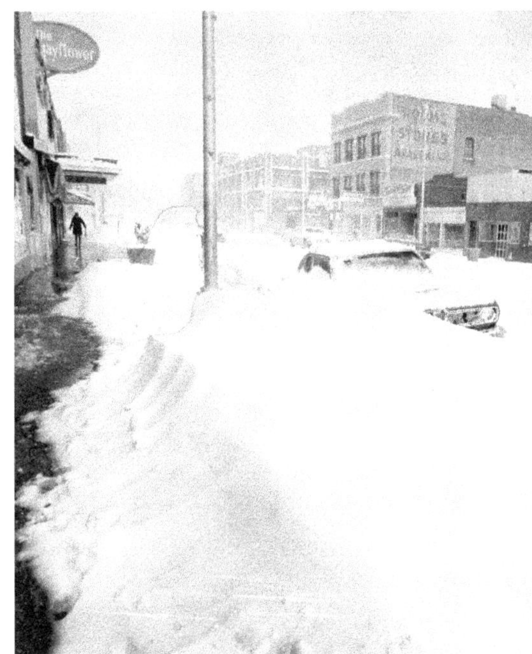

Left: Seventeenth Street, Cheyenne, Wyoming, after the blizzard. *Francis Steele Brammar, courtesy of Wyoming State Archives.*

Below: Blizzard-stranded Northwestern students are greeted after their arrival back to Northwestern University. *Courtesy Northwestern University Library.*

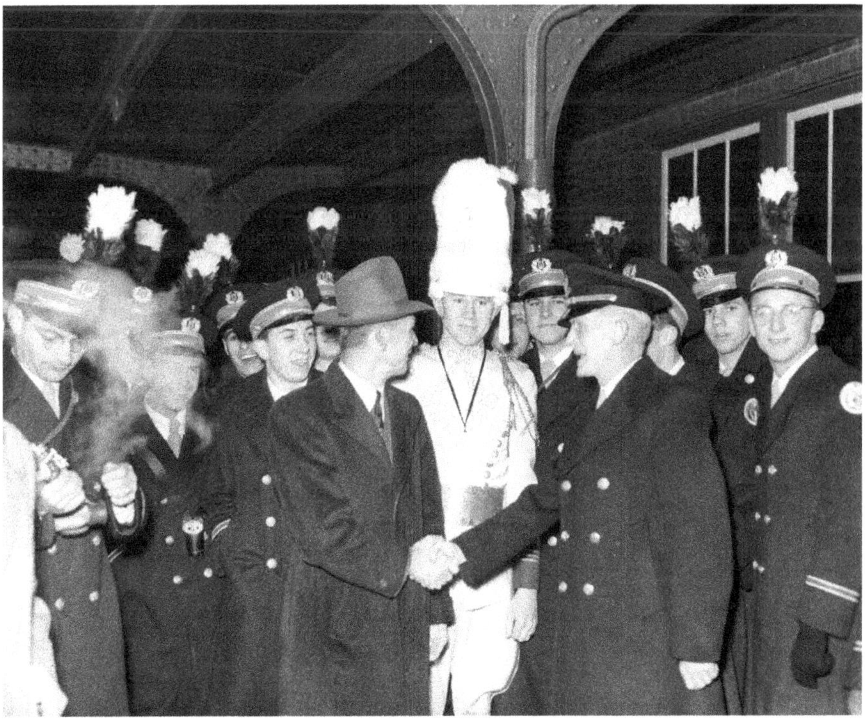

of the paper's publication, which was approximately 11:00 p.m. Eastern Standard Time, the storm had still not subsided.

George went on to say that radio reports indicated Cheyenne was completely isolated from outside communication. George said these reports were true, as he had observed the snow, drifts and wind blowing through the streets of Wyoming's capital city. The stranded passengers, however, were comfortably enjoying the western hospitality, which the students graciously accepted during their time in Cheyenne. Not only were the residents of Cheyenne assisting those stranded, but Union Pacific also provided free meals to those aboard the train. Even with this many people consuming food and water, George indicated there was no food shortage.

With not much to do to occupy their time, the students found entertainment in three of Cheyenne's local theaters: Lincoln Theater, Paramount Theater and Strand Theater. George indicated that the students had visited each of the theaters to view the movies that were showing. In fact, they were so bored they went back to the theaters at least twice. At one point, the students pleaded with Lincoln Theater manager Tom P. Brennan to see a sneak peek of the following day's movie. The owner was apologetic as he told the students he would be happy to, but the movie was in Denver, and it would not be delivered until well into the following week with the weather conditions. The students did not have to worry that their train would depart without them as they watched the films. If a train departure came up, the theater flashed a message on the screen informing them of a schedule change. With no messages telling of departing trains, there were more movies and a big party at the Plains Hotel. Not only did the movie theaters and hotels take advantage of the large number of students, but shop owners did as well. George stated, "Gift shops attracted us and soon the Wildcats in Cheyenne were easy to spot. We were the only ones in town wearing cowboy hats." Once it was realized that there were no new movies coming, the students created their own entertainment as they put together a talent show. George, Jack Hamilton and Dave Rogers set out to write the script for the upcoming show. After the boys had the script written, a call for talent was sent out. Of course, it was soon realized, as George said, that "everyone wanted to get in on the act." George was quick to the tell the paper the script was "pure corn," but the show was something that helped distract five trainloads of passengers, as well as a few Cheyenne locals who were in attendance. Northwestern University students Warren Richardson and Ed Jones, the "Sunshine Boys," performed a parody of the university's Waa-Mu Show for the audience.[55] Students George Gilbert and Dick Lane represented the

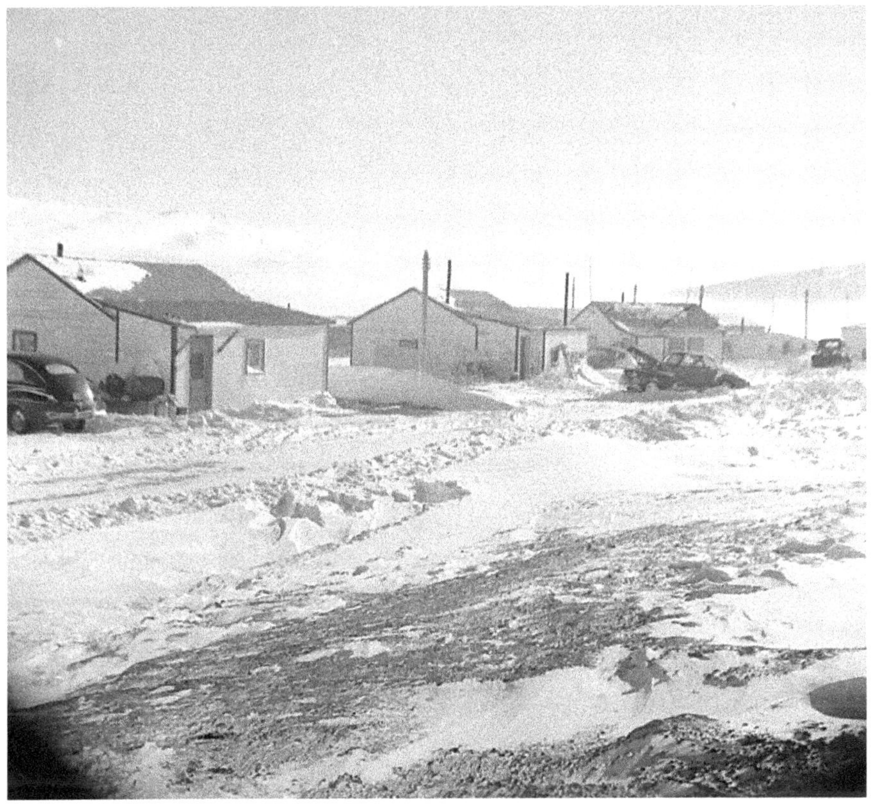

Wind-swept landscape from ground blizzards and clear skies above. *Courtesy of John Moyer.*

University Theater and radio, while Marilyn North and Rusty Hoefle came up with a skit where they pretended to be college students going to class at Northwestern. Of course, the fun did not stop here; the party continued in Cheyenne until the wee hours of the morning.

George said Cheyenne liked the college students, and they, in turn, liked Cheyenne. The Plains Hotel allowed the use of its ballroom for the students to dance as long as they did not charge admission. This, however, turned into what George considered the only unpleasant part of the entire trip. It was decided among the students that they should do something for the band members who played the numerous songs to which the students danced. The idea of passing around a hat for donations for the band seemed the best plan. The band member who received the hat after the students had passed it around got the wrong idea and placed himself at the entrance of the ballroom and charged those who came in to dance. All was going well, as

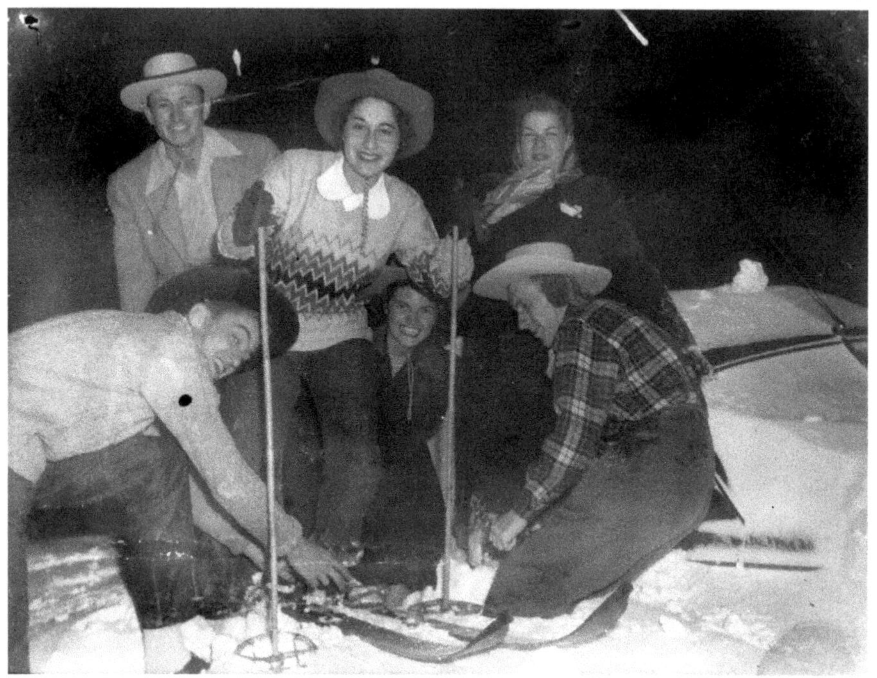

Northwestern University students on top of cars in Cheyenne posing for the infamous Wyoming press photographer Francis Brammar. *Francis Steele Brammar, courtesy of Wyoming State Archives.*

those came in paid their entrance fee of fifty cents. However, unbeknownst to the "hat-man," hotel manager Howard W. Hanson wanted to attend, but when asked for his money, he promptly refused, thus ending the party since the agreement had been broken.

Undeterred, the students sought out other forms of entertainment. Employees of the Paramount Theater took to the basement to see if there were movies the students could view. Success was had, as several movies were found, including *Fig Leaf for Eve*, *Urubu* and *The Payoff*, the fifteenth and final chapter of the 1949 Superman series, replacing the movies the students had viewed several times.

Not deterred by the weather, the college students offered their services to bring additional entertainment to students and other stranded passengers. The Northwestern students sang musical numbers, including "By the Sea" and "Temptation." The students not only brought entertainment to the Lincoln Theater but also caught the attention of Francis S. "One-Shot" Brammer, the *Wyoming Eagle* photographer. George said he and others posed

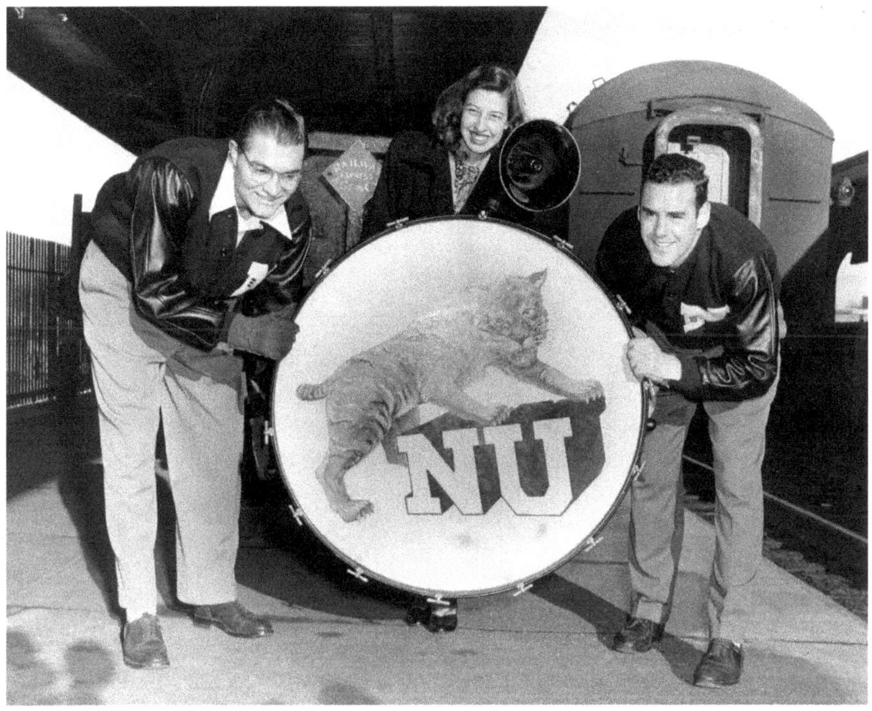

Northwestern University Band members. *Courtesy of Northwestern University Library.*

for Brammer dressed up in cowboy hats and carrying skis. Of course, to steal the show, the students took off their coats and earmuffs to pose atop a snow-covered car.

By January 5, the students who had been in Cheyenne for two and a half days now were not only participating in local entertainment, but a group of the students attended a Wyoming legislative session where they participated in adopting a resolution to mend a leak in a roof. Even newly elected governor A.G. Crane, who could not come out to meet the students since he was snowbound at the Governor's Mansion, called the students by telephone, greeting them on their unexpected visit to the Cowboy State.

A resident of Cheyenne and student at Northwestern, Mary Lee Rogers took time to speak with George regarding her snowbound predicament. Mary Lee told George she had dinner guests over on Sunday, and they were still there due to the blizzard and impassable snowdrifts. George said the students agreed most everything related to their stay was good and no complaints really could be brought up. Of course, the students enjoyed not being in class and the absence of studies. George concluded with the fact that the balance of men and women in the group weighed heavily for the men, but the few young women present were spreading their charm among those on the train.[56]

George Likeness was not the only stranded student who told of his blizzard adventure in Wyoming. "The situation is great here in Cheyenne," Ted Kinnamen (Mu '50) conveyed by phone to the *Daily Northwestern* newspaper staff. Kinnamen, a baritone in the band, said, "I hope we stay here awhile, we are handicapped by lack of women, but we can't have everything. We aren't doing much to solve the problem, since we are held up here; no one can get in, and no one can get out. The band didn't play in the show [talent show at the Lincoln Theater presented by the Northwestern students] because there was no way to transport the instruments back and forth."

Not only did Kinnamen have the opportunity to speak with the *Daily Northwestern* reporters, but Eldon Milroy (Mu '52), a trombone player, spoke with reporters as well. Milroy, who was from Rockford, Illinois, stated, "So far, it isn't so bad. We are still getting fed, and still sleeping. Meals on the diner car are rationed somewhat, but they are still generous portions and good. There's no menu, just one meal because the railroad officials are taking no chances in the running out of food. However, meals are still free. Four other trains are stranded here in the station with us. All of the trains are warm."[57]

Even with sixty-mile-per-hour winds and enormous snowdrifts, the only thing in Cheyenne stalled were the trains. The students and band members from Northwestern were not discouraged by the storm, which had restricted all travel to and from Cheyenne. Bill Buxton, a reporter for the *Daily Northwestern*, relayed to readers that the blizzard occurring in Wyoming was the worst storm in the state's history up to that time. It was communicated to the paper that it had been snowing since Sunday, January 2, and phone calls that he had received from Cheyenne indicated "the snow was coming down so hard one could not see across the street." On Monday, a day after they arrived in Cheyenne, the students dined at what at the time was considered "the city's finest hostelry," the Plains hotel. Sometime around 4:00 a.m. on January 4, the students boarded their trains as they anticipated their trip back to Illinois. Reports were coming from newspapers across Illinois that the trains stranded in the blizzard would be "hours late" and were not expected to arrive in Illinois until later in the afternoon. However, late that night in Cheyenne, the trains had still not left the depot en route to the East as expected. Assistant publicity director

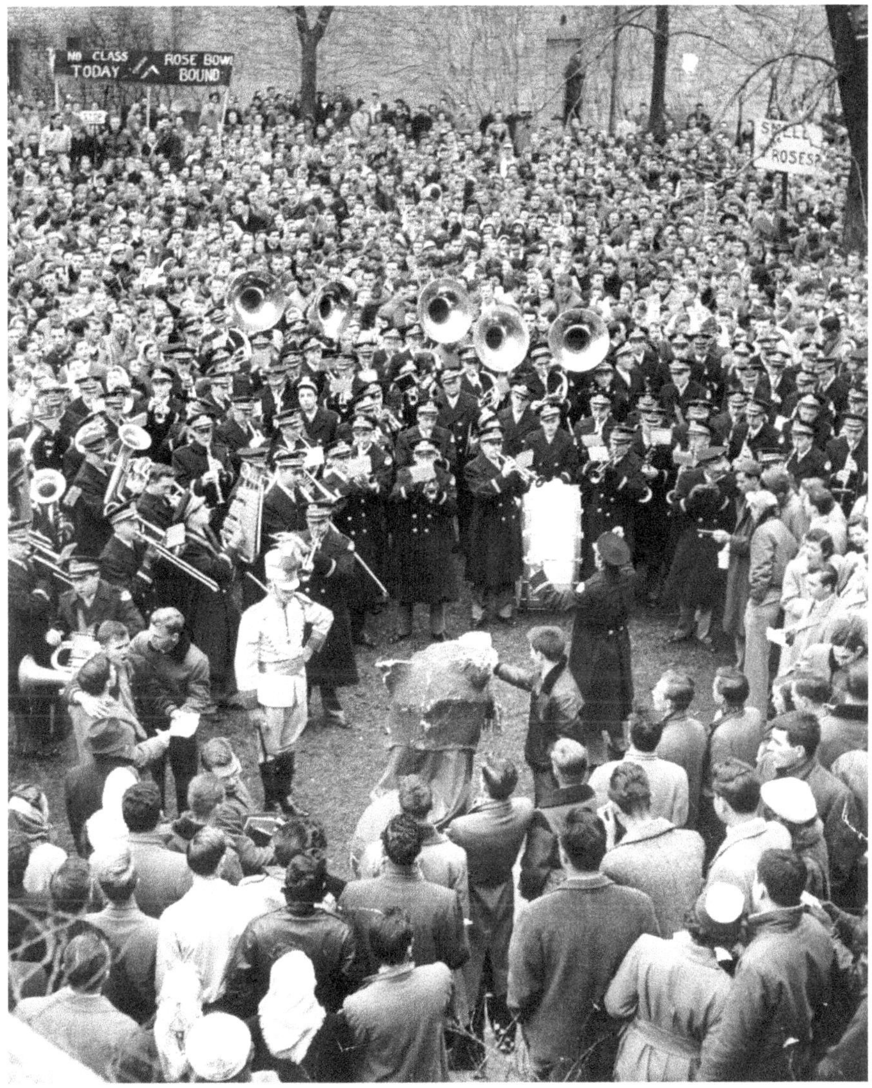

Northwestern University Band at Rose Bowl, Pasadena, California. *Courtesy of Northwestern University Library.*

Quentin Lambert told *Daily Northwestern* reporters that the Union Pacific office in Cheyenne had reported winds up to sixty miles per hour and snowdrifts had reached eighteen inches in height. He did not venture a guess as to when the trains would be leaving the city.

On January 4, team members and personnel of the athletic department, along with the president of Northwestern University, Franklyn B. Snyder, arrived at the Dearborn Street station in Evanston, Illinois, around 9:30 a.m. The Evanston police had to cordon off streets near and around the train station to assist with crowd control as hundreds of Northwestern Wildcat fans waited to greet the Wildcat students. Buses were chartered in Evanston to bring players and students back to the Northwestern campus. Of course, due to the blizzard, those students who were stranded in Wyoming could not make any planned victory rallies at the university. The director of student affairs, Joe Miller, told the *Daily Northwestern* that all plans for a victory rally were to be temporarily suspended until all of the Wildcat students had arrived on campus. There were pictures from the Rose Bowl game in Pasadena that were headed to the school; however, no one was exactly sure where they were or when they would arrive.[58]

CHAPTER 3

BUSINESS AS USUAL

The death of people during the blizzard was minimal, but the loss of cows, sheep and wildlife was devastating to ranchers and the state of Wyoming. The *Wyoming State Tribune* told of a horrific accident involving a Union Pacific train and a herd of antelope. West of Rawlins, a discovery was made by Deputy Game Warden Jim Underwood and Lynn Banker of Rawlins while they were out hunting. The two men found about one hundred dead and dying antelope that just twelve hours earlier had been plowed over by a train at the Union Pacific right-of-way. Upon examination of the animals, it appeared they had been eating well prior to the accident and were not malnourished. Although it was a significant loss, it gave hope that Wyoming's antelope herds had come through the blizzard better than previously assumed.[59]

For many weeks, attempts were made by ranchers to locate lost cattle across the vast plains of Wyoming. The task was complicated, as drifts buried cattle or enabled some cattle to traverse over fences that once had confined them to a specific area. One way the ranchers located these missing cattle was from the air. Pilots would take to the sky and search for cattle from the sky and report to those on the ground the location of cattle they could see from their vantage point. One such pilot was John Fryback from Wheatland, Wyoming, who earned the nickname the "Flying Cowboy." One story noted in the newspaper was that Fryback and his partner, Fred Wilson, made an emergency flight to Denver with two-year-old Roger Hansen and his mother, Mrs. Donald Hansen, of Casper, Wyoming. Mrs. Hansen and her son were

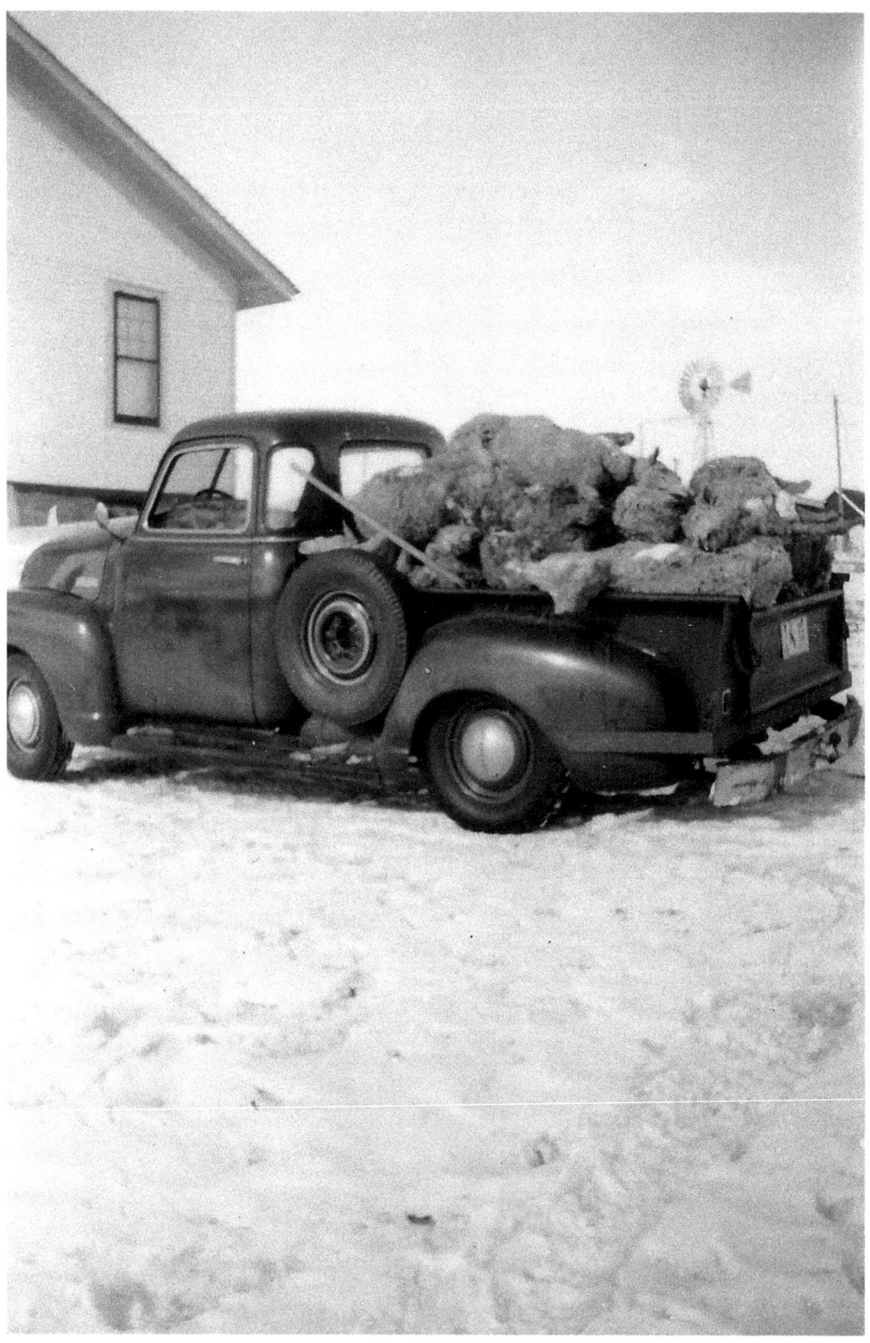

Hauling out the carcasses of the dead sheep found in and around the ranch. *Courtesy of Senator Fred Emerich.*

headed for Denver from Casper by bus when the storm hit, stranding them in Wheatland, Wyoming. Fryback and Wilson flew the boy and his mother to Denver, where Roger was admitted to the Denver Children's Hospital and treated for a breathing difficulty caused by a peanut that had become lodged in his lung. Returning home after their visit to Denver, Mrs. Hansen and her son became stranded in their home Wednesday of that week, preventing them from returning to the hospital for further treatment for the young boy. Bill Prendergast, chairman of the Red Cross, planned with both Fryback and Wilson to once again take Mrs. Hansen and her son back to Denver.[60]

Within days of coming to the aid of the Hansons, Fryback once again came to the rescue of those in need on a return mission in the Goshen Hole region after the storm. Fryback spotted a man leading a horse carrying a woman and child. Instinctively, Fryback thought this did not look like a good situation and felt he needed to investigate. He was able to bring his plane close to the couple and shut down the throttle so he could call out to them and see if there was indeed a problem. Based on their brief conversation, Fryback landed his plane just a short distance from the couple, quickly learning the child was ill and the parents were headed to find medical attention.

Wasting no time, Fryback loaded the infant and mother into the plane and flew them directly to the Torrington airfield, where the mother and child left by ambulance to the Torrington hospital for medical assistance. Later on, the couple was identified as Mr. and Mrs. Darl Blain Hacker, who lived on a ranch southwest of Yoder, Wyoming, in Goshen County. It was fortunate they were spotted by Fryback when they were. They were only a short distance from their ranch when Fryback saw them from his plane. The Hackers were making their way to the highway, which was approximately eight miles from the ranch. There was no further information in the article on the outcome of the child's hospital stay, but it is likely that Fryback's keen attention and quick response assisted in saving the child's life, as well as that of the family. Fryback, according to the paper, was busy, as he continued to fly many more missions to areas that were inaccessible to vehicular traffic.[61]

Livestock across the state were in danger of starving to death if food was not provided for them quickly. Due to the snow, packed areas and drifts, it was extremely difficult to get food sources to the cattle that they were accustomed to having. However, it was not only the horses, cattle and sheep that suffered and needed assistance in getting food after the blizzard. In Wyoming, some twelve thousand elk trapped by the snow were fed by the Wyoming Fish and Game Commission. The ferocity of the storm caused treacherous conditions throughout the western mountain

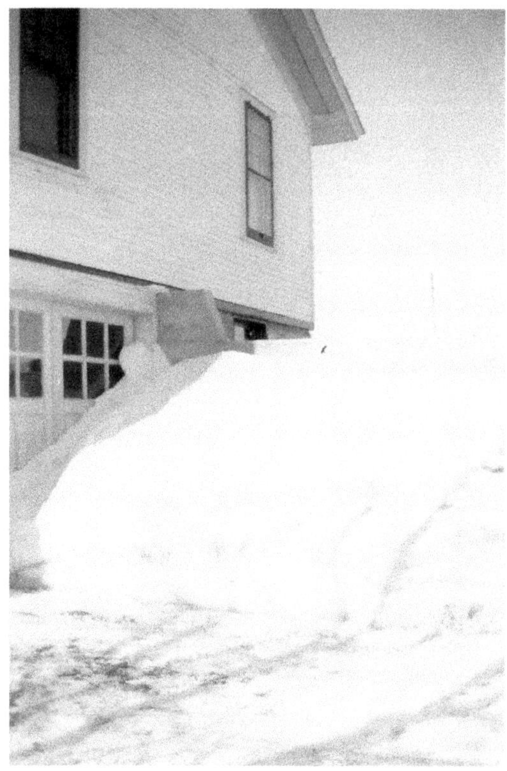

Drifts cover the cement wall near the garage. Carl Emerich went out into the blizzard to check on the sheep. The wind and blinding snow pushed him in the wrong direction, and he realized he was going the wrong direction when he bumped into the wall. Had he not bumped into the wall, he would have walked farther away from the house. *Courtesy of Senator Fred Emerich.*

canyons and valley areas where many of the state's elk resided. Hay and concentrates were dropped in these areas to assist in supplementing the elk's diet where there was little to no food available.

Statistics released by the Wyoming Fish and Game Commission in Cheyenne were staggering, as they informed the community of the amounts of food and cost it took to sustain the elk population. Lester Bagley, a representative for the commission, in a statement to media said, "To feed its many 'boarders,' 2,020 tons of hay and two-hundred and six tons of cottonseed cake representing an aggregate evaluation of $84,202.50. Of the total tonnage, five-hundred and sixty tons were held over from last year, and 2,460 tons during the year were purchased." Bagley further stated, "Elk do better on natural feed than on a diet of cured hay."

The fish and game commission had entered into a cooperative agreement with the U.S. Fish and Wildlife Service, administrators of the Jackson refuge, whereby the refuge management allowed the meadow grass growing on the reserve to stand and cure as natural feed instead of cutting and storing it as formerly done. The commission, in turn, supplied hay for feeding for

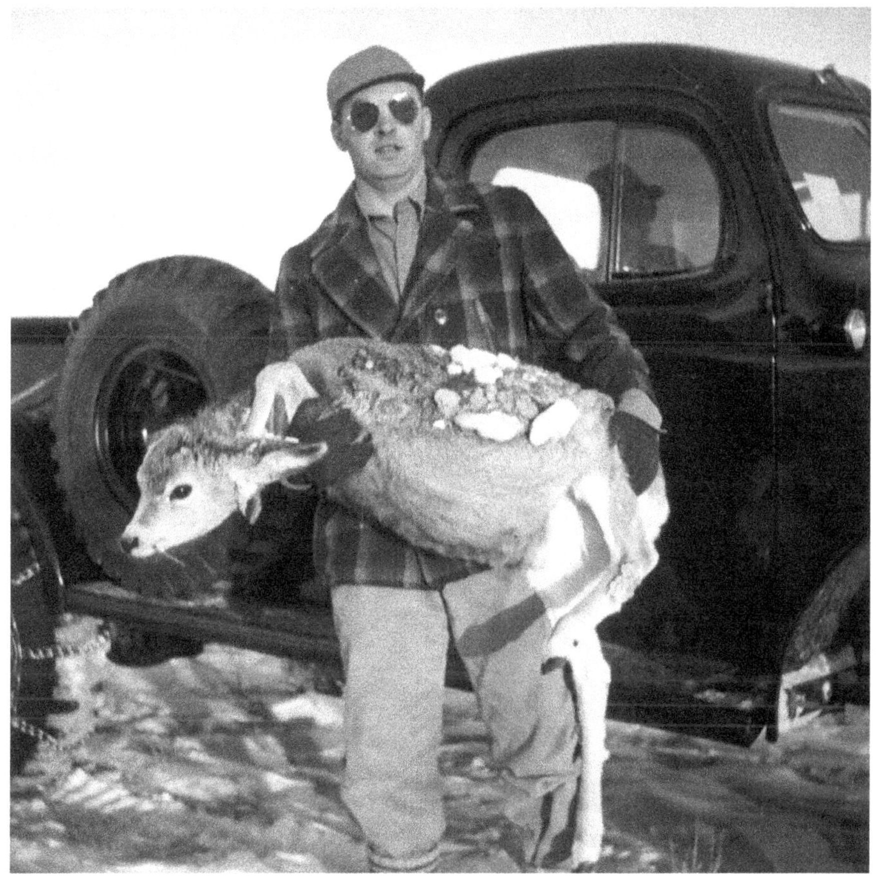

Orville Mayer, deputy game warden, rescues a snowdrift-caught deer, which was brought to town and revived. The deer was released near the east end of the mountain near Little Gooseberry Creek. *Courtesy of Chuck Morrison, Morrison Collection, Casper College Western History Center.*

emergencies such as this one on the refuge. The success of the policy is pointed up by the previous year's experience, in which there was no feeding at all on the Jackson refuge. Even though the elk would feed on the surrounding area, natural grass was not available to these animals.

"Also during the abnormally harsh winter, feeding on the refuge was delayed more than a month after the boarding program was under wap [*sic*] in the outlying elk areas."[62] According to Bagley, the hay and cake in storage in emergency use were distributed as follows: Jackson Hole area, 2,176 tons of hay (exclusive of the 5,000 tons of government-owned hay in storage on the federal refuge) and 129 tons of cake; Green River area, 357 tons of hay and 50 tons of cake; Star Valley, 343 tons of hay and 20 tons of cake; Big Piney, 140 tons of hay and 6 tons of cake.[63] Through the efforts of local, state and federal agencies, the elk population in Wyoming was saved with the programs previously established and the distribution of the hay and supplements for the elk in the region.

With the snow on the ground, temperatures well below freezing and winds blowing, the University of Wyoming did not close enrollment for students attending the six-week course as part of the university's College of Agriculture classes beginning the first week of January 1949. In fact, thirteen students faced the challenges of the blizzard and enrolled in the short course, which focused on crops and farm management, according to the director, Harold W. Benn. Of the attendees, ten were from Wyoming and three from Montana. Those from Wyoming were Milton Sundin, Pine Bluffs; Merrill Yorgason, Burlington; Ted Ondo, Worland; Riki Shimogaki, Basin; Bruce Berner, Bosler; Harold Davis, Buford; Raymond Tanner, Mountain View; John Ertman, New Castle; and Robert Hughs and Olyn Allbert, Riverton. The three from Montana were Bill Currie, Matthew Brown Jr. and Charles Skorupa, all of Bridger.

The article pointed out the second portion of the shortened course would cover up-to-date methods of livestock production, disease prevention and control, livestock judging and training other phases of efficient livestock operations, which would begin in the upcoming weeks. Students who had not enrolled during the blizzard, as did the thirteen brave students, also had the opportunity to enroll for the second portion of the course. The article also mentioned the College of Agriculture would be offering a favorite wool short course again at the beginning of February, which was an attraction to sheep men and students from many different states each year. It was clear that these students were concerned more about their education than a blizzard. Many of these men went on to serve in the United States military during the conflicts in Korea and Vietnam.

During the blizzard, neighbors continually came to the support of those in need, and the Bell family was no exception. The Alton Bell family owned a ranch near Little Bear, Wyoming, north of Cheyenne.[64] The newspaper mentioned the Bells related to the cliché "a friend in need is a friend indeed," as their neighbors were willing to assist them at their ranch since they were stranded. The Bells were at their daughter's home in Careyville Acres in Cheyenne and had been stranded from Sunday, January 2, until the following Saturday, January 8.[65] The Bells were bringing their grandchildren back into town after they had spent the holidays with them

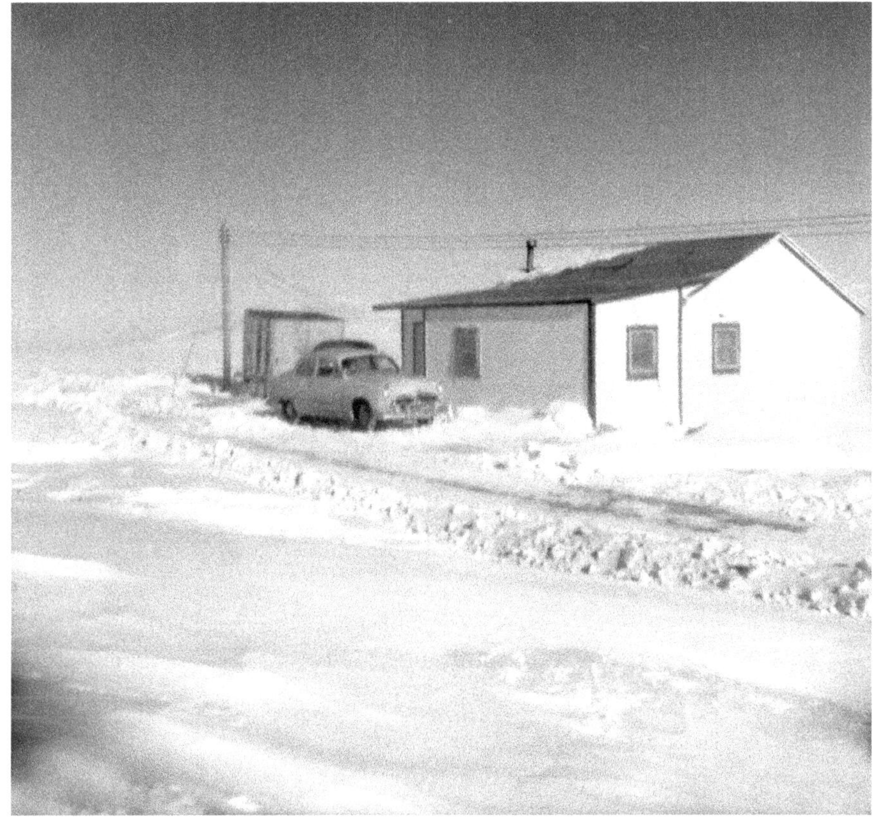

Upside of the mining camp relatively clear of snow. *Courtesy of John Moyer.*

at the Bell ranch. The plan was to drop them off on Sunday morning and drive back later that morning, but the storm's intensity hindered them from making the trip back to Little Bear. On Wednesday around noon, Mr. Bell made a call to the Swinbank ranch to see what the weather conditions were like back home. There were twenty people stranded at the Little Bear Inn, along with Paul Gustafson, the proprietor, who was listening in to the weather conditions. At the inn, the lights had already gone out several days before the call by Bell, water pipes were frozen, butane and food were running low and the only source of news from the world outside the inn was calling others by telephone. Mr. Gustafson overheard Bell telling Swinbank his sheep would not survive on their own unless someone could reach them and turn them out. Gustafson quickly rounded up three others, and with the aid of truck and walking, they reached the Bell ranch, where

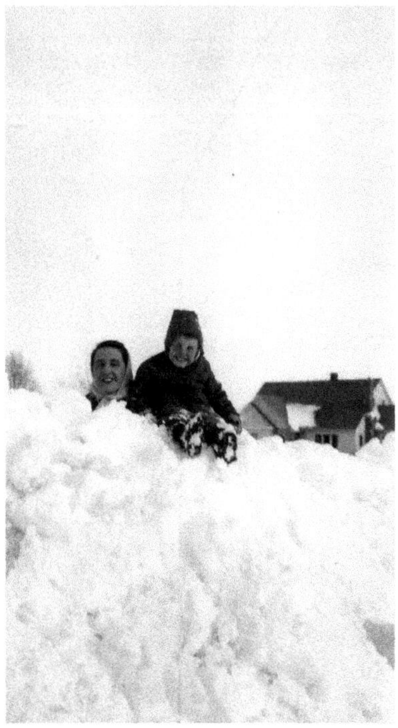

Anna McDermott and child on a snowdrift. *Courtesy of Mary Kay Koroulis Albrechtson.*

they fed and let out the sheep that were alive. Unfortunately, many of the sheep did not survive. Much of the herd had made its way down into the barn, where the horses had trampled them, while others grouped against the fence, becoming buried under the snowdrifts. Of the sheep, approximately two hundred were presumed dead. Another one of Bell's neighbors, Hugh DuVall, came to the aid of the sheep on the ranch when he realized the Bells were not home. DuVall cared for the sheep while he continued a search for his stray animals after the blizzard.

With all the chaos going on outside with the sheep, Bettie Gustafson with her five children kept the Little Bear Inn running. As she did all the cooking for those guests who were stranded, she continually reassured those who were fearful of the blizzard and its outcome, since some had not been through a weather phenomenon such as this. Of the stranded guests, there was a three-month-old baby who survived on a chocolate mixture given to him and, according to the article in the *Wheatland Times*, cried when given milk dropped off by the American Red Cross. Until Thursday evening, candles were the only source of light, and water had to be pumped and carried in to the group due to the frozen pipes. Resourcefulness and kindness always seemed to come first with those who were stranded together during the blizzard. Neighbors and even those who were not neighbors came along and made things happen to survive and make it through the blizzard. Indeed, a notable example to follow!

For a historian, attempting to capture an event that happened nearly seventy years ago can be difficult because so many of those who lived through it have passed and are no longer here to tell their story as it happened to them. However, there are times when people who lived through an event ensure future generations can relive those moments because they took the time to write down what happened and what they experienced during that moment in time. One story comes from Goshen County, Wyoming, where a teenage girl documented in her diary the events seen through her eyes. Peggy Ann DesEnfants lived in Goshen County just six miles south of Van Tassel. Although the *Torrington Telegraph* was running the story, Peggy's diary had taken a long trip to finally come back home to Wyoming. Jess Willard, who lived in Los Angeles, sent a clipping from the *Los Angeles Times* to friends in Lusk when he saw the printed copy of Peggy's diary in the newspaper. Later, it was found out that Peggy's uncle Charles DesEnfants was a member of the accident investigation division of the Los Angeles Police Department and had received a copy of the diary from friends in Wyoming. Charles wasted no time in sending a copy to the *Los Angeles Times* to be published. Peggy went into great detail of what happened during the blizzard as she wrote these events in her diary.

On January 2, as the storm began in 1949, Peggy's memoirs indicated that activities on the farm were typical and not out of the ordinary. She wrote that her brothers Bill and Billie had started feeding the cattle sometime around 10:00 a.m. By 3:00 p.m., the storm was in full swing, and Peggy stated, "Guess it is what they called a good old 'northwester.'" The next day, January 3, the storm intensified as Peggy said it seemed worse than the day before. Her brothers made a valiant effort to go to the barn to attend to the animals inside, but their efforts were useless against the snow and wind. Later in the day, the boys made a second attempt to rescue the chickens. Making it to the chicken coop, the boys pulled the chickens from the snow and trudged their way to the granary, which was a better building for the chickens. Due to a large drift, the granary door was shut tight. Billie improvised and climbed atop the drift, tossing the chickens in through a window leading into the granary. With animals to tend to, Peggy continually monitored what was happening both outside and inside as she reported that the phone lines had just gone out as the day was ending.

Not much took place on January 4, as Peggy penned in her diary that nothing had changed regarding the weather. There was nothing they could do about the calves, and the cattle were standing in place due to the drifts and high winds that prevailed. The only thing Peggy observed that particular day was that the best thing they could all do was to worry.

On January 5, Peggy and her family appeared to be much better, as Peggy noted, "Has cleared." She explained that the wind continued and the drifts grew higher across the farm. Peggy's Uncle Jack and Aunt Bea made their way from their home to the DesEnfants residence seeking shelter. The gas tank at her relatives' home had run out of fuel, leaving them without heat.

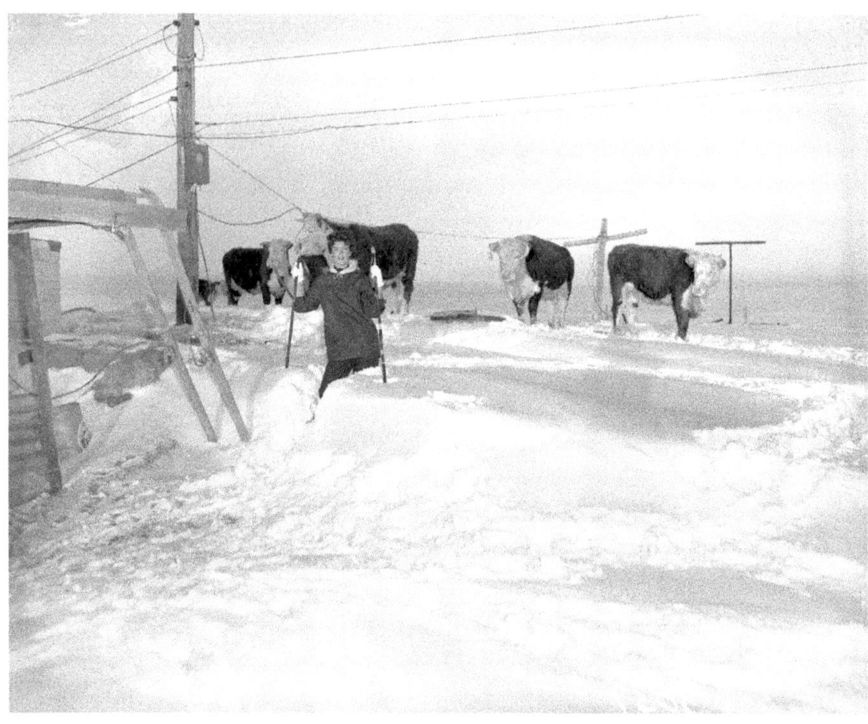

Mrs. Jack Welsh with ski poles walking with cattle; notice the tops of the power lines behind the cattle. *Francis Steele Brammar, courtesy of Wyoming State Archives.*

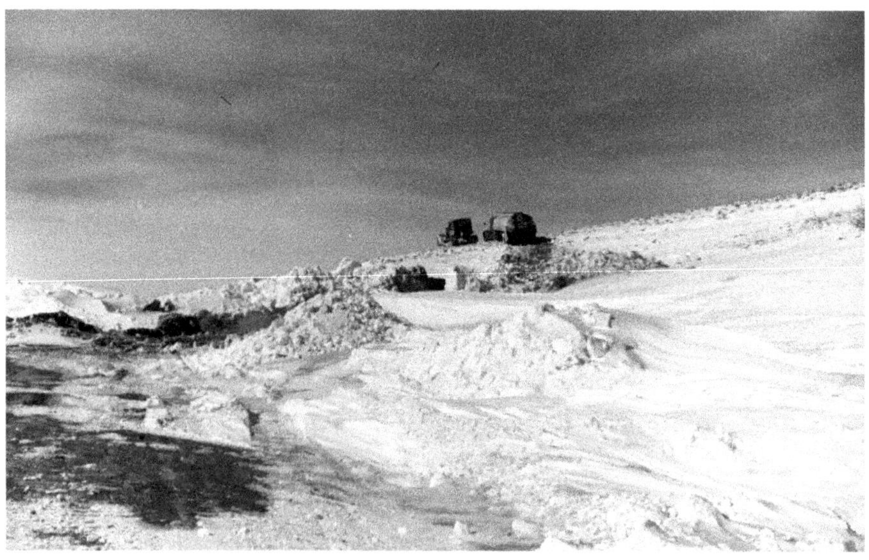

Assisting a fuel truck that became stuck in the snowdrifts. *Courtesy of John Moyer.*

Peggy pointed out that her family was running low on provisions, and now with two additional people to feed, this supply would quickly diminish. Even on that particular day, Bill and Billie were able to get out and feed the calves. They took a jeep to locate lost cattle but went about a mile from the farm and had to turn back because of the insurmountable drifts that covered the area. Per Peggy's account, this was the fourth consecutive day and night the cattle had gone without feed.

By January 6, it is obvious that the conditions were dangerous where Peggy and her family lived. Peggy's brothers took the jeep and the tractor, driving for over an hour to get their Uncle Jack and Aunt Bea back to their house only a half mile across the pasture. Once the boys had dropped off their aunt and uncle, they once again started looking for their cattle. With one boy in the tractor and the other in the jeep, it took them over three hours to cross the farm looking for the cows. In their search, they located four dead cows, while the others found were in pretty bad shape. They heard from their uncle Jack that he had recovered three of his cows on the roof of his barn. To get the cattle back into the barn, Jack cut a hole in the barn and hoisted the cattle down one by one. Bill and Billie got their cattle back to the farm, along with several bales of hay, but it was well after the sun had gone down when the boys returned to the house. Peggy told how her uncle Jack and aunt Bea had assisted a neighbor, Ramona Coffey, because her husband was stranded in the snow and could not get back to Wyoming. Peggy ended her daily journaling with "Boy is the food running low." This is an indicator that either Peggy was very observant of what was going on or the food had become scarce and was being rationed out to the members of the family. It is difficult to imagine how terrible it may have been in those conditions.

Life started getting back to some normalcy the following day, as Peggy reported, "Cold and clear." The men in the family started breaking away at the ice on the water tank, but not before they dug it out of a six-foot snowbank. Peggy stated the snow had drifted over the windbreaks and feed racks. In fact, the snow had blown into all the buildings and drifted up to the rafters. With the need of feed pushing them, Peggy and her brother Bill headed out to the Petersons', where they bought ten pounds of flour and Bill hooked up the phones and once again restored communication lines between neighbors and those beyond Torrington. Being the reporter and storyteller she was, when Peggy returned home, she picked up the family's party line and listened in to all the problems from nearby neighbors.[66] Ranches and farms all around them had lost livestock: Cy Roby, 65 cows; Edwin Crapes, 50 calves; Keith Newman, 17 cows; the Coffeys, 8 cows and a few sheep; Mahlon Peterson, 70 sheep; and the Van Tassel Ranch, 175 cattle. Peggy, as she wrapped up the adventures of the day, made mention that she had started seeing planes fly over the area. She mentioned her family had considered placing an F on the ground indicating they were low on food.

The blizzard was harsh on the DesEnfants family, but by January 8, Bill and Billie had taken the tractor and headed to the schoolhouse. After they had finished with their school lessons that day, they brought food back to the ranch. Apparently, Peggy kept up with the news around the ranch as well as in town, as she reported that Bill McKelvey had walked to his home from Lusk, Wyoming, which was thirty miles, only to find out that he had lost ninety-six cows. Finally, Peggy ended writing in her diary that a Mr. Otto York had lost seventy head of cattle.

After such a tremendous storm, Peggy found a valuable lesson on January 9 in the problems and issues her family and others dealt with during the blizzard. She mentioned she was feeling lucky because her family had only lost five cows and one calf so far. Peggy appeared to understand the complexity of what was going on and how such a small loss seemed to be a blessing compared to the losses of most of the other ranches that were so close to her family's. The wind continued to blow and cause problems for many. On January 10, Peggy wrote nearly everyone's home was full of blowing snow, and it was still coming with no end in sight. However, she said her house was the only house not filled with snow from the winter blast.

It was soon realized that a ten-pound bag of flour would not suffice for Peggy's family. So on January 11, Billie Suitcase, Jack (Peggy's uncle), Bill and Billie DesEnfants and Bill and Tommy Coffey prepared two four-wheel-drive jeeps with chains and headed for Lusk, Wyoming. They arrived sometime around 3:30 p.m. and, according to Peggy, cleared the stores out of food. The caravan headed back from Lusk around 9:30 p.m. with supplies and food. As the story progresses, it becomes apparent that Peggy was not a fan of shoveling snow. On January 12, she stated, "Shoveled snow and worked like sin all day!" Here Peggy enlightens her readers, as she conveyed that Uncle Jack and Aunt Bea did not make it back to their house as she had indicated on the sixth; she wrote that Jack and Bea had finally made it back to their house that particular day. "Same old story…WORK, WORK, WORK!" Peggy was fed up with shoveling snow and would rather have been writing. Once again, Peggy tells of a neighbor who traveled to Torrington, which took them all day; it was only thirty-five miles away. Little was happening, as the only journal entry for January 14 was to note that Foley Calhoun had tried to break through drifts to get out to the main road.

The first storm had just stopped when another storm hit, which Peggy's family may have known about but is unclear in Peggy's diary. She writes, "The wind started blowing again, and Bill went and tried to care for the cows. As the storm worsened, Bill could not see his tracks in the snow, so he decided to abandon the jeep and make his way back home." As with many who survived the Blizzard of 1949, Peggy's final entry characterizes what many felt across the state: "Everyone is wondering will there be any more cattle left in the morning because it is another 'northwester.'"[67]

Death occurred many times with cattle, sheep and wildlife during the blizzard, but there were rare moments when miracles happened and these animals eluded death, managing to survive. Two miles north of Veteran, Wyoming, at F.E. Courtney's ranch, many boasted it should be "Courtney versus Ripley's Believe It or Not" when workers made an amazing discovery. As work began on digging out sheep pens from under the snowdrifts, a sheep was found buried under the snow. The sheep had been buried in snow for thirty-three days, and the astonishing part was that the sheep was still alive and in good condition for what it had undergone. Courtney told the paper they had found small bits of hay near the ewe and a large melted cavity in the snow, enabling the animal to breathe. The breath of the ewe had, amazingly enough, melted an air vent through the nearly six feet of snow that was directly above her. According to Courtney, this was one of his best ewes, and to the rancher's surprise, she was quite active when they discovered her. Courtney explained her hind legs appeared to be somewhat paralyzed but did not give the impression of being frozen. At the time of the article, the ewe was making a speedy recovery.[68]

The misery suffered by the cattle and other animals on the range was horrific, as thousands died from exposure to the elements during the blizzard. With cattle and sheep being a source of revenue to many across Wyoming, the government understood this was something that had to be addressed quickly. On January 27, 1949, the Wyoming Relief chairman told reporters that three hundred tons of hay would be flown from Fort Riley, Kansas, to Casper, Wyoming, to assist in feeding the starving cattle in central Wyoming. Ralph E. Barton, the Natrona County emergency chairman, organized for U.S. Army Air Force (AAF) hay to be delivered to Casper because feed supplies in the area were minimal and near depletion.[69] Russell Thorp, a pilot with the military, flew hay into the Casper airport. From there, ranchers from central Wyoming could come and pick up the necessary feed for their starving cattle. Thorp indicated that due to the blizzard, the flight would not even leave Kansas until the end of the week, delaying the distribution of hay to the livestock. The air transport of the hay would not have been part of the plan had it not been for Barton. Once he realized the train shipments of hay did not meet the need for the livestock, Barton petitioned Thorp to assist in getting an AAF transport authorized. Even as the article went to print, snow continued to fall in central Wyoming, causing large drifts, which thwarted road crews from keeping county roads open and ranchers from reaching feeding pens for their stock. The central Wyoming region, according to officials, was the worst and the last remaining area in Wyoming under emergency services in the state. The paper described other places across the state dealing with clearing blocked roads and stated that getting food to those short of supplies was "progressing fairly well."[70]

Ranches across Wyoming took a major hit when the blizzard came through in January 1949. Both cattle and sheep ranchers lost devastating numbers of animals from starvation, freezing and suffocation, as many were buried under snowdrifts. Firsthand accounts of the work of these ranchers are a rarity, but when they are found, the amazing fortitude these men had as they labored to save and protect their assets is astonishing. Percy Cooper, a sheep rancher from Casper, articulated his story with letters to his wife during the blizzard and the days after, along with his own experiences he penned after the blizzard. His account, along with the letters he wrote, spotlights a time when saving his business was dependent on grappling with Mother Nature and continued long after the blizzard had moved on.

Percy and his father, Tom, headed out on the morning of January 2, 1949, to Casper. The storm had already started, and a north wind was fiercely beating down. The pair headed out to Sandhills, where they drove out to the sheep camps, checking on the herders and sheep before heading back to Casper.[71] The sheepherders were camped out in different places across the plains. One herder, Dan Gallegos, was camped at the "slat fence," while Jake Lavato was camped on the south line near Lester Armagast's ranch. The following morning, Percy and Tom went back out to check on these herders and the sheep. Dan had lost his sheep, and Jake's sheep had drifted toward Armagast's. As Tom and Percy headed back to their camp in Sand Springs Creek after checking in on the herders, they found themselves stranded in the snow near Fred Cottman's ranch, forcing them to spend the night there. The following morning, after enjoying a warm place to sleep. Percy borrowed a horse from Fred and rode over to his ranch headquarters on Bobcat Creek, bringing back two saddle horses for him and his father. On Thursday, January 6, Percy and his father headed out to locate the lost sheep. Although a ground blizzard out of the southwest came upon them, they were able to recover a few of the sheep. On Friday, they headed back out to look for the other sheep, this time with great success. They found a large number of sheep with twelve other black sheep (markers).[72] Once again, they headed back out to the Armagast ranch in search of their sheep. Percy said it started storming bad out of the north, but they were able to get back to Cottman's ranch without any problems.

After hauling feed out to both sheep camps, Percy and Tom realized they would need another team and wagon to do the job efficiently. That night, both Percy and Tom rode back toward their ranch headquarters. Percy headed east of the camp to the Senora bedground, where he was able to locate additional horses, returning to camp well after dark. Tom rode down the west side of Bobcat Creek looking for extra horses to borrow but was unable to locate any along the creek. He arrived back to camp headquarters late that evening; however, with such limited communication, Percy had been unable to inform him that he had found the needed horses. The next morning, they headed out to the Sandhills with the wagon and horses. Tom took the wagon and horse, while Percy took the ranch's old pickup truck. The truck had been parked too close to the house, and the engine was frozen and would not start. Percy had to take a piece of tin, start a fire on it and put it underneath the truck to melt the frozen snow and get the truck started once again. Once they left the house, they encountered large drifts and had to utilize the team of horses to pull the truck through. Once they reached the top of the divide, they were pleased to see that the Amerada Oil Company had plowed the road. Tom, who was seventy-seven years old, began to have problems with his feet from the severe temperatures. The two men continued moving Jake and his sheep to the Twin bedground, where they found him the next day enjoying a good day from the storm. They once again headed back out to Armagast's ranch after being able to find one hundred head of Jake's sheep. By January 15, the storms had started back up, bringing another ground blizzard from the north. This time, Percy was able to feed hay to Jake's sheep they had relocated back to the ranch headquarters just days before.

Now, with Jake and his sheep moved, Percy made the decision to move Dan to the Sagebrush bedground, where they counted a total of twenty-three black sheep. With a hard wind blowing from the southwest all the next day, they were still able to get haystacks out to Jake's sheep near the creek and also get hay to Dan's bunch of sheep at Sagebrush. On January 22, another ground blizzard kicked up from the north around ten o'clock in the morning. They were able to get hay to Dan's sheep as the storm continued well into the evening. The next day, however, was a different story, with snow coming down and the temperatures still well below freezing. Due to the poor weather conditions that day, they were only able to feed Jake's sheep; it was impossible to get hay to Dan and his sheep.

When Percy was finally able to get hay to Dan, he used his lariat to drag bales of hay with the assistance of his horse out to the sheep. After Percy had finished getting hay to the sheep, he then headed back to his headquarters. Upon his arrival, it was clear that the condition of Tom's feet had gotten serious. His toes were frozen, and they had not improved even after coming in from the snow and frigid cold. Percy knew that Tom needed medical attention, so he took his horse and headed to the Cole Creek oil field, which was about twelve miles away. Once there, Percy used General Petroleum's phone to call for assistance. Bob Grieve, another rancher in the area, had called and spoken with Trula, Percy's wife, letting her know about the bad storm her father-in-law and husband were dealing with. With this news, Trula had contacted Roy Lamereaux with his plane to head out in the direction where Percy and Tom where. Roy—who piloted a Cessna 170, which was equipped with skis—landed near the Sand Springs Creek, picked up Tom and flew him back to Casper to see a doctor. That evening, Percy sat down and wrote his wife a letter:

> *Dearest Trula,*
>
> *While I wanted to fly with Roy Lamereaux and Norman French, I thought it best to send father because he does need rest and change. Everything you sent was fine, and you certainly must have moved fast this afternoon. When I called you from Cole Creek I was alone in the office, but men began coming in to eat their lunches, and it was rather hard to talk, which accounts for some notable omissions in my conversation. We have not done so bad with the sheep, but I am worried about the cattle. The herders naturally play out under these conditions, they need good weather as bad as the sheep. If some people along the river should pick up our cattle, ask them to feed the cattle for us until we can get to them and we shall pay all the costs, etc.*
>
> *I hope Joe* [Bailey, a trucker] *can bring the feed from O.T.'s* [O.T. Evans] *and the hay & misc. items to Stevenson road turn-off as soon as he can, that is after going to Dan's camp as is scheduled for tomorrow. We have cotton cake, but can only feed about so heavy with it, therefore need the other feed. The Northern Lights are very bright tonite* [sic], *greens and reds, so it seems more like the Arctic than Wyoming*

Brooks Headquarters 2:00 p.m. January 26th

I am going to send this in with Houston Lamb (Brooks Co. foreman). I have been [d]*own here all day waiting for hay. Roy Lamereaux stopped and told me he had left a man to help me at our camp. He is sure to find about helping out. Everyone seems to be getting hay but us. I am in a hizzy about what to do when this hay doesn't show up. I have lost about a day waiting down here, and both bunches need help, sure a mess. I have heard of some cattle today & Donovan's* [neighbor to the south] *are feed*[ing] *some of our calves.*

On January 26, Roy Lamereaux flew Art Morrison, who was a government trapper, to assist Percy with the ranch. Although Art was a trapper, he failed to bring warm enough clothes and nearly froze, according to Percy. Now that the road near the ranch was open, Percy rode out to the B.B. Brooks Co. Headquarters, where he met up with truck driver Joe Bailey. With a truckload of hay, Percy rode with Joe, leaving two bales of hay at the Stevenson's turnoff. The following day, six inches of new snow fell, but Percy and Joe made their way with hay to Dan and his sheep at the Twin bedground. That same day, Roy Lamereaux flew someone out to help with additional ranch duties. Roy brought in Mary Hester Nicolaysen, who took Percy's horse and rode a half mile back to the headquarters camp. Mary did this so Percy could fly back out with Roy to check on some bulls that were near that area. As Percy and Roy approached the area where the bulls were, they had to land the plane into the southwest winds and navigate over and through rough drifts. They had loaded some hay on the plane, which they dropped to a lone bull they saw as they flew over the ranch. Percy said dropping the hay to the bull was of no avail, as the bull later died from exposure, as did the other bulls they were hoping to rescue and feed. Percy had left what he called a "bum" group of weak sheep in a tin corral at the ranch. It was assumed that these sheep would not survive the cold because there was no way they could get back to them due to drifts. However, it was discovered that the sheep, in fact, could take care of themselves, as they walked out onto the high drifts and ate from the haystacks in the corral.

Help continued to come from friends and neighbors. Julius Begonia, a friend of Percy's father who had worked for Tom in the 1920s, attempted to make his way out to the ranch, but the ground blizzard had gotten so bad that he could not find his way off the creek with his team and wagon. Percy took his truck, headed back into Casper and was stranded

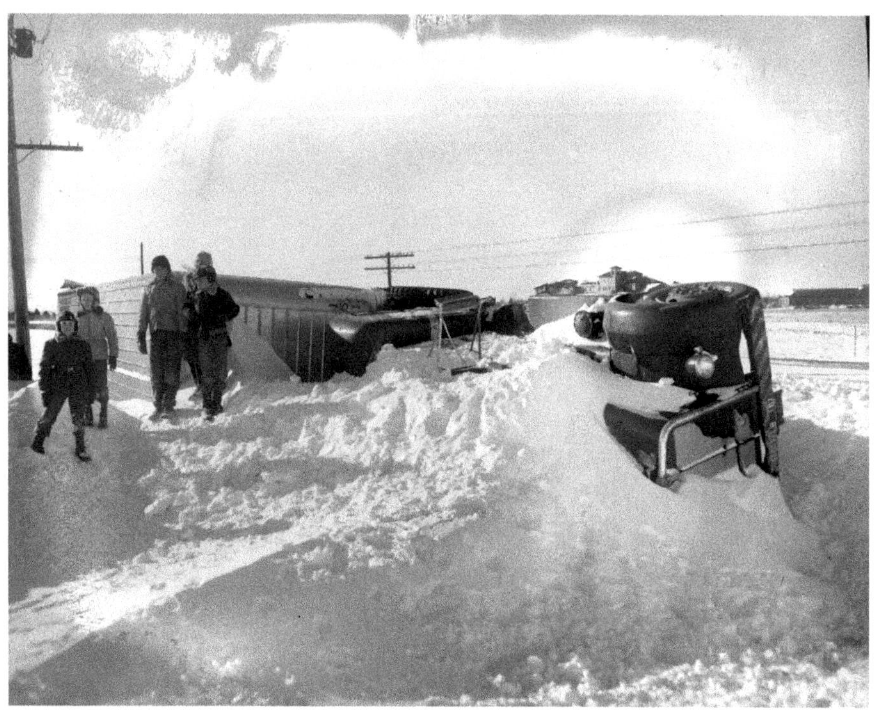

A semi-truck turned over in the snowstorm. *Francis Steele Brammar, courtesy of Wyoming State Archives.*

by yet another snowstorm that rolled in. Percy's truck had stalled on the highway, but as fate would have it, he was picked up by a neighbor rancher, John Burke, who attempted to get Percy back to the ranch. The storm became so intense that they got as far as the Wardwell Airport, where the road was blocked, and they could proceed no farther. Members of the Wyoming National Guard were directing stranded motorists to take shelter in the airport hangar until the road was cleared. The U.S. Air Force was flying hay from Kansas into Casper because of the condition of roads into Casper as well as the blocked railroads. Percy alluded that it wasn't going to do much good trying to get hay to the cattle because the hay was snowed in at the airport. Air Force leadership at the airport came up with a plan. The proposal was to drop the hay directly to the cattle on the ranches. Two planes were able to get out with their cargo. One plane took off in the direction of Mark Davis's outfit, while Percy rode along with the second plane, guiding it to his ranch. When Percy's plane reached its destination, they made their first attempt to drop the hay. The crewmen, with the assistance of Percy, untied a load of hay as they prepared to throw it to the sheep they had spotted. The pilot took the plane down into a slight dive and pulled up to level off. When the plane made this maneuver, all of the supplies and hay slid to the back of the aircraft, pinning Percy and other crew members. The crew were prepared for such an event, as they were all wearing parachutes. This, however, was not the case for Percy; he was simply tied into the plane by his waist so he would not fall out the back of the aircraft. On their second attempt to drop the hay, they were able to throw out a few bales, but as the hay went out the back of the aircraft, it hit the plane's stabilizer, which did not make the pilots happy as they were attempting to maneuver the plane into position. Finally, on their third attempt, they figured out how to drop ten bales at a time as the pilot circled the aircraft closer to the ground. They continued this same cycle until they had delivered seventy-five bales of hay to the starving animals. When they returned to the airport, they learned that the other plane was unable to drop its hay due to poor visibility.

Percy's wife, Trula, did not sit idly by while others on the ranch were working hard to save sheep and cattle. She ensured that when pilots headed out to the ranch to bring additional help or take Tom to the hospital, they brought back needed clothes and other essentials for Percy to battle the blizzard. It is evident in the following letter from Trula to Percy that not only was she working to assist Percy, but she was also coordinating with the Air Force to get additional planes with hay out to their ranch.

Dearest Perk,

I naturally was very depressed when I heard that things are so tough. I knew they must be bad but of course hoped that we wouldn't have too big loss, please take care of yourself. Take some of that medicine [Dicoumarol] *for Tom's feet (I sent that time) and put it in your ears. I am sending you a chamois mask for your face, one of the Air Force men gave Mary, Nic and me each one; I hope it will help a little. Also, I will send you another silk scarf. Tom said he had left a muffler there so you might find it. I will get one or may two Air Force planes on Monday if they can fly.*

Do you need coal urgently? I'll send you a few sacks with Roy. What about gasoline? Shall I send a drum with the pickup, which I can get it out? I'll put a notice on the 6:15 p.m. newscast as soon as I know when they can open the road. The Air Force will get right on it, and I will talk with Captain Ginrey tomorrow when I go to the base.

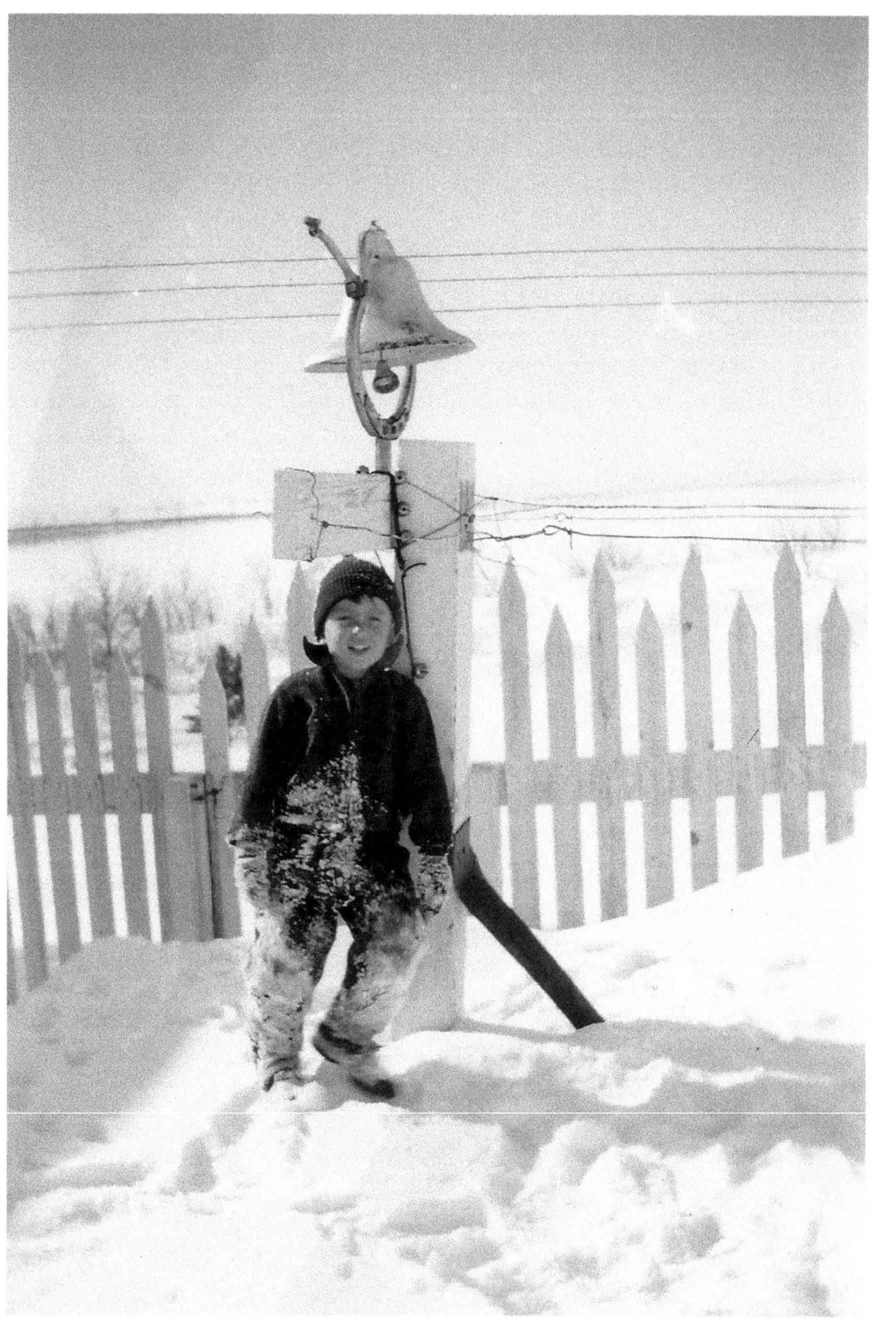

Fred Emerich poses for a picture near the clothesline and ranch bell. *Courtesy of Senator Fred Emerich.*

Tom gets so excited, and he left this morning without letting me know so I could send you a little word. It is rougher in Carbon County if that is any consolation.

I have been going out to the base and working as they are short of workers, and it is a cold place, and I wouldn't let Grandmother [Sue, Tom's wife] *go. I'll try and get two planes out tomorrow. I'll have one for sure.*

Gerry Nic is flying hay to the 8 Mile ranch, and he still hasn't been able to get our cows. However, a cow and two yearlings came in, and he is feeding them.

I told Tom to check the truck and get all the things out, but he only saw the meat. [The truck had been abandoned at the turnoff from the highway where it had stalled.]

Gerry Nic just called and said he had 20 head of our cattle, mostly calves, and yearlings and they didn't look so bad, he is feeding them now. His sheep were gone, but he hopes to get them back and is losing a few every day and who isn't.

We are all fine; the girls and Don are all in school. I know how you must feel to have the animals suffer and hope it won't be too bad, at least we won't be paying much income tax.

With all my love,
Trula

Even as January came to a close and Percy and his family had survived the blizzard, February held much of the same. The cold temperatures and snow continued to drop as the month rolled in. Fighting to feed the sheep and cattle was unrelenting, but ranchers and Airmen continued to fly missions across the area, dropping hay and supplies.

Just like a rerun of the events in January, the roads to the ranch were once again opened, and Percy headed that way. Temperatures in the area had dropped to twenty below zero that morning, making the drive back to the ranch a cold one. Jake Lavato was unable to get his sheep out to graze because of the enormous drifts that continued to build. Percy headed out to the Cottmans' ranch, while Art Morrison went into town to attempt to locate a bulldozer that had been sent out to clear the paths and roads around the ranch. The following day, Percy was able to locate the "Cat," which was able to break through to a trail, after which Percy and those assisting him began hauling hay. "Speck Henry sent the Ohio Oil Co. [now Marathon] out with a truck loaded with hay. (The oil field hands did not attempt to stack the hay and pushed it off the truck anyway they could.) The catskinner spent the night at our camp letting the dozer run all night because of the extremely low temperatures."[73] Of course, the wind the next day had blown shut the path that had been cleared just the day before, but they were able to feed 125 bales of hay to a large group of sheep. After dispersing the hay out to the sheep, Percy headed back into town. As they were heading back, they came upon a stranded trucker. Percy and the other members of his party dug the trucker out of the snow and followed him back to Casper. The next morning, Roy and Percy flew back to the ranch in hopes of locating lost cattle that were still unaccounted for. They were able to locate some of the cattle, but the roads were again blocked, making it impossible for Percy to drive back to the ranch camp. On February 6, one of the worst storms during the blizzard came up. A ground blizzard started with winds blowing at over seventy miles per hour. In what Percy said was the worst day yet, the ground blizzard became so intense that he could not get out to Roy's airplane at the Evansville Airport. Sometime later, Roy was called into service to rescue a seriously ill woman at Midwest, Wyoming, about forty-three miles north of Casper. Percy was waiting at the Evansville Airport for Roy's arrival. Upon Roy's arrival, the wind was blowing something fierce. Percy was instructed to run out and hang onto the plane's strut, as the wind was attempting to tear it off. Roy was able to taxi directly into the airport hangar with the ailing woman. Returning to Casper following the ambulance transporting the woman to the hospital, Percy and the ambulance crew had to shovel themselves out of drifts several times enroute to Casper. Unfortunately, the woman died after they reached the hospital.

As he had done many times throughout the blizzard, Percy flew back out to the ranch to locate and feed his sheep. He was able to gather up Dan Gallegos's sheep and bring them in from the range so they could graze; however, the following day, the wind blew hard yet again, which caused Jake Lavato's sheep to pile up, resulting in the death of about twenty-five sheep. Of course, the following day the wind was back again, causing additional problems with the sheep. The storm was bad all night long, with snow falling that was wet enough for the sheep that they developed what ranchers call "wool blind."[74] With all the sheep blind, the only hope for both sheep and Percy was warmer temperatures, which, gratefully, came the next day. This was short-lived, as another six inches of snow fell the next morning. Fortunately enough for Percy, another Air Force C-47 dropped additional hay for his sheep. It took Percy until 2:00 p.m. to hunt down Dan's sheep again and move them to the creek, where they mixed in with the remaining

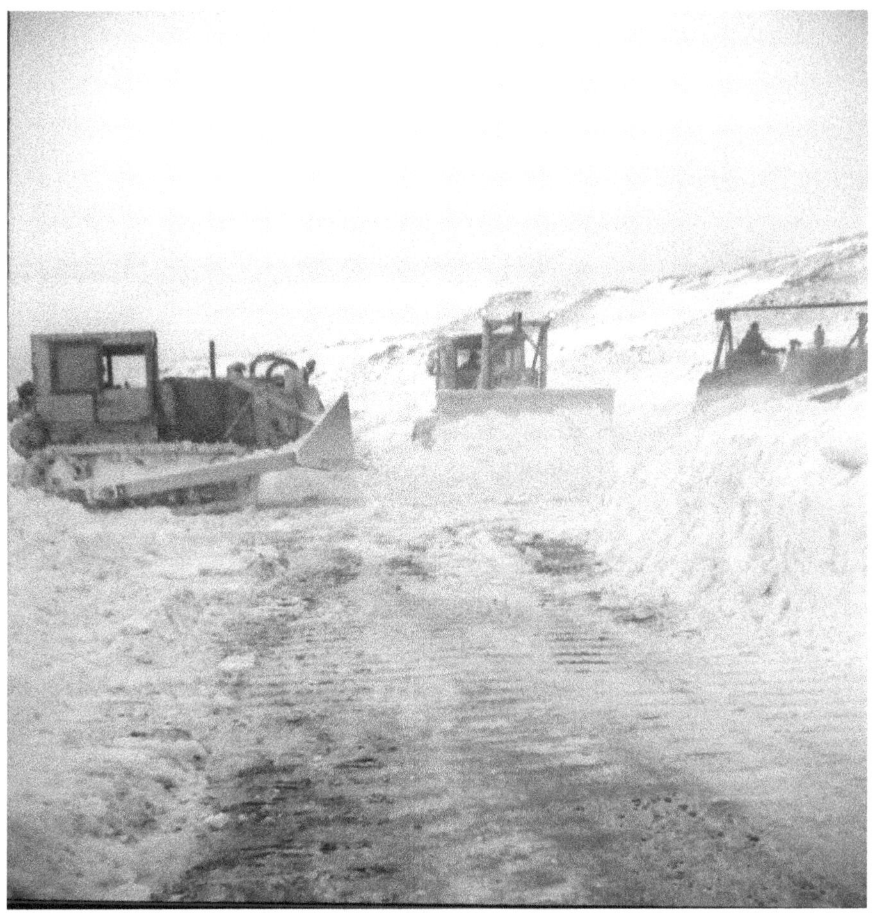

Covers were built on the Caterpillar bulldozers to protect the operators from the frigid temperatures. *Courtesy of John Moyer.*

sheep Jake had. That evening, Percy headed back to the Cottmans' ranch, where temperatures reached thirty-four degrees below zero. The weather that night forced Percy to stay at the ranch. He had to sleep in one of the sheep wagons without a sleep roll, but a rolled-up canvas kept him protected from the freezing temperatures.

On February 15, Tom and Fred Cottman assisted in guiding one of the C-47s out toward theirs and Percy's ranch with more hay. Not realizing the speed of the aircraft, by the time Tom and Fred began to look, they were near Pine Ridge, which was over 150 miles from Casper. Realizing their mistake, they had the pilot turn back around and head back in the direction

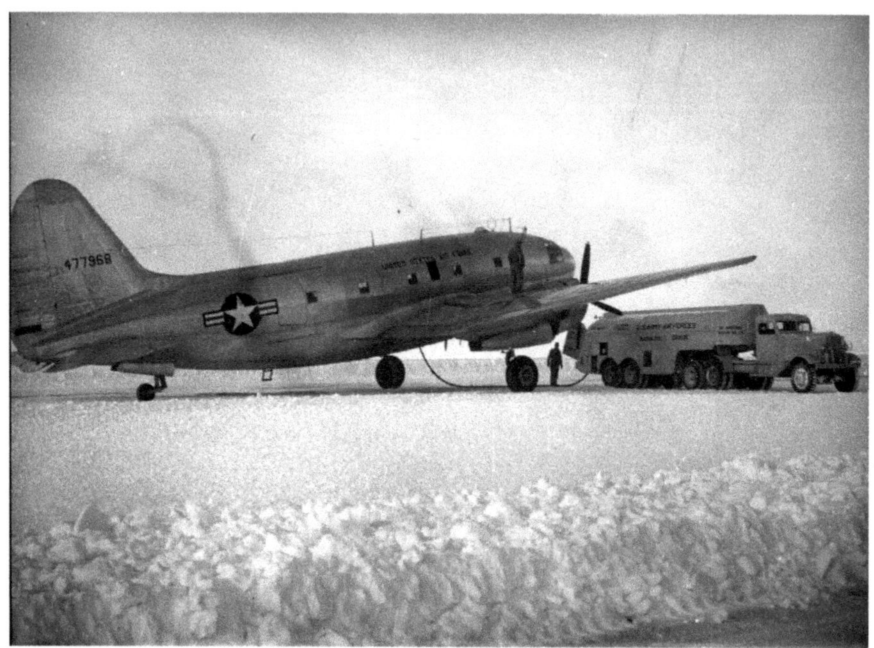

Refueling operation, January 1949. *Courtesy of Chuck Morrison, Morrison Collection, Casper College Western History Center.*

of Percy's ranch, where they found a large group of sheep and dropped hay to them, with many of the bales breaking apart from the fall. It was recognized sometime later that the sheep they had dropped hay to were not Percy's but those belonging to Pat Murphy, whose ranch was farther west. Many of the sheep in that direction had slowly migrated because of the wind and snowdrifts, which made it easy for sheep to leave their corrals and fences. Percy was able to feed nearly all of the sheep during the two- or three-hour window in which the sheep would feed with the hay supply dropped the day before. Having a decent morning the following day, Percy headed out to find more sheep to the east and south of his ranch. The day turned out to be great when an Air Force C-47 flew over, dropping additional hay to the sheep. On January 18, after Roy had flown Tom out to the ranch, a convoy of trucks came out to the ranch following United States Army Cats that broke open a trail. Another C-47 came by and dropped several more bales of hay, which was a wonderful sight for Percy and neighboring ranchers. The military worked hard to clear the roads leading up to Stevenson's ranch; however, because of a large draw filled with snow, they were unable to reach the ranch and had to stop about three-quarters of a mile from Stevenson's residence, where they left the hay they were bringing in. Percy said that Ed Stevenson was mad because they did not bring the hay all the way to his house.

The day the C-47 dropped hay out to Percy's ranch, he had headed into Casper to have a short visit with Trula and get what supplies he could in his truck. Percy left early the next morning to search for more lost sheep and cows to the east of the ranch. He was able to locate six cows near the Nicolaysens' ranch on Cole Creek, where he spent the night before heading back to his ranch. After a night's rest, Percy headed back out looking for his animals. With the snow beginning to melt, he headed out to Middle Fork of the Cheyenne River, where he was able to recover twenty cows. Heading back to his ranch with the cows, he now ran into more problems with the sheep. Since all of the corrals were filled with deep snow, they had to improvise and build corrals out of fence slats and wooden gates. These makeshift corrals met the purpose for which they were intended, as Percy and his ranch hands were able to cut out three hundred strays from their sheep the first day after the corrals were built. Organizing a sheep roundup with other ranchers, Percy and his fellow ranchers covered over 150,000 acres to find everyone's sheep. They started their roundup on the Cheyenne River Breaks, where they were able to find two hundred sheep with a variety of brands, bringing them back to the corrals.

As February now turned into March, Percy continued looking for cattle and sheep, as he had been doing since the storm had come through during the first week in January. Now the search was for the B.B. Brooks Co.'s sheep. Percy spent three days searching and sorting over 10,000 sheep. Among the sorted sheep, Percy was able to bring home 178 of his own sheep; however, by the time the searching was over, 20,000 sheep had been sorted, ensuring they were back at the correct ranches. When the group worked with Stevenson's herd, Percy was able to gather 17 of his head. Taking a plane on March 5, Percy decided to continue his search from the air. This was profitable since he was able to locate five cows from the Armagast ranch, as well as 8 calves from the Donovan ranch and even 15 cows that had wandered to the Bobcat Creek, which was near the ranch, making it easier to get them back. As the weather begin to improve, operations around the ranch started to become somewhat normal. With this good weather, Percy was able to move all of his cows back to the ranch headquarters. As they finished up with moving the cattle, they started moving the sheep back north of the winter range by the end of March.

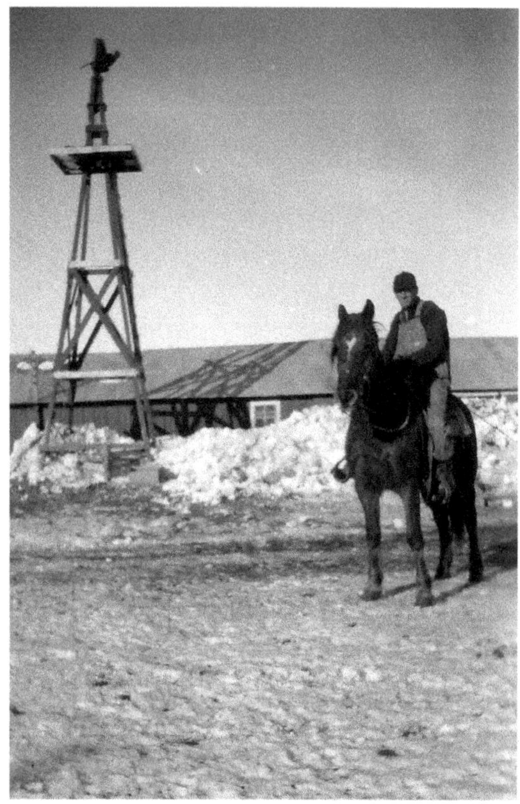

Carl Emerich on a horse as he heads out to search for sheep and cattle from the ranch. *Courtesy of Senator Fred Emerich.*

For three months, Percy and other ranchers worked nearly every day to rescue, locate and feed the cattle and sheep. Not once did Percy complain about his current situation; instead, he forged ahead and continued to work. Ranchers were aware Mother Nature did not pick favorites when metrological events such as a blizzard occurred. This was a terrible storm where many animals perished and ranchers lost money; however, for so many of the ranchers, this was certainly not the first blizzard they had endured, nor would it be the last.

As always, Trula wrote to Percy to give him the latest updates on what was happening in town and her efforts in getting needed supplies to both him and the sheep. Trula's ability to coordinate and work with the U.S. Air Force pilots to get the hay and supplies to her ranch was amazing. What was even more impressive is that just like so many others who were part of the blizzard, she was assisting other ranchers in getting food and other necessities out to them as well, as she explains in the following letter to Percy:

Thurs.

Dearest Perk,

The Army, of course, has started out on the road and should reach you tomorrow. Tom thought you could meet them and have them cut a road past Cottman's Head Quarters, keeping on the North side of the creek.

Tom was with me at the Airbase, so I couldn't tell you all I wanted to. We [got] *the groceries and got them to out to Roy L's* [Lamereaux] *Monday morning. Roy Smith took out the 170* [Cessna] *to George Taylor's and turned it over. No one was hurt, but it isn't fixed yet. Tuesday, they promise to bring out the stuff in a 140, but it* [wind] *was blowing to hard, but Dorothy* [Lamereaux] *told Tom that Roy took some things on Tuesday. He flew Gerry* [Nicolaysen] *Tuesday afternoon because Gerry is looking for a whole bunch* [of sheep] *which has disappeared.*

There was no coal in town, so I got a few sacks from CB&Q [Chicago, Burlington and Quincy Railroad]. *Joe* [Bailey] *sacked it, but believe it or not, told Fred* [Cottman] *he could have a little as he needs a bit.*[75] *Should I send a barrel of gasoline on the truck if I can send it out or can you get away in? What else do you need? What shall I do about the groceries out at Roy's?*

Guess Joe Burke lost a bunch of sheep in a pile-up at a fence corner. Mary Jane Strand said Herman Werner is looking for 5,000 head of sheep and lost cattle. Am sending this with Joe, hope you get it.

All my love,
Trula

Meanwhile, back at the ranch, Percy followed up with a letter the following Saturday:

Saturday 18, 10:00 AM

Dearest Trula,

Your letters and fudge were very, very welcome. I have been so busy I could not make connections with the plane or truckers to get a letter to you such as you deserve. Hope I can get in soon. I have the Air Force boys here with their Cats this AM again, and they are nice boys.

We have some of Morey Young's sheep (not many), green brand Crescents. Pat Murphy's also Cottman's, Brooks and Stevenson are so we have quite a herd now. I shall try to get the cattle at Gerry's [Nicolaysen] *soon as possible. You might call Mrs. Young and tell her about the sheep. We will try to gather them all if they are not too far away. Many of Dr. Stuckenhoff's* [sheep] *are scattered around here, but they are so weak and so numerous we cannot handle them with ours. You might call Mrs. Murphy also unless Father has done so previously, we had some 200 of the Murphy sheep, but they have been dying fast and are scattered now. I am going to have the Army open the road to Stevenson's, and then Stevenson can come back to our hay pile at their turn-off and get all he wants there with their truck. You could call this to Mrs. Parker or Evans.*

Tell Gerry N. [Nicolaysen] *that there were about 60 of Stuckenhoff's sheep at the Bill Hawk's place on Jan. 18th, they are probably in Gillett by now, he will get a kick out that.*

Be sure to keep a lookout for all the people who have been helpful in this storm so we can do something for them. Must go now.

Love to All,
Perk

Percy told his perspective as he viewed it from the ranch where he and his fellow ranchers struggled to survive and feed both sheep and cattle as often as the blizzard would allow. With Trula in town, she had her own assessment of how things were and what she endured during the time she and Percy were apart.

Trula had just gotten off the phone with Bob Grieve, as he had called to inquire about Percy and what was happening at the ranch. Bob informed Trula that there was to be a meeting of all the local stockmen there in town, which both Trula and Mary Hester Nicolaysen attended. The men in attendance could see something was going to have to be done regarding the current situation with the sheep and cattle in the area. From where Trula was sitting, the meeting seemed to be going nowhere until Mary Hester stood up and told the group they needed to contact Governor A.G. Crane and have him ask for additional assistance from the United States Army. After Mary spoke, the men got on the phone and, within a matter of minutes, had everything arranged.

On the day that Percy had put Tom on the airplane to the hospital for his feet, Trula was there to meet him at the airport and get him to a doctor.

Tom was seen by Dr. Morad, who had Tom's foot placed in a boot-like contraption that encased his entire foot to include his toes, which, because of the attentiveness of Dr. Morad, were saved from frostbite. Tom was not the only member of the Cooper family during the blizzard to seek medical attention; all three of Percy and Trula's children—Sue, Merriam and Donald—came down with chickenpox.

Even with Trula feverishly working to get aid to her husband, she still found ways to help others along the way. When the U.S. Air Force members came in from a mission hauling hay to the ranches, Trula would be at the airbase, which is now the Natrona County International Airport, and cook meals for the troops. The Casper County sheriff would pick up Trula nearly every morning, taking her and her family out to the base. Trula did not have much, but she utilized everything she had available to her to make a hot meal for those Airmen. In the kitchen, there was a hot plate, an electric stove and a potbellied stove. There was running water in the building but no hot water. Using the water, she had available, they would heat the water on the potbellied stove to use for washing dishes, boiling food or whatever was needed. The people of Casper were generous, as they brought food in that would be used to cook the meals for their military guests, even though many themselves were running low on everyday supplies.

Trula recalled some of the great adventures and misadventures when she worked the airbase. One evening when the roads were closed due to the drifts, she opened up the kitchen to Mrs. June Forgey and another rancher's wife since they could not go home and there was no other place for them to stay. Another morning when the sheriff came to pick her up, their vehicle was struck by an oncoming snowplow, which made them jump with fright as it took off the rear fender of the police car. Of course, what made her chuckle with delight was the time when one of the crew members of the C-47 accidentally had his ripcord snag a nail on the wall, and his parachute blew open in the room where she was.

Before their arrival in Wyoming, many of the young Airmen had been flying near the Aleutian Islands and were certainly not impressed with the weather they were now encountering.[76] Upon their arrival, they were griping about being sent on this assignment; nevertheless, when they grasped the gravity of the situation, they quickly changed their minds about being in Wyoming. They did contend that Wyoming was much worse than Alaska after experiencing the intense winds and ground blizzards nearly every day.. The Airmen were sent to Wyoming so quickly from their last duty assignment that they had no money with which to purchase lodging, food and other necessities. Trula said the town picked up the tab at the Henning Hotel where they were staying with the money earmarked for the hay being purchased to be dropped off at the ranches. Trula took it a step further when the crews headed to their ranch. She would tell them before leaving to go to the Riverside restaurant and have their meal charged to her and Percy.

It was obvious that Trula was concerned about Percy and the needs at the ranch. Percy had told her that he was in need of hay hooks. Trula searched in town to locate the hooks for him. Unable to find the hooks, Trula, in desperation, made the decision to order them from Montgomery Ward. She was pleasantly surprised when they arrived in just a few days, and she was able to have them flown out to the ranch.

Smart thinking and improvising by a local rancher saved nearly all of his livestock. Art King, proprietor of the King Corriedale Ranch located six miles west of Happy Jack Road, used an old ranching trick to save the lives of hundreds of sheep on his ranch. Art and several ranch hands had heard the blizzard warning on Sunday, and they wasted no time in herding in the stock to a safer area. King moved his sheep into large sheds and corrals on Sunday just as the blizzard was advancing into the vicinity. As the storm moved in, King and his ranch hands kept a close eye on the sheep and kept them traversing through the snow so they would not tire and stop or become buried in the drifts. The plan King had devised worked, and other than several sleepless nights, only two sheep fell victim to the storm.[77]

There are numerous eyewitness accounts of the Blizzard of 1949; however, many of those individuals are not with us today. Those who lived through this amazing weather event have since passed on their stories to children, grandchildren and in some cases great-grandchildren. One such story was passed on by Michael Dykhorst, grandson of Clarence William Weber. Michael told how his grandfather so many times recalled how he and his family worked to survive and save the farm they lived on in 1949.

Sometime in early January 1949, Clarence's parents decided to venture out and visit friends in nearby Guernsey, Wyoming, where he and his parents lived on their farm. When Clarence and his family left, the sky was dark and gray, and near the horizon, it was nearly black as the storm was approaching. While his parents were visiting with their friends, Clarence and his brother played outside to pass the time. As the wind began to blow, the temperature began to fall, and although Clarence and his brother were dressed warmly for the winter, they did not stay outside long before they headed back in the house to warm up. As the day wore on, Clarence's dad said to their friends,

"We still have to do the chores and deliver milk to the store tonight, so I guess we better be getting on home."

As Clarence and his family drove back to their farm, the sky appeared cold and dark. Upon their arrival, Clarence assisted his father in moving all their stock into the corrals and proceeded to move the milking cows into the barn so they could milk them. After they were finished separating and bottling the milk, they made their way back to Guernsey to make their deliveries to the store where they sold their milk. As Clarence drove into town, he said they did not see any snow floating through the air or even the appearance of snow hitting their headlights. As Clarence described it, there were wisps of "snow snakes" moving across the road as they traveled. As they drove, Clarence's father stated, "Anyone who goes out on a night like this is a damn fool." The milk delivery was made, and father and son made their way back to the farm and went to bed for the evening.

The following morning, Clarence and his brother were awakened by his father, who said, "Come here, I want to show you something." As they made their way through the house, Clarence's father took him out to their closed-in porch. Attempting to look through the porch's screen door, all Clarence could see was a blank sheet of white. Clarence said in the past snow would catch to the screen and make it look like this, but when his father opened the door leading out to the yard, the blank white sheet of snow did not disappear as it had many times before. Now he could not even make out the corners of the door because of the amount of snow. "Get dressed warm, but don't go outside until we are all ready; then we will go together," said Clarence's father. "Hold onto each other and don't let go; you could be lost in ten feet," was the warning given as they headed out into the snow.

They worked their way to the corrals and eventually to the barn. With drifts over three feet deep, they dug their way to the cows to milk them. After milking the cows, they made it back into the corral to locate the other cattle and horses they had brought in the night before. Shoveling their way through the corral to the other livestock, Clarence said as they moved through the snow they would occasionally see a cow open her eyes and they could make out the brown spots of the cattle against the white snow. Near the corral, there was a windbreak made up of Russian olive trees on the north and west sides of the farm. Although this assisted in seeing a little better, the visibility was limited to only a few feet in front of him. Whether by coincidence or fate, days before the storm they had taken all of the oats they had shocked in the field and had stacked them in a stack-lot just inside the corral fence. The horses had huddled in the lee of the stack, and despite

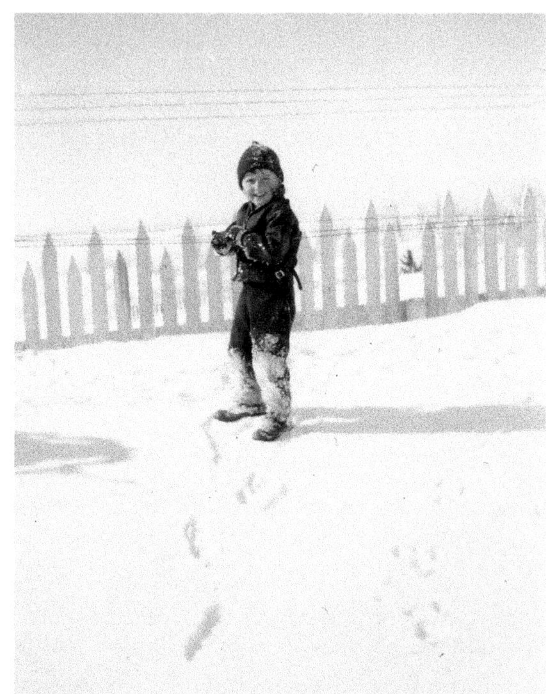

Right: Fred Emerich playing on drifts in the front yard of his home. *Courtesy of Senator Fred Emerich.*

Below: A family on top of a tall snowdrift in front of their house. *Francis Steele Brammar, courtesy of Wyoming State Archives.*

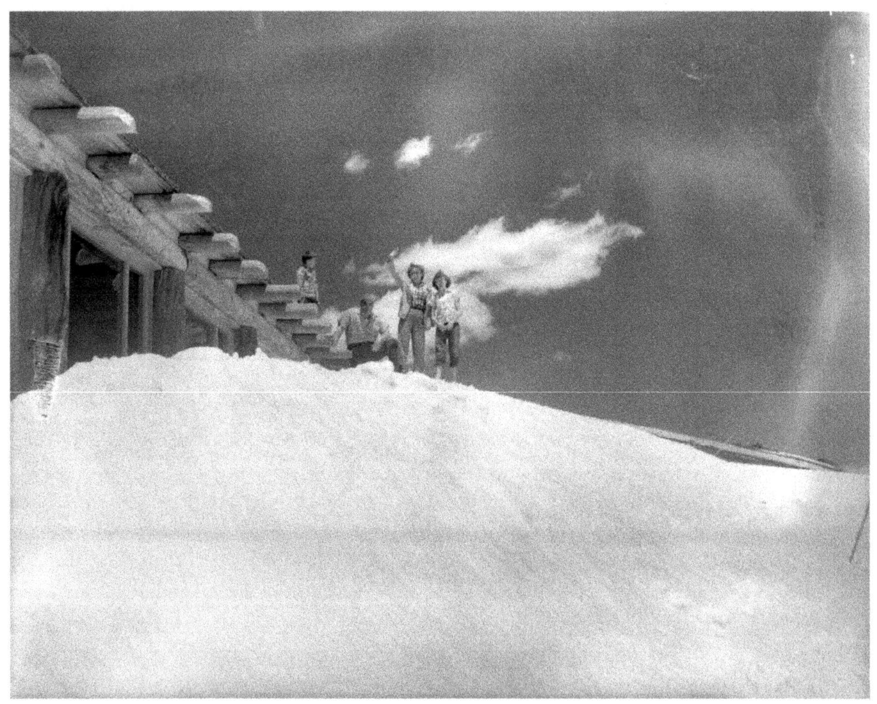

the weather conditions, they were doing well. Once the cows were milked, Clarence and his father ensured that the milk cows and other farm animals were as protected from the elements as they could be and then proceeded back to the house.

Not having the convenience of indoor plumbing in the farmhouse, Clarence's father strung a rope between the house and the outhouse, which was located thirty feet away, fearing someone could become lost in the blizzard while heeding the call of nature. With the cattle safely in the corral, it was a waiting game for the family now. The family and Clarence's Uncle Ted passed the time playing cards. The group grew tired of playing, but there was a never-ending supply of other games Clarence's father either knew or made up to help in passing the hours.

No one ever left the house unless accompanied by someone else. The snow continued for several days as the family stayed safely in the house. Clarence's mother informed the group early on she was not going to cook or make something whenever someone decided they were hungry. She willingly agreed to cook the family supper, but anything else was left up to that person. This, according to Clarence, was when he first learned to cook.

The group consisted of Clarence, his father, his mother, his brother and his dad's brother Ted. Between the adults, they came up with enough games and activities to keep Clarence and his brother from suffering from cabin fever, but amidst the games and other activities, there was the hourly trek out to check on the animals, after which they came back to the house to rest and warm back up.

Across from the farm was a cornfield that had recently been picked with the aid of corn-picker, which left lots of shelled corn lying around. The area, which was known to be a major duck flyaway, had attracted a large number of mallards to field as they swarmed in to eat the corn left from the recent harvest. The family cats had already found this source of food and had filled the farm manger with a bed of feathers from their excursions for food. Clarence and his father also hunted the ducks as a source of food for the family. They would work their way over to a ditch bank with their .22 rifles but would only shoot at the ducks if they were able to line up two heads with one shot. Clarence's mother baked duck, roasted duck and devised several different ways in which to serve duck as the main course. Of course, after several dinners consisting of duck, a change had to be made. Clarence's mom then started covering the duck dish in consommé, giving the meal a different taste, and once again duck became the meal of choice.

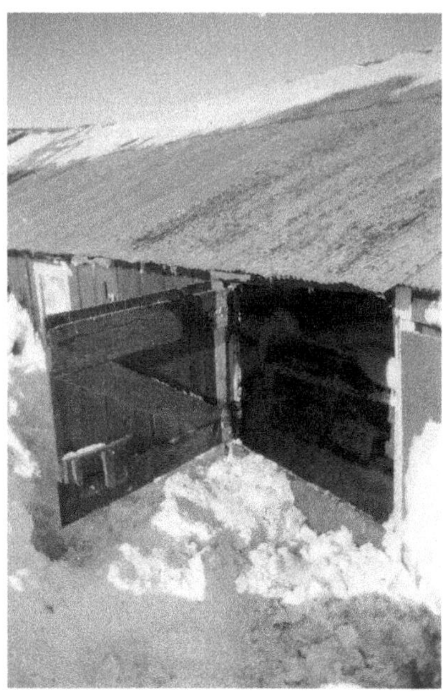

The farm gate door is freed from the snowdrift. *Courtesy of Senator Fred Emerich.*

Even with what seemed to be an endless supply of duck, the larder was getting low, and it was realized soon they would have to make their way into town for more supplies and staples to sustain the family. After nearly a week, the storm had abated enough that they could see the telephone poles for quite some distance. This break in the storm seemed to be a good time to make a trip into town for the needed provisions. Clarence, his brother and his father dressed and ready themselves to make the journey into town, which was a mile and a half from their home. The trip into town was not bad, as the wind was on their backs and pushed them toward town. As they made their way back home, the same wind that had pushed them was now in their faces, making the trip back extremely hard. The wind was blowing so hard it almost seemed it was sucking the breath from their mouths. Each would take a turn leading the caravan while the other two hunkered in behind the leader to get a reprieve from the elements. Every twenty or thirty yards, they would switch, with the leaders giving one other a break. The trip back from town took nearly two hours, but even with all of this, they continued to survive as a family in what would soon be considered the storm of the century.

After several more days, the storm finally subsided, and it was time to venture out and survey the damage. Due to the eight-foot board fence on the north side of the corral, as well as the natural olive tree snow fence, the cattle survived quite well during the blizzard. The guinea hens on the farm did not fare as well, as most of them were dead. The poor fowl met their demise from the cold, as the snow encased their heads, likely killing them from asphyxiation or simply freezing to death. The horses were not in the corral, but upon further investigation, tracks were found that indicated they had simply walked over the eight-foot fence that had drifted by now and were gone. Clarence said they were easy to track through the snow, as their hoofprints stood up in the snow and did not sink as they normally would have done. The combination of the horses' weight and the snow blowing away from the tracks presented a trail leading to where the horses had wandered off. As Clarence rode off with his own horse searching for the other horses, the temperature was somewhere around fifty below zero, not including the wind chills, which were significantly lower. As his eyes began to water from the bitter temperatures, he blinked to get the water out, but when the wind hit the water, his eyelids froze shut. Unable to see, his only hope was that the horse knew the way back to the house. Miraculously, his horse took him back home, where he groped to find his way back in. Once in the house, he was able to let the heat thaw his eyes open once again. After his eyes opened and he had rested, Clarence headed back out to locate the horses. Once again, he followed the trail of hoofprints left by the horses to their location. He was able to locate all of the horses, but one horse did not make it, as she had fallen in a ditch on her back and was unable to free herself, which ultimately led to her freezing to death.

The road leading out was covered in an eight-foot drift, which had solidified and was hard as a rock, so this would not be the way out. They used hay-saws to cut through the drifts located on the west of the farm buildings, making their way into the open fields. The drifts seemed to be formed by even the slightest blade of grass in the field, which resulted in an eight-foot drift. If the drifts were thin, they could either break or saw their way through, making their way finally to their neighbor's adjacent fields and eventually the main road. The main road had been cleared by the time the Webers were digging out, but access to the road was only feasible by a tractor, as no car would be able to traverse the still snow-packed roads. For the next several days, the task at hand was to dig out from the storm and get back to the normal chores of farm life. It would be a couple more weeks before the road leading up to the farm would be cleared. The county was utilizing D-8 Cats (Caterpillar D8 bulldozers) to help with snow removal, but the drifts were at such an angle and frozen solid that the bulldozers slipped off into the ditches. Clarence also recalled that the town of Guernsey had purchased a big V snowplow. At the time of purchase, many in the town complained that it was overkill and the town never received enough snow to warrant the purchase of something so frivolous. Now that there was the amount of snow to utilize this piece of equipment, it had become frozen to the point it could not be moved from where it was originally parked.

Finally, after several weeks of work, the roads were clear of snow. However, on each side of the one-lane road were six-foot drifts. As the snow began to melt, Clarence said the mud on the road was something to behold as

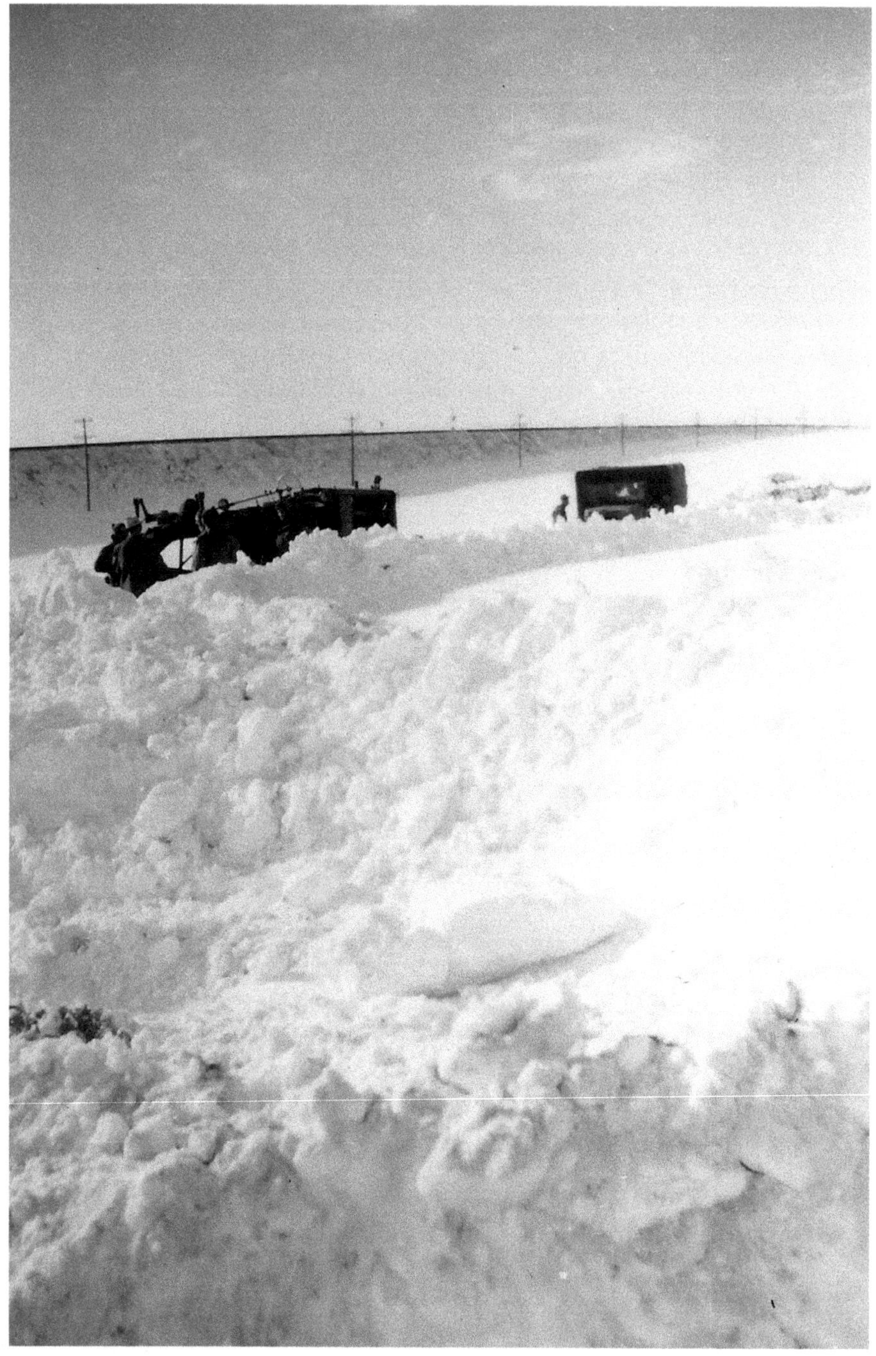

Wyoming National Guard members plowing Railroad Road. *Courtesy of Senator Fred Emerich.*

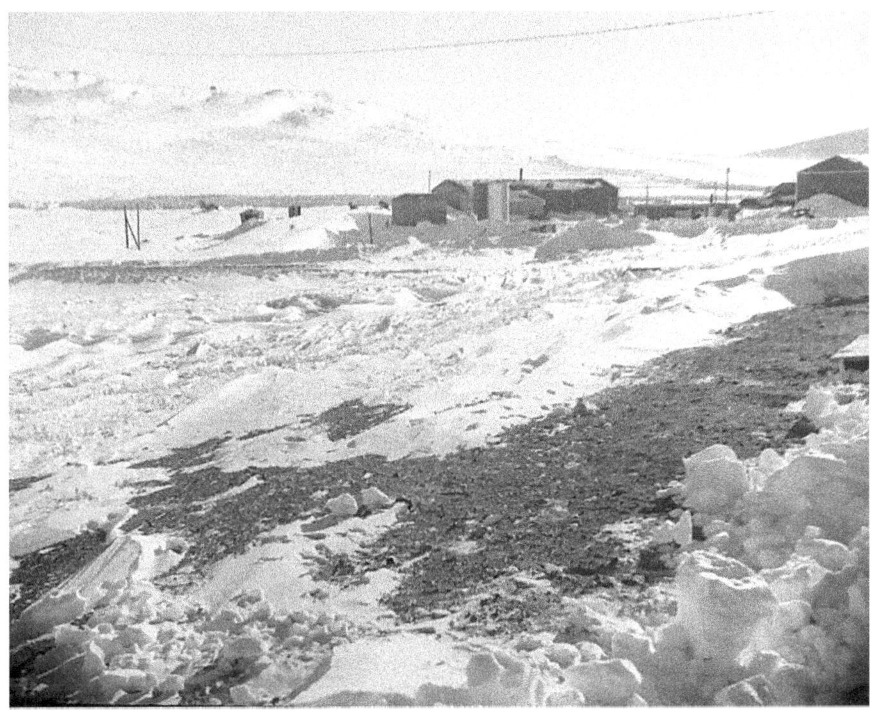

Roads clear but snowdrifts continue to cause a problem in the mining camp. *Courtesy of John Moyer.*

the road became saturated with the snowmelt. As any young man might do, Clarence took the family Buick on inspiring mud road races down the muddy lane in a series of what he called "grasshopper jumps." Finishing up his story regarding the Blizzard of 1949, Clarence stated, "It had to be a good car to take that kind of abuse, but it did and kept rolling." Clarence and his family, like so many others in Wyoming, made the best of a situation as they survived on the supplies they had and sought out other sources to assist with their family's well-being as they waited out the storm.[78]

CHAPTER 4

NEIGHBORS HELPING NEIGHBORS

Throughout the blizzard, lives were saved by heroes and heroines alike. Just like any situation when others are in trouble or danger, people quickly to come to the rescue. The Blizzard of 1949 proved this over and over, as was the example in Cheyenne, near the Cheyenne Veterans Administration Hospital just east of town. Daniel Ryman, forty-one from Cheyenne, had left his house headed to the grocery store to, as he stated, "collect a bag of vittles."[79] As Ryman headed back, the storm quickly overtook him, and per Ryman, the temperature had dropped to zero. He told the Denver paper he was stumbling around for an undetermined amount of time, "I don't know how long, bumping into telephone poles and fire hydrants. Soon all the houses seemed to have disappeared as the wind picked up. I got so scared I started lighting matches to keep warm, but they kept going out, finally, there were no matches left." Exhausted, Ryman fell to his hands and knees in the snow and began to yell for help, hoping someone would hear his pleas. Although his story was covered nationally, the efforts of the man who rescued him went unnoticed except by the *Wyoming State Tribune*, which ensured he received the credit he deserved for his heroic efforts that day. Lee Weidum, who served as the chief of the Vocational Rehabilitation Program at the Veterans Hospital, heard Ryman's cries for help. Weidum searched in the blowing snow and drifts for twenty minutes until he located Ryman in a field approximately a quarter mile away from the hospital. Once Weidum located Ryman, he made his way back to the hospital for medical supplies and came back to Daniel to treat him for his

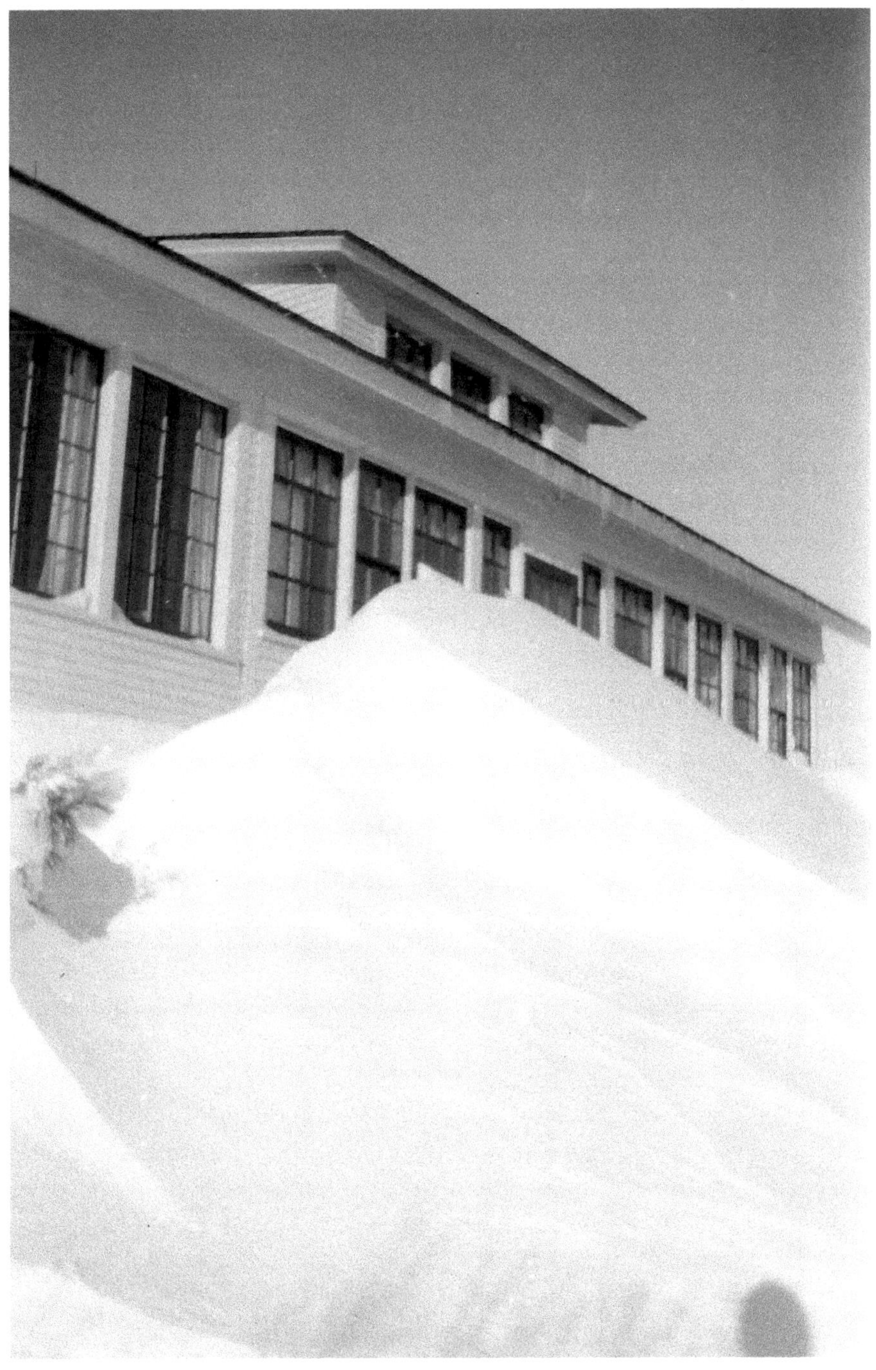

Drift reaching the second floor of the Emerich residence. *Courtesy of Senator Fred Emerich.*

exposure to the elements. After Weidum had treated Ryman, he assisted him in moving to a nearby house owned by Dr. W.A. Olinger.[80] After further examination by Dr. Olinger, it was determined that Ryman's feet and hands were severely frozen. Weidum's willingness to brave the blizzard and treat Ryman demonstrated courage, and of course Dr. Olinger opening his home to a stranger to stay and recover shows the level of hospitality of people when disaster strikes.

Even during the blizzard, many of the Cheyenne military veterans showed perseverance and rigidity as they were forced to wait out the storm at the Cheyenne Veterans Hospital located just outside town. The colorful description given by the paper summed up the blizzard these veterans were stranded in: "Cheyenne's bombastic blizzard proved this week that the Veterans' Hospital, despite its nearness to the city, is not as close as it may seem, when it takes from Tuesday to Thursday to get a snow plow thru."

Soon after the storm broke, street crews were out working to clear the roads that led out to the hospital. They understood that critical supplies of milk and bread had to get through to those who needed them. Nevertheless, with massive drifts and one snowplow that broke down, progress to clear the highway was becoming an arduous task. The newspaper reported the staff and patients were getting along quite well, although they had been together for four days.

One nurse, Margerie Thompson, who had recently transferred from Bay Pines, Florida, kept many of the patients in a happy mood. She explained to the patients each morning, "Just close your eyes and imagine you are in Florida, and tomorrow you will wake up with the storm gone and the sun shining." It is feasible other nurses picked up on Margerie's weather humor and decided to utilize it to keep up the spirits of the veterans. Other nurses started each morning, asking the veterans, "Shall we go rabbit hunting?" Both nurses and staff worked hard to not only meet the needs of the patients but help them through the blizzard as well. Dr. Francis K. Burnett was there during the storm, and Dr. Arnold C. Balk, who was on duty from Tuesday to Thursday, worked continuously with nurses and other staff who were unable get home. The ones who had the worst responsibility during the blizzard were those who manned the kitchen in the hospital. The cooks and mess attendants were on duty from Sunday until Wednesday before relief was given to them. Another staff member who pushed through the drifts each day to get to work was John Gaut, the hospital registrar.

Not only were patients and staff stranded, but several who had been visiting family at the hospital were in the same situation. According to the

Plows clearing roads outside the mining camp. *Courtesy of John Moyer.*

newspaper, three wives, including one who had a small child, were visiting their husbands at the hospital when the storm struck. The hospital staff took great care of the four extra "patients" until the arrival of the snowplows. By Wednesday, the first car made it to the hospital. Of course, the car did not use the conventional way by the highway but had to access the hospital through the fields that surrounded the hospital. However, by Thursday, snowplows had made it through and supplies had made it to the hospital, and people were able to get back home and to other places they needed to go. Now the nurses were confident they would be able to soon get their patients out for the rabbit hunt they had promised.[81]

The Cheyenne newspapers knew there were heroes out there in the storms working hard not only to assist people but also to save lives when necessary. The newspaper noted, "There is a prompt human responsiveness, even from the most indifferent. Cheyenne pointed out this fact in the fighting blizzard." The paper gave several examples of the heroism many showed in Cheyenne as many neighbors and friends sought assistance from one another during the blizzard. The newspaper noted:

> *These included businessmen who sent food and fuel trucks into sections where the larders were running low; men and women who trudged thru blinding snows to take milk to a baby in a neighbor's house or medicine to someone who was sick; those who joined in the search for the missing. Rescue missions which plunged out into the country to reach the stranded; druggist who voluntarily filled desperately-needed prescriptions; telephone and power linemen who kept those vital services functioning; society matrons and Army colonels who pitched in as "kitchen help" at overcrowded hotels; radio announcers who worked overtime to keep up the flow of vital information; soldiers and military equipment which helped at hundreds of places and countless others.*[82]

The city of Cheyenne indeed went far beyond what many might expect a town to do for others, but these acts of kindness show the closeness of not only this Wyoming town but of many across the state who pulled together to survive the storm. There was not one person who saved the day but a group of individuals who came along and worked as a team to help their neighbors who were in need, ensuring they received the help they needed during, through and after the storm.

Communication during the blizzard was crucial, but the problem was the telephone system could not handle the barrage of phone calls that came through the switchboard. One form of communication that assisted during the blizzard was amateur radio. With the powerful winds and relentless snow, transportation and communication in Wyoming came to a grinding halt. R.E. Williams, one of Rawlins's three ham radio operators, announced that a relay of shortwave radios in the area would be set up to handle emergency calls for residences. Williams explained that the shortwave radio system was part of the American Radio Relay League, formed to assist highway and government officials in transmitting messages when regular forms of communications had failed or, in the case of the blizzard, their systems became overloaded.

Cheyenne telephone officials were now only accepting official phone calls through their switchboard operators because of line interruptions in several areas throughout the city of Rawlins. Williams indicated that he had already handled several messages for residents because of the phone company delays. Williams stated that since the storm, he had retained contact with ten different cities that were affected by the blizzard, including Cheyenne, Wyoming; Greeley, Colorado; and Gering, Nebraska, at no charge. Williams also stated, "We will handle any message."[83] Williams indicated the work

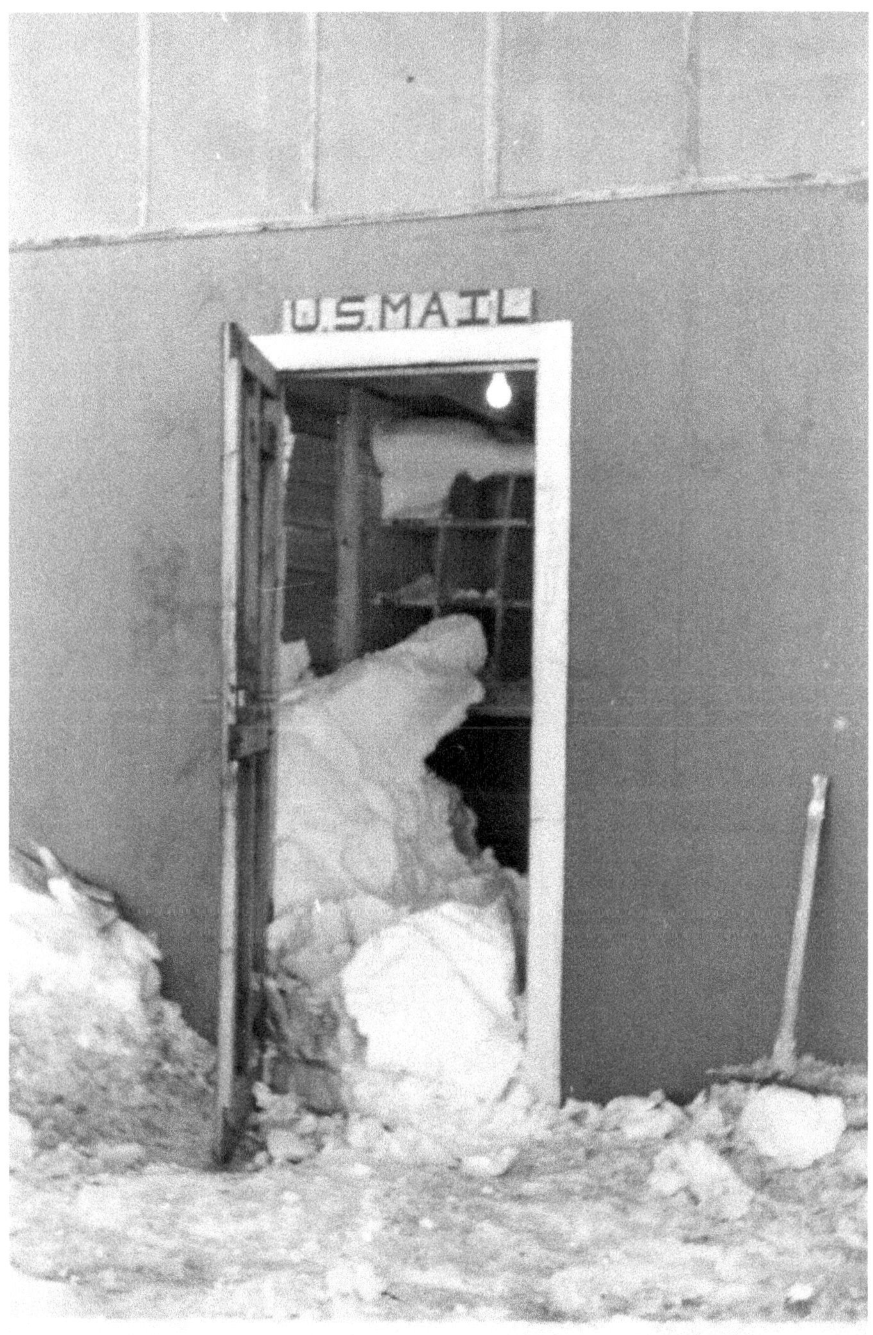

Snowdrifts in and around the door of the U.S. post office in the mining camp. *Courtesy of John Moyer.*

of the nonprofit organization over the last few days had been mainly radio operators receiving distress calls from stranded motorists and other individuals in western towns across the states who were traveling on trains and buses. The group also assisted the Wyoming State Highway Department in coordinating truck and snowplow movements.

Williams himself was instrumental in finding several people in Baggs, Wyoming, who were sought by a stranded group of travelers in Cheyenne. Williams's amateur radio station, W-7-MUG, was the answer to a family's prayers as he was able to locate Carol Oberholtzer, the daughter of Hennan and Mary Oberholtzer of Rawlins. As any parent would be, Carol's parents were apprehensive and informed Williams she had to be near Cheyenne or possibly Greeley. Williams continued to contact his fellow radio operators to locate the girl. Radio operators in both Greeley and Cheyenne informed Williams that Oberholzter was among those stranded at Rockport, Colorado, where there were several stranded buses with nearly three hundred passengers. The press had recently reported a massive influx of stranded passengers due to buses that could not continue their journeys due to the blizzard.[84]

The citizens of Cheyenne made a point to give themselves a pat on the back for their efforts not to price gouge those stranded in town due to the blizzard. Newspapers reported at least one roadside tavern and two gas stations that had raised their prices as motorists sought shelter during the storm. The article stated these business establishments were no longer welcome in Cheyenne because of how they had treated those stranded. Motorists passed on stories that these establishments charged thirty-five cents for a cup of coffee when it typically cost a nickel. It was not only the coffee being overpriced but meals as well. The paper was bold in stating, "Jacking up the prices under such conditions is surely trading on human misery." The article noted that selling merchandise at the going rate was acceptable, but that was as far as it should go when it came to moving prices up during a crisis. Of course, the city was said to have been very hospitable and did its best to lay out the red carpet for those stranded within the city limits. It was understandable that the city was limited in what it could do in welcoming visitors to town because many of those who could assist in making a visitor's trip to Cheyenne more enjoyable were themselves stranded at home and could not get out to come to work and help. Many consider a respectable job was accomplished despite the weather conditions that had brought so many to Cheyenne. The article concluded that residents were pleased to see that merchants and others in Cheyenne did not attempt to get their hands into the pockets of those who, upon no choice of their own, were brought to Cheyenne.[85]

Those living in the city limits had access to many of the necessities needed during the blizzard and after to survive. However, those living in the rural areas of Wyoming on the open ranges were not as fortunate and waited for days and in some cases weeks before assistance got to their locations. One particular incident involved a widow and six children who were down to their last two pieces of coal to stay warm and an ill woman who was alone on a sheep ranch feeding one hundred sheep. These individuals were among several found northeast of Medicine Bow by a Red Cross mission.

On a three-day mission was a party consisting of four Wyoming Army National Guardsmen, an Air Force first aid expert and Mel Lynch, the Carbon County assistant agent. The group discovered numerous families

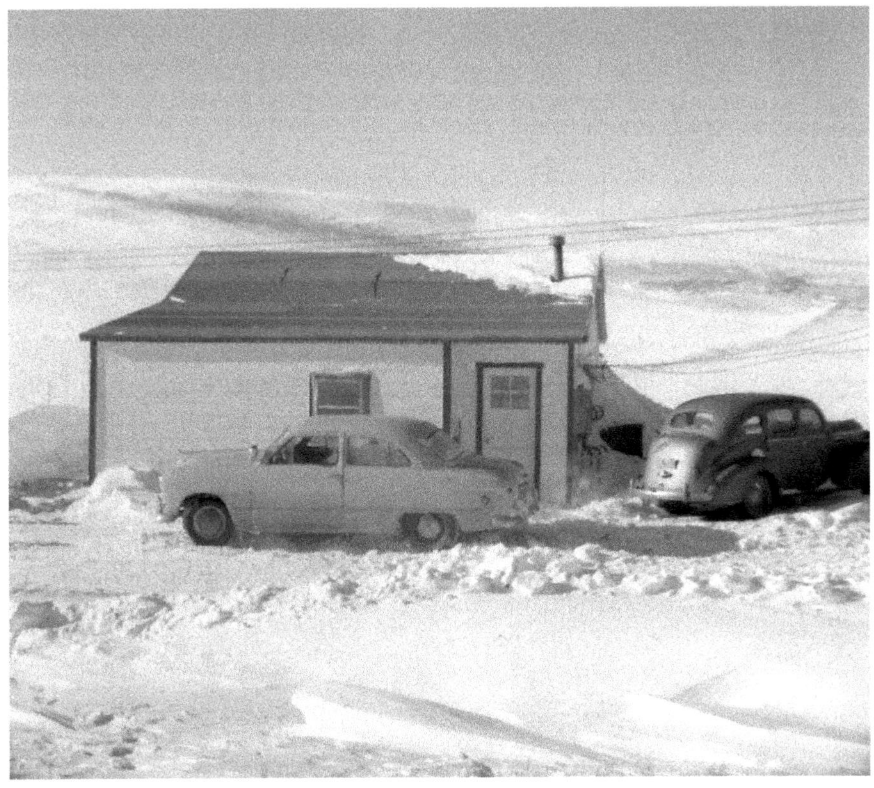

Confined to the house because of snowdrifts. *Courtesy of John Moyer.*

who were suffering from adversities that included cold, hunger, exhaustion and frozen extremities. Mrs. Carl Matson and her six children were down to only a small amount of food and two pieces of coal described as "about the size of footballs and would have lasted about one hour." The Red Cross workers were able to give the family about twenty-five dollars' worth of food but were unable to provide them with any coal to assist with staying warm. They indicated that coal would be flown to them as weather conditions permitted flights to their region.

Mrs. Mark Meer, the ill woman who was aided by the rescue mission, was found tending one hundred sheep on her ranch near Pedro Mountain north of the Shirley Basin in the absence of her husband, who had left the weekend before to seek assistance and started the Red Cross relief mission in motion. Lynch reported from his observation over the three days that livestock conditions in the region were bad. Ranchers like the Meers and others were suffering heavy losses in their sheep. Lynch stated, "They are not dying from starvation, but from the cold and stormy weather." Lynch also reported the cattle loss was not near what the sheep was. The reason for this difference was that many of the cattle would lie down in the snow after their legs had become cut by the razor-sharp edges of the hard-crusted ice. Not only was Mrs. Meer suffering, but so were her employees on the ranch. Bob Ellis, a sheepherder for the Meer ranch who, according to Lynch, was about eighty-two years of age, was discovered with a fractured rib at the Lawrence Sullivan Shirley Basin Quealy ranch. Ranch manager Lester Cheesbrough was with Ellis in the ranch house, where the Red Cross learned they had food and fuel, which had sustained the pair throughout the blizzard.

For the next two days, the crews of the Army weasels traversed across what the paper called a "storm-lashed" country before taking a reprieve. On Tuesday, January 4, the crews spent the night at the Cottonwood ranch owned by Joe Burke.[86] The following morning, the crew continued to Medicine Bow and eventually made its way back to Rawlins across a snow-packed U.S. Highway 30. The crew covered an astonishing 130 miles, which required over 120 gallons of gasoline for the trip through the Shirley Basin and Medicine Bow. Although the weasels were the first into many of these areas, it was a team effort, as a convoy of trucks loaded with supplies made its way into the area behind yet another convoy of bulldozers out of Cody supplied by the Taggart Construction Company. The convoy pushed through enormous snowdrifts averaging fifteen to twenty feet in height as it left Medicine Bow on Monday. Mrs. Burke, who was expecting a child, was going to ride with the convoy from Medicine

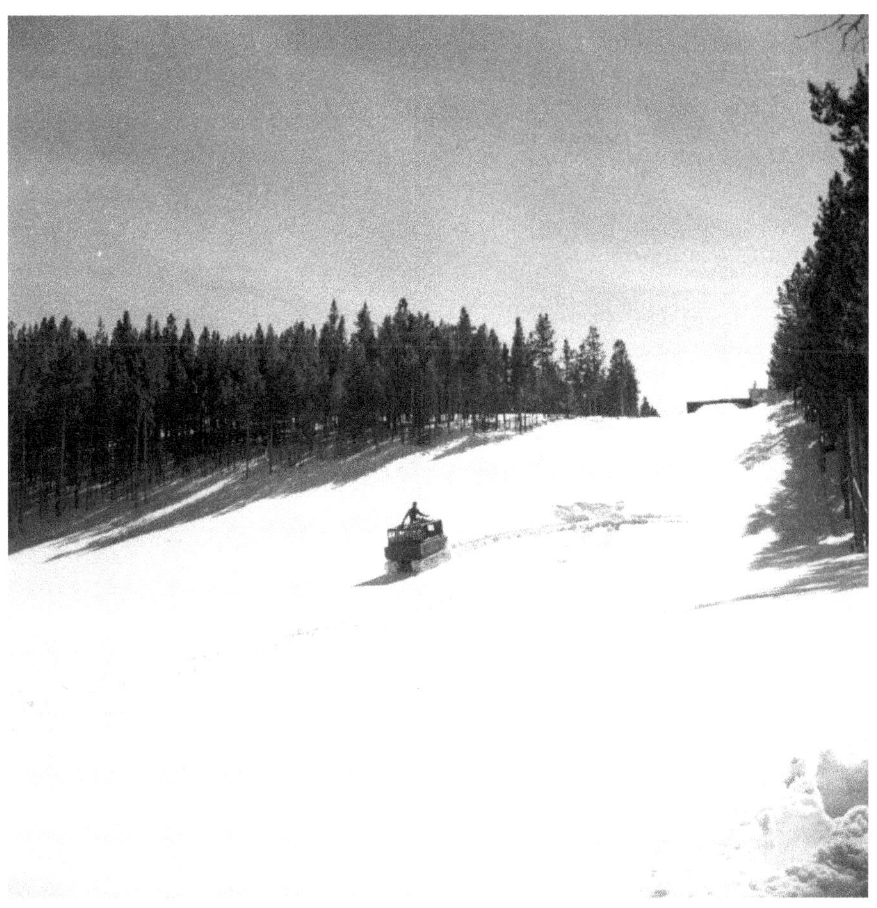

A snow-covered hill, possibly Casper Mountain, with a large belted vehicle to move through the snow. *Courtesy of Chuck Morrison, Morrison Collection, Casper College Western History Center.*

Bow to the hospital in Laramie. She was not the only individual in the Medicine Bow area needing assistance, as Lynch stated, "More help is needed in the Medicine Bow area."

The Red Cross general field representative, Harry Williamson, made an announcement that there were going to be additional missions with Army weasels to the northwest part of Carbon County, which was known to have been hit hard by the blizzard. Even as Williamson was announcing the upcoming mission, preparations were being made to get the weasels underway to go and check on the welfare of those in Little Medicine Bow and Marshall Counties, as well as check on their overall health and the amount of food they had on hand. The Red Cross team had a complement of Wyoming National Guardsmen that included Sergeant Delbert Benskin and Sergeant Otto Sherman, who were both from Cheyenne. These two young men manned the Red Cross food truck that made a sixteen-hour trip to the Willows, which is north of Rawlins, behind the heavy equipment as they plowed through drifts assisting motorists stranded along the highway.

The men who made the long trip across the frozen tundra were only able to travel between eight and ten miles an hour through snowdrifts and lost their directions from time to time through the Shirley Basin. The group included Sergeant C.J. Anderson, Sergeant J.P. Chocas, Corporal W.P. Lemoine and Corporal Jack R. Babcock, all from Cheyenne. Babcock vividly remembers that trip to the Shirley Basin. He said a rancher had come to the temporary base in Rawlins, where the National Guard was stationed for "humanitarian relief." The rancher said his wife was ill and he needed to get back home to his ranch to check on her. Babcock said the team loaded up supplies and equipment along with the rancher and headed out into the blizzard. The team stayed on course as it headed along the highway. However, once they started cross country toward the ranch, the men became disoriented with the severe blizzard conditions. Not only were they battling the conditions, but the Army weasel they drove continually threw its track. Babcock said

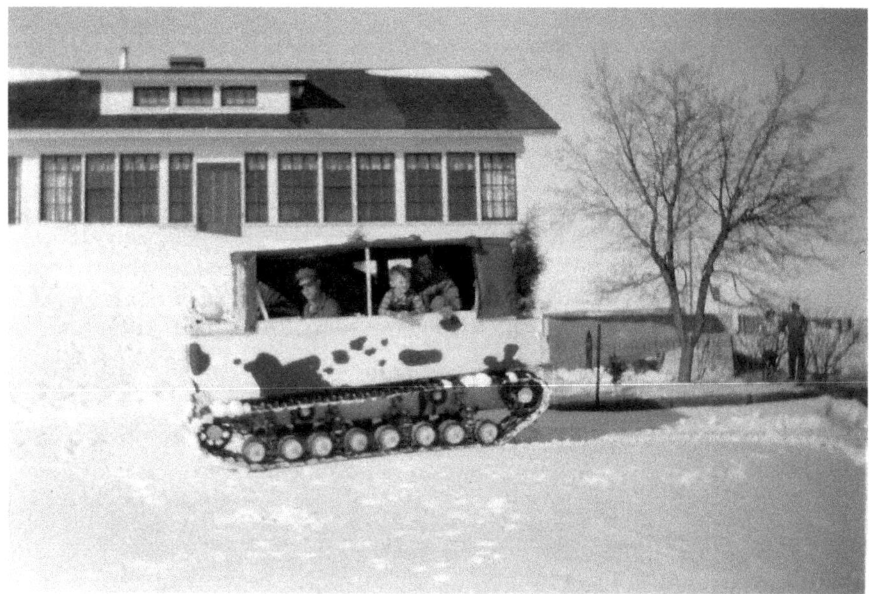

Fred Emerich gets a chance to ride in a U.S. Army weasel. *Courtesy of Senator Fred Emerich.*

this took several hours to fix in the frigid temperatures and furious winds. After the repairs, the team was able to get underway and continued toward the ranch even through the night. As the sun was starting to rise, the rancher made an unusual request of the soldiers. He said, "Just let me out here, I have a band of sheep I need to check on." The team quickly replied, "What about your wife?" To which the rancher said, "Aw, she's all right!" The team let him out and continued to the ranch, where they found the rancher's wife doing chores. Babcock said she was very pale and sick, but she was still on her feet and taking care of things on the ranch. Babcock and his team were responsible not only for rescuing those who needed medical attention but also hauling crews to and from the bulldozers, and Babcock said he also remembered that one of the crews taken by the weasel crew was made up of personnel working for the railroad.

One of Babcock's final stories about his weasel crew was that they traveled to Saratoga and Encampment to pick up two mothers who were very close to delivering. They transported both women to the Rawlins hospital so they could be at the hospital to deliver rather than stranded at their homes. Babcock said his team followed the highway to both places, but the snow was so fine that even the slightest bit of wind made it difficult to see and in some cases almost impossible.[87] In addition to these weasel crews assisting those who required the services of medical personnel, they also assisted in getting the needed supplies to stranded residents. The weasel operators took two weasels to Wamsutter, Wyoming, along with four bulldozer operators. These operators worked with others to plow the snow from Wamsutter to Rawlins, bringing supplies such as food and medicine to some seventy residents who lived in four railroad camps along the route and were now isolated by the deep snow.

Williamson of the Red Cross indicated to the *Rawlins Daily Times* that seven more weasels were en route to their location along with additional National Guard personnel who were assigned to the Rawlins disaster center. He also stated that although he was unsure, either ground support or air support or potentially both was soon to be arriving to assist in taking food to those families who, from reports, were out of food in the Sailor and Austin Creek area just north of Hanna, Wyoming. Two families, those of Scott McNees and John Anaylas, were among those who had reported that they were completely out of food. On Monday before the article, most of the C-17 Operation Haylift sorties had been canceled due to the weather, but one aircraft was in operation and was able to fly into Wamsutter to bring in Albert "Shorty" Terrill, a local sheep company employee who was suffering from a frozen foot.[88] The Wyoming National Guard, along with the Red Cross, played a significant role in saving the lives of many across the state during the blizzard. It was a community effort in which many came to see what they could do. No matter the circumstance or challenge, Wyomingites met the challenge of the blizzard head-on, facing adversity and many times dangerous situations to assist others who were in need of medical assistance or were stranded.

Many across the state lent a hand when it came to helping those in need. One such person was Ben Nelson, from Cheyenne, who was one of the many train passengers stranded in Green River, Wyoming, on his way back from the Rose Bowl. Nelson was not just a passenger but also the mayor of Cheyenne. Upon his return to Cheyenne, he wasted no time in assessing the effects of the blizzard. After his arrival on Saturday, January 8, he and City Commissioner Leo Water and County Agent Wilber Brettell boarded a Wyoming National Guard C-47 equipped with food and medical supplies and headed out to assist in delivering essential items to marooned individuals.

After the mayor returned to Cheyenne from the aerial mission, he toured the city to assess the damage inflicted by the blizzard. He was quick to thank the police and fire departments, the sheriff's office, the Red Cross, the National Guard and both Commissioners A.W. "Art" Trout and Leo Water for their outstanding work during the first intense days of the storm in his absence.[89]

Commissioner Trout's exploits were published for those in Cheyenne to spotlight the excellent job he and his crew were doing to clear the streets and alleyways as quickly as possible. The *Tribune-Eagle* stated that automobile traffic was only possible down one or two streets in Cheyenne in the early morning hours of Wednesday. By Sunday, January 9, Commissioner Trout announced motorists could access any road within city limits. The *Tribune-Eagle* stated, "That represents an improvement we didn't think possible of achievement as we walked to work three days ago. It shouts the fact that somebody 'knows their way around' in the matter of snow clearance and removal."[90]

That person, of course, was Commissioner Trout, whom the paper referred to as a blizzard-fighting veteran, and his street and alley crew. According to the paper, Trout came up with a plan of action in advance to clear and remove the snow, and when the blizzard hit, his crews took to the streets with "vigor." To clear the city in the timeframe it did took, on average, sixty men arriving each day, working fifteen-hour shifts, manning twenty-five pieces of heavy equipment and thirty-five trucks. Trout stated,

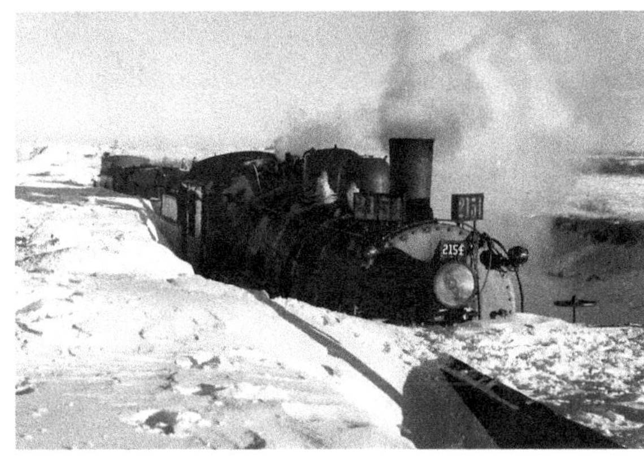

A steam engine stalled in a massive snowdrift. *Courtesy of Mike Kampa.*

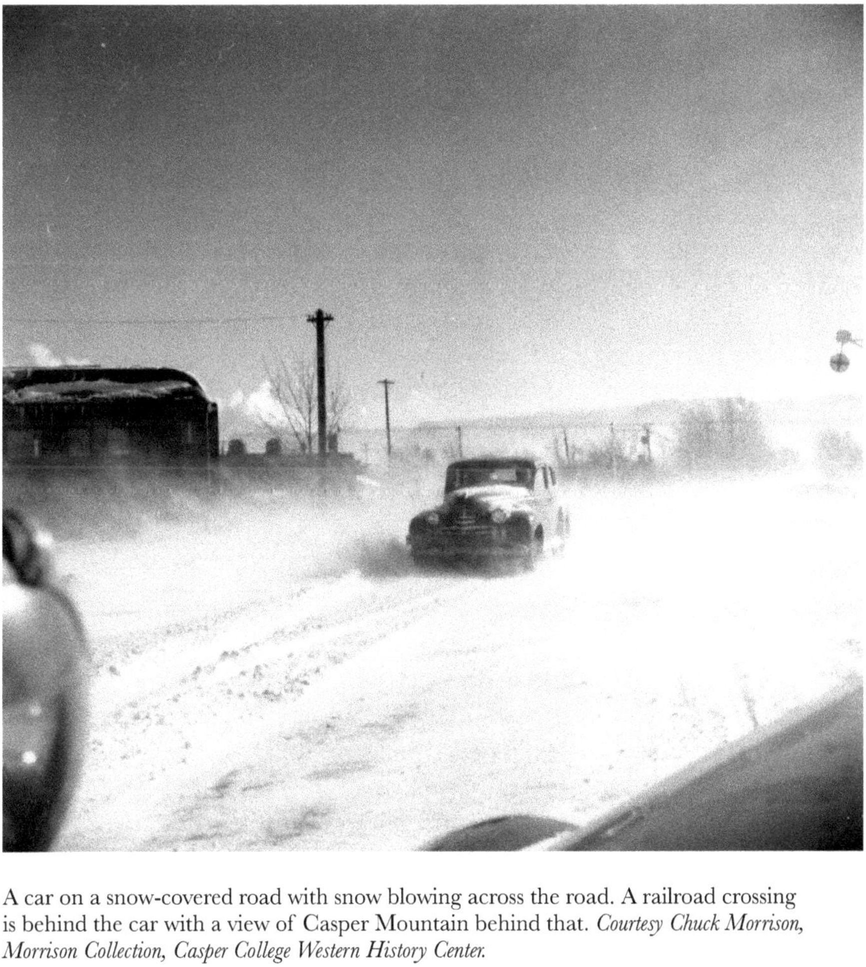

A car on a snow-covered road with snow blowing across the road. A railroad crossing is behind the car with a view of Casper Mountain behind that. *Courtesy Chuck Morrison, Morrison Collection, Casper College Western History Center.*

"The present-day conditions is complicated by a large number of cars which are always caught on the streets." The paper noted that twenty years earlier, the car problem was not an issue, as there were fewer vehicles on the street than in 1949 and the mobility of the public not only in Cheyenne but across the state was restricted. Commissioner Trout reflected on some of the blizzards he remembered, saying this storm was "up with the worst I have seen." He did add that this particular blizzard was "sharper" than others he had seen but nothing worse than the ones he could recall from 1912, 1913 and 1920.[91]

Despite the blizzard, several harrowing acts of kindness, bravery and courage were shown. On January 5, 1949, three days after the blizzard hit, a young mother was in desperate need of getting to Memorial Hospital in Cheyenne to deliver her baby boy. Private First Class Arthur Phillips and his wife, June, were expecting their child but had not planned for the storm that hit on Sunday. Arthur had phoned the base asking for help in getting his wife to the hospital so she could deliver the baby. Robert E. Clizbe, an interviewer for the Wyoming Employment Service, reported to the *Wyoming Eagle* that Wayne Landis (a Cheyenne city patrolman), a military policeman (MP) from Fort Warren and Don Roman (who resided at 2216½ Pebrican) were those who assisted June to the hospital that Tuesday night. The unidentified MP and Patrolman Landis slowly made their way through the snowdrifts and driving snow. As the Airman and Landis slowly made their way down Twenty-Second Street, they became stuck in a drift and were unable to continue, making it within just a few short blocks of William and Violet Clizbe's home, where the young Phillips family were renting the upstairs loft. Now being stranded, the men felt they would not be able to get to June Phillips and move her to the hospital. As fate would have it, another Cheyenne citizen, Don Roman, was out working his way through the drifts nearly four blocks from his residence when he came up and saw the two men stuck. Roman volunteered the use of his truck, and the party continued toward their destination. Just as they thought they would make it, Roman's truck became stuck in yet another drift, this time only one block from the Clizbes' home. This, however, did not discourage the party from getting to Phillips. The three men left their vehicle and forged ahead through more snowdrifts to reach the family. These same men then carried Phillips from her house back one block to the truck and miraculously got her to Memorial Hospital, where she delivered a healthy seven-pound, twelve-ounce baby boy.

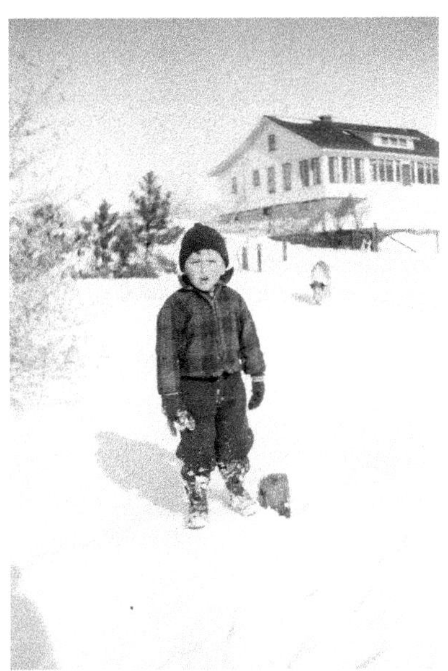

Fred Emerich down below the family residence on a snowdrift that covers the fence; notice the post beside Fred. *Courtesy of Senator Fred Emerich.*

This is yet another example of the fortitude of Wyomingites in their effort to aid fellow citizens in their time of need. The spirit of the community certainly shined through each time someone was rescued, food was dropped to cattle and even strangers who had no place to go were fed and lodged. Understandably, the Phillipses were relieved that they were able to get to the hospital, thanks to those in the community who responded to their appeals for help.[92]

Throughout the state, the Wyoming National Guard assisted in the rescue of stranded and marooned individuals. The Torrington National Guard unit gave the *Guide-Review* in Lingle, Wyoming, a detailed report of its work throughout the blizzard. Accolades continued for two Wyoming units: the 960th Ordnance MM Company, located in Torrington, and men affiliated with the 960th out of Guernsey. The paper pointed out that these men were on duty the entire time. However, they were not compensated for their work, other than the knowledge of knowing they were responsible for assisting and saving so many in Goshen County.

The *Guide-Review* contacted the unit asking what the men had done during the blizzard. A day-to-day report of the units was given to the paper by Sergeant Emilio R. Gomez from Cheyenne. The weekly report gave a snapshot of each day from January 3 to January 10 detailing the tasks completed by those guardsmen who participated in rescue missions in the area. On Monday, January 3, the day right after the storm hit Torrington and surrounding towns in Goshen County, fourteen guardsmen reported for duty. These men stayed on duty throughout the day and into the night, staying at the armory, ready to respond to emergencies as they arose. That Tuesday morning, January 4, a 4½-ton wrecker, 2½-ton truck and ¼-ton jeep were deployed along with five guardsmen and Dr. Loren Morgan. The group was headed to Huntley, Wyoming, just ten and a half miles south of Torrington. Their mission was to reach the ranch of Robert Sittner, whose wife was pregnant and in need of medical attention. The men were only a few miles outside Torrington when they encountered a fifteen-foot drift. Starting at 5:30 p.m., the men began to dig through the drift to continue to Huntley. They made it as far as the Henry Jones corner, which was six miles from the Sittner ranch. It had taken them four hours to make it to this point from Torrington. Their work concluded at 11:30 p.m. The following day, the guardsmen continued their battle with the drift but were unable to make it to the ranch. The baby had been born the night before, and reports were that mother and baby were doing just fine.[93] Ironically, twenty miles away, just between Hawk Springs and Yoder, Robert's brother Ed was in the same circumstances: his wife was in labor with a child. Efforts were being made to reach Ed and his wife, but to no avail. Ed realized he was not going to receive any medical assistance with the birth and used his farm tractor to pick up a few neighbors who could assist with the delivery. On Thursday morning around 5:15 a.m., the baby was born. Dr. Cutler from Scottsbluff, Nebraska, was flown in by ski-plane to the area and reported that mother and baby were doing just fine.[94]

That same day, a call was received from Dr. Leo Kennen to have a truck dispatched. The National Guard's efforts continued as it assisted in saving the lives of a family in Torrington who nearly died from carbon monoxide poisoning. Sent to the location were two 2½-ton trucks—one truck carrying the needed oxygen for the family and the other to push through the drifts along the route. The William "Woody" McHodgkins family narrowly escaped death early on Wednesday, January 5, when snowdrifts choked out the home's chimney, which was also believed to be full of soot, causing additional issues. The family of three showed minor signs of poisoning, but it was the quick reaction of the National Guard and sheriff's office that saved their lives. The guardsmen, upon notification of the incident, rushed to aid in getting oxygen provided to the McHodgkins family quickly. Mrs. McHodgkins seemed to get over her symptoms rather quickly and stayed with her sisters for a few days. Their son Robert reported no effects from the gas. Since Robert had slept with his window open that night, it is believed the fumes may have dissipated before reaching him. Mr. McHodgkins, however, had taken in more of the toxic gas than first assumed. The guardsmen were able to get the oxygen delivered; however, as soon as they returned to the armory, they were immediately sent back to the location to retrieve members of the family and bring them back to Torrington for medical treatment. With signs of the poisoning manifesting, McHodgkins was quickly admitted to the Platte Valley Hospital for treatment. On the morning of Thursday, January

6, McHodgkins passed away at the hospital, despite the efforts of the doctors and those of the guardsmen.[95] Dr. Keenan praised the guardsmen for their precision and abilities in aiding the McHodgkins family.

On Wednesday, January 5, the guardsmen were back at it again on another rescue attempt. Fifteen guardsmen along with ten men form the Holly Sugar Corp. made a second attempt to get through Huntly Road to get medical attention to Pauline Dick, who was critically ill and needed immediate attention. While guardsmen were working to assist Dick, another group headed to the Torrington airport with two 2½-ton trucks to clear the runway. The group worked hard on Wednesday to clear the runway. However, the blowing snow made it impossible, and they had to return to the armory.

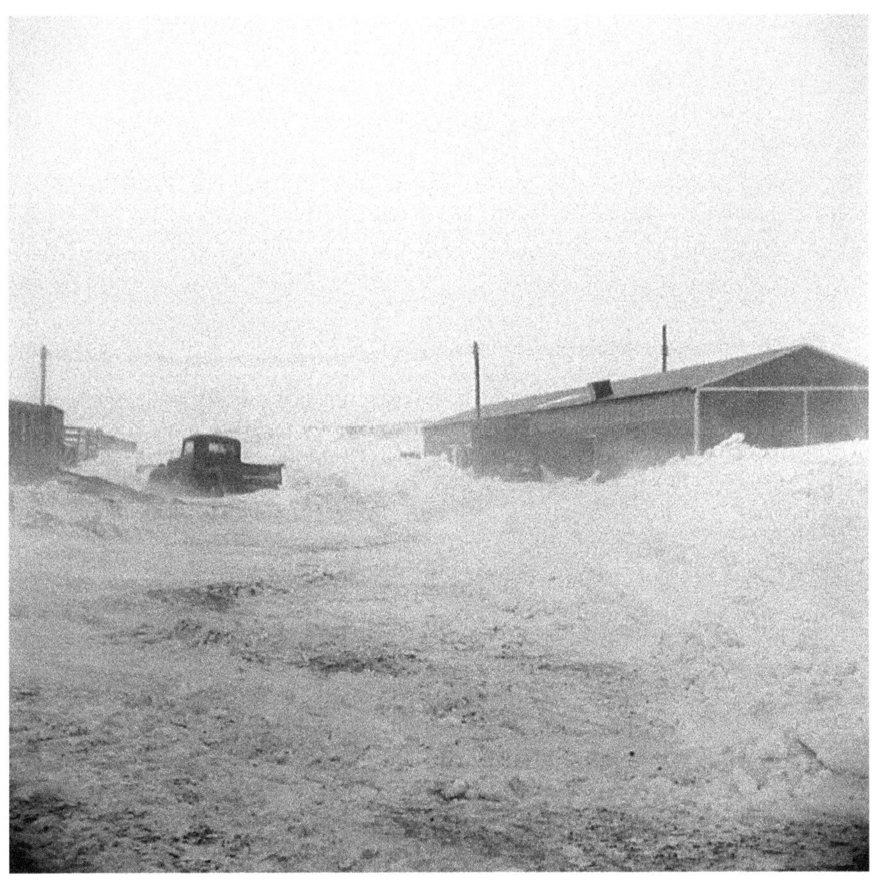

Roads are cleared, but snowdrifts continue to build. *Courtesy of John Moyer.*

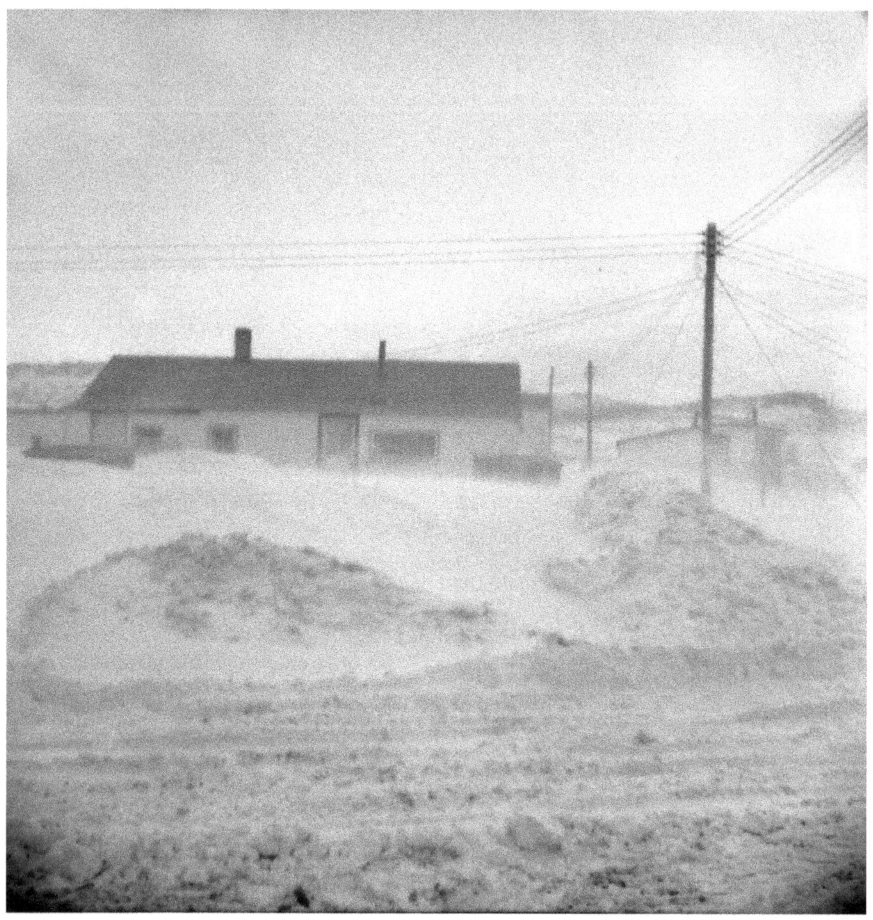

Blowing snow continues. *Courtesy of John Moyer.*

On Thursday, January 6, work efforts began to show progress as the guardsmen started to see their efforts paying off. That morning, the group that had gone to the airport to clear the runway returned and was successful, but this time the men had a bulldozer helping remove the snow and massive drifts that had grown overnight. Fifteen guardsmen also left the armory with a 2½-ton truck, with everyone given a shovel to help highway crews clear Highway 85 toward Cheyenne. As the sun set, three 2½-ton trucks were sent out with twenty-five guardsmen to support Torrington firefighters as they worked to break through heavy drifts to Frank Baumgardner's ranch. Family members stranded at the ranch were running low on food, and others needed medical attention. The guardsmen

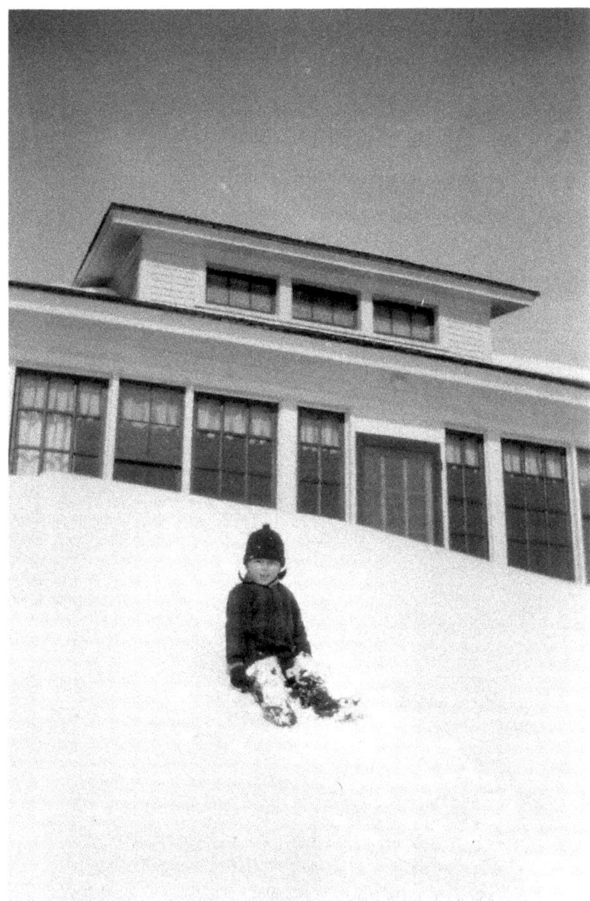

Young Fred Emerich on top of a large snowdrift that is near the windows of his family's two-story home. *Courtesy of Senator Fred Emerich.*

arrived the following morning at 6:00 a.m., having worked through the night to reach the ranch. Once they had everyone loaded for the return trip, they arrived at 11:00 a.m. back to the armory with all those who required aid from the ranch.

As day four rolled in, endeavors continued to clear roads of snow. Twenty-five men left the armory to once again assist the Highway Department in clearing the freeway to Cheyenne. Another fifteen guardsmen were left back at the armory to field any emergencies that might arise. As Friday turned into Saturday, rescue missions continued through the weekend. At least ten guardsmen loaded up fuel oil on one of the half-tracks they had and headed to the residence of Fred Moirike just south of Torrington. Another ten men from the armory assisted Charles F. Calhoun in freeing a snowplow stuck at the Goshen County Fairgrounds. As the guardsmen were digging the plow out, men from the Holly Sugar Corp. joined in the operation and eventually pulled the snowplow free of its frozen encasement.

Sunday unexpectedly became a day of respite for the guardsmen. The phone was silent, as not one emergency call came into the armory. That morning, forty men reported for duty, spending their entire day at the armory without even the smallest bit of assistance needed in the community. About 5:00 p.m., the men were released and sent back home to deal with their own issues related to the blizzard. On Monday morning, there was one call recorded in the report, which was the last of the entries. The armory sent out two 2½-ton trucks to assist Charles F. Calhoun once more. This time, the group helped Calhoun break through a road to the Burge Schoolhouse. The

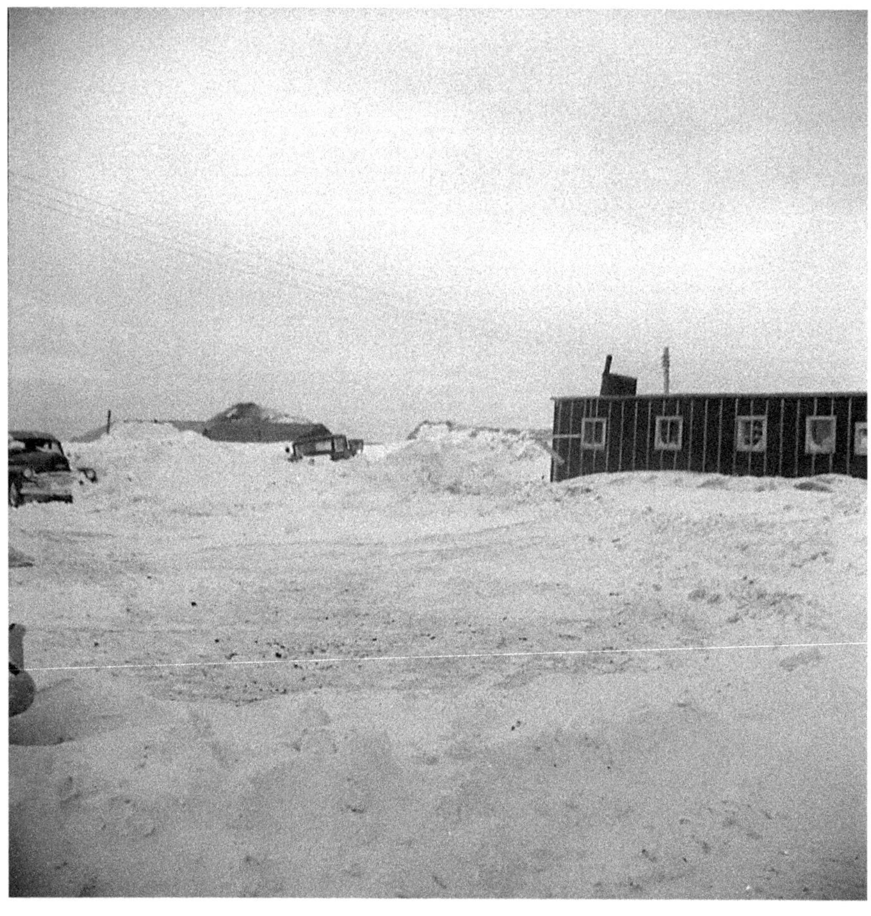

A cook shack at Elk Mountain Coal Company mining camp and vehicles buried in drifts. *Courtesy of John Moyer.*

Torrington guardsmen deserve accolades for the endless hours and their endurance as the blizzard came through. These men continually reported for duty even though the tasks exposed them to harsh temperatures and oftentimes insurmountable tasks that took hours and sometimes days to complete. Their efforts show the sacrifice that so many men and women make in our military ranks today.[96]

As mentioned, the military worked hard to assist where they could during the storm. The Naval Reserve unit in Cheyenne was no exception, as eighty-three naval personnel were stranded at the Naval Armory located at 3596 Evans Avenue. Just as with any military group, they worked hard when needed but found time for entertainment. Those stranded produced a regular stage show to pass the time. The show, *Snow Bound Review*, was written by Corporal Jerry Connors and Private First Class Richard E. Plain, both of whom were stationed at Fort Warren Air Base in Cheyenne. The show included a Hawaiian hula dancer, a tap dancer, a comedy quartet, movies, boxing, a number of vocal solos and a poem written and recited by Connors. The arrangements and entertainment of the guests fell to Commander Dhuyvetter, Yeoman First Class Bud Huber and Chief Quartermaster Tom Crane, who ensured that all of the Navy's guests were accommodated as best as possible during their forced vacation with their military bunkmates.

Hale Newcomb, a Navy radio operator, contacted the *Cheyenne Tribune* and relayed news that those who were stranded were not only military personnel but also many mothers and babies. He also told the *Tribune* that many of those taking shelter were individuals the Cheyenne police had brought in from stranded trains and vehicles stuck on the roads close to the armory. Per the *Tribune*, Newcomb also stated the local police and National Guard had brought in most of the food to the armory, but the Red Cross had paid for the groceries after the first day and a half. Of course, preparation of the food was essential. This was taken on by two military personnel, A.L. Daniels and W.W. Schenk, a gunner's mate first class, who cooked the meals for those stranded. These two men spent over thirty-six hours cooking food for the masses and preparing baby formula for the children. The job was so strenuous that the day the article ran, Daniels was taken home to recuperate. While these guys were cooking to keep so many going, there were others taking on numerous other tasks as needed.

W.B. Hagger, a chief pharmacist mate, did his part and took care of many of the sick babies who had colds and even made house calls to those residents he could reach in the frigid temperatures. Of course, with so many stranded in one place, it was a certainty many families were worried about the whereabouts of their wives, husbands and children. The Navy personnel quickly set up a shortwave radio to inform the community who had family members marooned at the armory. With the number of people, a shortage of food, blankets or some amenity was sure to happen, and it did. Soon a lack of milk became evident, and Lloyd Langley, who was the owner of a local store, the Jack Frost, came down around two o'clock in the morning to bring milk. The Owl Inn donated milk as well to the children. Not only did the business owners step up, but the chairman of the Cheyenne Chamber of Commerce, R.J. Hoffman, acquired cots from several different locations and also obtained blankets from the Frontier Hotel.

The Red Cross throughout the blizzard came to the aid of many in Wyoming. On January 5, volunteers came to the rescue of Helen West and her seven children. Helen and her family were marooned within the Laramie city limits. With the storm's continuous battering, the West family found themselves stranded and unable to go to Laramie for provisions. Their home at Twenty-Fifth and Sheridan was running low on both fuel and food. The day before, on January 4, members of the Albany Red Cross had made their way through waist-deep snowdrifts to take supplies, which included coal and food. On January 5, a ten-member ski patrol made its way back to the family with more supplies. The children in the West family varied in ages from two to seventeen, and even though their home was within the city, they were cut off from any chance of reaching supplies or other necessities needed to survive the storm.

The Albany Red Cross continued its work in Laramie, as it supplied cots and mattresses for forty to fifty people who were stranded on the trains there. The passengers were housed at the local Knights of Pythias Hall at 214 Ivinson. Many of those marooned were bus passengers who had gone as much as forty hours without sleep. The Knights of Pythias graciously offered their hall as a respite for the weary travelers, and cots were secured by Dr. W.R. Nesbitt, who was head of the University of Wyoming health service.[97]

CHAPTER 5

CONCLUSION

The Blizzard of 1949 is a part of Wyoming history that will go down in the annals as one of the hardest experienced by those in the state. Although the loss of life was minimal, the devastation experienced by ranchers and farmers placed a burden on the economy for several years. The tenacity shown by those who lived through the Blizzard of 1949 makes for a remarkable story that continues to amaze those who hear the memories of the ones who experienced it. This part of Wyoming history has long since passed; however, the phrase "Wyoming Tough" is illustrated by those who survived the storm.

NOTES

Preface

1. *Moberly Monitor-Index*, "28 Below in Wyoming," December 22, 1948.
2. *Los Angeles Times*, "Train Blew Over by 90 Miles an Hour Gale," December 21, 1948.
3. *New Castle News*, "Fair New Year's Day Is Forecast for Most of U.S.," December 31, 1948.
4. *Mt. Vernon Register-News*, "Illinois Roads Slick, Blizzard Brews in the West," December 28, 1948.
5. William H. Klein, "The Unusual Weather and Circulation of the 1948–1949 Winter," *Bulletin of the American Meteorological Society, Journal of Atmospheric Science, Journal of Physical Oceanography* 77, no. 4 (Winter 1949).
6. Ibid., 99.
7. Blue Hill Observatory was founded by Abbott Lawrence Rotch on February 1, 1885. It holds the record for the longest continuous weather record in North America.
8. Klein, "Unusual Weather and Circulation," 99.
9. *Arizona Republic*, "New Blizzard Rides on Gale into Midwest," December 21, 1948.
10. *Salt Lake Tribune*, "More Snow in Wyoming Adds to Winter Moisture Store," December 10, 1948, 13.
11. *Long Beach (CA) Independent*, "Big Winds Ditch 6 Train Cars," December 21, 1948; *Tennessean*, "East Digs Out," December 21, 1948, 8.

12. The Siberian Express hit in 1933 as the Great Depression was coming to an end. The storm started in Russia and blew across the United States, bringing the coldest weather on record in the Northern Hemisphere. "Snow Day! The 6 Worst Winter Storms in US History," Shmoop Blog, blog.shmoop.com/2010/02/18/6-worst-winter-storms-history.
13. *Wyoming Eagle*, "The Storm," January 5, 1949, 2.

Chapter 1

14. *Missoulian*, "Montana Takes Fourth Place," January 1, 1949, 5.
15. *Minneapolis Morning Tribune*, "Snowbound Hamline Pines for 'Mild' Minnesota Winter; St. Mary's Off," January 6, 1949, 19.
16. E-mail interview with Kerwin Engelhart, September 17, 2016.
17. Vern Mikkelson was awarded a trophy as "Outstanding Player of the Tournament."
18. *Minneapolis Morning Tribune*, "Snowbound Hamline Pines," 19.
19. *Eugene (OR) Guard*, "Rotary Hears of Events When Train Marooned in Blizzard," January 19, 1949, 9.
20. *Goshen County News*, "Local News," January 6, 1949, 8.
21. Today, West Highway is where Highways 26 and 85 converge into one. This highway stretches between Torrington's west side and Lingle, Wyoming. It is the second-busiest road in Wyoming behind Dell Range Boulevard in Cheyenne.
22. The Holly Sugar Cooperation Factor was established in 1926, later becoming the Torrington Sugar Factory, which is still in operation today.
23. *Goshen County News*, "Mayor Calhoun's Wrecker Helps Many in Storm," January 6, 1949, 1.
24. *Torrington Telegraph*, "County Snow Plow Breaks Way to Hospital for Sick Woman," February 17, 1949, 12.
25. *Rawlins Daily Times*, "Mercy Plane Carries Food to Marooned Family," January 19, 1949, 1.
26. Ibid.
27. *Rawlins Daily Times*, "Rawlins Citizens Express Appreciations for Cleared Streets, Donate $13," January 19, 1949, 10.
28. Salom Rizk, aka "Sam Risk," authored the book *Syrian American*. Rizk's book won critical praise in the *New York Times Book Review* for the "vivid and earnest" portrayal of his life. From 1938 to 1958, he traveled to the United States, sharing his life's story and impressions with nearly one

million high school and junior high school students. His lecture tours were sponsored by *Reader's Digest*.

Chapter 2

29. AM Network: Affiliated Radio Stations, 1949, *Broadcasting-Telecasting Yearbook*.
30. The A.G. Andrikopolous family owns one of the largest oil companies in Wyoming.
31. Mary Carroll (Rahm) Johnson, e-mail message to the author, October 28, 2017.
32. Gallagher Transfer and Storage Co., based out of Denver, Colorado.
33. *Wyoming State Tribune*, "42 Marooned in 4-Room Ranch House Had Little to Eat; Slept in Relays," January 6, 1949, 4.
34. Ibid.
35. *Torrington Telegraph*, "Owner of Silver Tip Refinery Stalled in Torrington by Snow," January 6, 1949, 6.
36. Ibid.
37. *Tribune-Eagle*, "Storm Victims Ate Snow to Quench Thirst," January 9, 1949, 8.
38. *Goshen County News*, "Marv McIntosh Found Refuge in Farmhouse," January 13, 1949, 1.
39. *Goshen County News*, "Local Man Saved Persons from the Storm Last Week," January 13, 1949, 2.
40. *Goshen County News*, "Rancher Marlatt's Deed of Real Heroism," January 20, 1949, 5.
41. *Windsor Beacon*, "Party of 14 Marooned in Cabin-Reisig Family Survive Ordeal," January 13, 1949, 1.
42. *Torrington Telegraph*, "A Lucky Mistake Saves His Life," February 24, 1949, 3.
43. Woman's Medical College of Pennsylvania in 1949 was only the second medical college that trained only women in the field of medicine. Founded in 1867, the college would not become coeducational until 1970.
44. VJ Day marks victory in Japan, the day the Empire of Japan surrendered, effectively ending World War II.
45. E-mail interview with Erik Magnuson regarding his father's experiences during the blizzard, August 10, 2017.
46. Albert W. Epperson, "On the Beam," *Morgan County News*, February 18, 1949, 3.

47. *Rawlins Daily Times*, "Snowbound Travelers Find Hardships Alleviated by Western Hospitality," February 11, 1949, 5.
48. Francis E. Warren was a highly respected individual, community leader, cattle baron and Wyoming's first United States senator.
49. Samuel K. Allison, an American physicist and member of the Manhattan Project, became director of the metallurgical laboratory at the University of Chicago, which in 1942 conducted the first controlled release of nuclear energy. He was sent to Los Alamos in 1944 as chairman of the Technical Committee. Allison's voice counted down the Trinity test in 1945. He later joked that his ability to count backward made him famous.
50. GI (Government Issue) is the abbreviation given to soldiers starting around 1941 during World War II. It is still in use today by someone identifying a military member.
51. *Wyoming Eagle*, "Wyoming Blizzards Best in World, Italian Woman Thinks," January 7, 1949, 6.
52. *Eugene (OR) Guard*, "Snow Oh No!," January 19, 1949, 13.
53. *Minonk News-Dispatch*, "Minonk Boys Marooned in Snow," January 1949, www.minonktalk.com.
54. *Mercury*, "Blizzard Rips Through Western States; Heavy Snow Slows Train and Motor Travel," January 3, 1949, 14.
55. The Waa-Mu Show began in 1920 when the Women's Athletic Association (WAA) joined forces with the Men's Union (MU) in a performance of original, student-written material. The show was traditionally a musical revue, consisting of Northwestern-inspired vignettes tied together by a theme. Over the last five years, the Waa-Mu Show has evolved into an original full-length musical. "About the Waa-Mu," waamushow.org.
56. *Daily Northwestern*, "Eyewitness Tells of Cheyenne Life," January 5, 1949, 1.
57. *Daily Northwestern*, "Snowdrifters Enjoy Life; Eat and Sleep on Train," January 6, 1949, 2.
58. *Daily Northwestern*, "Snow-bound 'Cats Devise Talent Show," January 5, 1949, 1.

Chapter 3

59. *Wyoming State Tribune*, "Many Antelope Killed by Train," January 9, 1949, 2.
60. *Wheatland Times*, "Local Men Fly Casper Child to Denver Hospital," January 6, 1949, 1.

61. *Wheatland Times*, "Wheatland Flying Cowboy Gives Aid to Sick Child," January 18, 1949, 1.
62. *Big Piney Examiner*, January 1949.
63. Ibid.
64. Little Bear, Wyoming, located on Little Bear Creek. Post office established May 24, 1877, Isaac Bard, postmaster, population 10. Discontinued May 15, 1955.
65. Careyville Acres was established on January 20, 1944. These units were built to house families of military personnel coming back from World War II. The housing area was located on East Pershing with an estimated 325 units. The actual number of units ended up being 180 for Careyville Acres. Fred Gish, *Cheyenne, Wyoming 1940–1955* (n.p.: self-published, 2016), 85.
66. Party lines were extremely common in the 1930s and 1940s in rural areas. The basic advantage of using a party line was that since each connection had to run a number of miles in order to reach the remote homes, a larger number of homes had access to telephonic services utilizing fewer number of wires. "How Party Lines Came into Existence," partylinecentral.com.
67. *Torrington Telegram*, "Goshenites Keeps Valuable Record of 1949 Blizzard," February 17, 1949, 1.
68. *Torrington Telegraph*, "Veteran Rancher Discovers Sheep Alive in Drift," February 10, 1949, 7.
69. The U.S. Army Air Force was still transferring units and equipment over to the United States Air Force, and the final transfer order (Transfer Order 40) was not officially signed until July 22, 1949.
70. *Rawlins Daily Times*, "300 Tons of Hay Being Flown to Casper Area," January 27, 1949, 5.
71. Sandhills was located about ten miles from Percy Cooper's ranch headquarters.
72. Sometimes, temporary identification is desirable in a sheep flock. Paint branding; marking crayons, sticks and rattles; and spray markers can all be used to identify sheep and lambs for periods of several weeks to several months. Marks from marking crayons will usually last for several weeks, whereas paint brands tend to last for many months.
73. A Cat-Skinner is an operator of a Caterpillar tractor, also called a "cat man."
74. Wool blind is when the snow and ice buildup on the wool around the face of the sheep causes them to be temporarily blind as long as the temperatures stay below freezing.
75. Trula had to climb down in a railroad car to get the coal she was sending to her husband.

76. The Aleutian Islands is a chain of small islands that separate the Bering Sea (north) from the main portion of the Pacific Ocean (south). They extend in an arc southwest, then northwest, for about 1,100 miles (1,800 km) from the tip of the Alaska Peninsula to Attu Island, Alaska. Brittanica.com.
77. *Tribune-Eagle*, "King Ranch Saves Stock," January 9, 1949, 6.
78. E-mail interview with Michael Dykhorst, grandson of Clarence William Weber, September 24, 2017, "Blizzard of 1949."

Chapter 4

79. Elliott Chase, "People Taught a Number of Things by Blizzard," *Star Press*, January 30, 1949, 4.
80. *Wyoming State Tribune*, "Cheyenne Man Is Found Nearly Frozen," January 4, 1949, 3.
81. *Wyoming State Tribune*, "Isolated for Days, Vets Hospital Made Best of It," January 9, 1949, 8.
82. *Wyoming State Tribune*, "Unsung Heroes," January 5, 1949, 6.
83. *Rawlins Daily Times*, "Ham Operators Offer Help in Communications," January 7, 1949, 4.
84. Ibid.
85. *Tribune-Eagle*, "No Gouging," January 9, 1949, 4.
86. The paper pointed out that the Cottonwood Ranch was formerly the Richards Place.
87. Eyewitness statement from Jack Babcock, Moron, Wyoming, August 8, 2017.
88. *Rawlins Daily Times*, "Mission Reports," January 4, 1949, 1.
89. *Wyoming State Tribune*, "Mayor Joins in Rescue Job," January 9, 1949, 2.
90. Ibid.
91. Ibid.
92. *Wyoming Eagle*, "Four Aid Woman in Battle to Reach Hospital," January 6, 1949, 8.
93. *Goshen County News*, "Guard Boys Did Much Good Work in Storm," January 6, 1949, 1.
94. *Torrington Telegraph*, "Two Sittner Babies Arrive," January 6, 1949, 1.
95. *Goshen County News*, "Family in Narrow Escape from Monoxide Gas Here Wednesday," January 6, 1949, 1.

96. *Guide-Review*, "National Guard Unit at Torrington Does Much in Relieving Distressed Persons During Recent Raging Storm," January 12, 1949, 1.
97. *Laramie Republican Boomerang*, "Red Cross Aids Marooned Family," January 5, 1949, 3.

INDEX

H

I

J

K

L

M

N

ABOUT THE AUTHOR

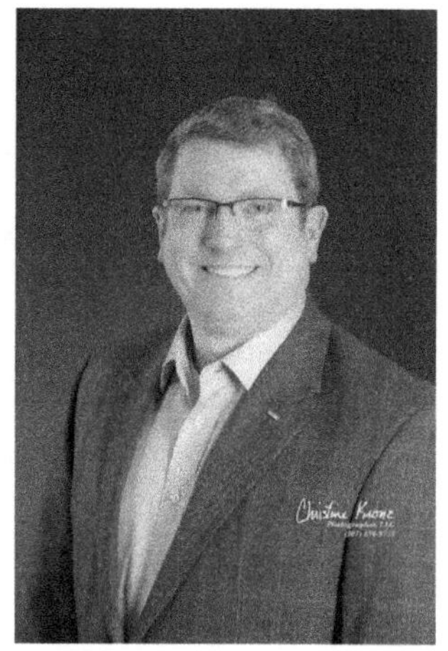

A native of Greenwood, South Carolina, James Conway Fuller was on born July 3, 1971. After a short stint in college, he joined the United States Air Force at the age of eighteen. During his time in the U.S. Air Force, he completed a bachelor of science in history from Drury University in Springfield, Missouri, and most recently a master of arts in American history with American Military University out of Charleston, West Virginia. James and his family fell in love with Wyoming—the people, the lifestyle and the natural beauty. After his retirement on January 1, 2014, they were proud to call Cheyenne, Wyoming, their "new hometown."

James is driven to preserve and perpetuate the history of Wyoming. He has had the privilege to work with numerous boards and nonprofit organizations that support those efforts. Through his business (Discovering History and Heritage, LLC, established in June 2014), James had the opportunity to provide all of the historical research for the Wyoming PBS documentary *Storm of the Century: Blizzard of '49*. That documentary was nominated for a Rocky Mountain Region Emmy Award and went on to gain national recognition with PBS.

www.ingramcontent.com/pod-product-compliance
Lightning Source LLC
LaVergne TN
LVHW052337100826
845147LV00020B/1095

* 9 7 8 1 6 2 5 8 5 9 3 5 8 *